AF455257

The Official Doctor Who Fan Club
Volume 1

The Jon Pertwee Years

by

Keith Miller

Pegimount Press

Dedicated to my Mum (1911 - 2009), Barry Letts' floozy

Published by Pegimount Press (www.pegimountpress.com)

ISBN 978-0-9573704-0-1

Foreword

Doctor Who fandom is like the series that gave birth to it: rowdy; uncontrollable and sometimes spectacular. It's intertwined with its parent show in a way no other fandom is, each informing the other. And as it turns out, the fandom is only a few years younger than the series. Keith Miller was there at the start, and it's somehow surprising that he's only just telling his story now. His book is an archaeological treasure trove for those interested in fan history, containing as it does set visits to the stories 'Carnival of Monsters', 'The Three Doctors', 'Planet of the Spiders', 'Genesis of the Daleks'*, 'Terror of the Zygons' *and 'The Masque of Mandragora'*. That material, largely unavailable elsewhere, would be worth the price of admission alone.

As someone who entered fandom in 1983, it's startling that this sort of thing was happening a decade beforehand, and few of those involved then were still around for the fan boom of the 1980s, so it's something of a secret history. The correspondence between the various production teams and fledgling fandom is fascinating, and shows a genteel connection only possible in an age of letters and photocopies, where the sudden appearance of an uncontrollable mob of fans, or even more than a handful, must have seemed a very remote possibility. Included here also is (unless you know different) the first *Doctor Who* fanzine, in its entirety.

Brilliant stuff.

One almost wonders how the contents of that first issue could be decided upon. Keith Miller was the first person to make those choices. He's the First Fan, the first person who considered what a *Doctor Who* fan life might be like. As such, he's a valuable resource, and we're lucky to have him, and this book.

Paul Cornell,

Oxfordshire, April 2011.

**in Volume 2: The Tom Baker Years*

"You sound so keen"

At the fag-end of 1971, I decided to find out if there was any kind of fan activity for Doctor Who. I wrote to the BBC and they sent me the address of one Graham Tattersall who was running the only official fan club in Bamford in Derbyshire. I duly wrote to him, and he replied saying he was no longer going to be running the club and offering his apologies. He had been running the club since 1969 and was to later tell author Stephen James Walker of *The Frame* magazine:

" In the end I found the whole project of running the Club not only expensive but very time-consuming. My job was taking up much of my spare time and I had no option but to give up the club. It was at that point, I believe, that Keith Miller took over as Secretary."

With the feeling that this really was "the right place at the right time", I wrote again to the BBC offering to take up the mantle as runner of the club, and almost by return came this reply:

BRITISH BROADCASTING CORPORATION
TELEVISION CENTRE WOOD LANE LONDON W12
TELEPHONE 01-743 8000 CABLES: BROADCASTS LONDON PS4
TELEGRAMS: BROADCASTS LONDON TELEX TELEX: 22182

30th December

Dear Keith,

I had my suspicions about Graham T. I am extremely pleased that you would like to do it from now on. I must first write again to G.T. and let him know what is happening and then I will write to you again and let you know how it all stands. But I hope that you will be able to run the Club as you sound so keen. You will hear from me, as soon as I get in touch with G.T. and have a reply from him.

Yours sincerely,

(Sarah Newman)

K. Miller.

"Welcome to the Doctor Who family"

BRITISH BROADCASTING CORPORATION
TELEVISION CENTRE WOOD LANE LONDON W12 7RJ
TELEPHONE 01-743 8000 CABLES: BROADCASTS LONDON PS4
TELEGRAMS: BROADCASTS LONDON TELEX TELEX: 22182

10th January 1971

Dear Keith,

Have had a reply from G.T. and If you are willing to be the Club Secretary we are very happy our end. If you sort of feel in a few years time or months that you have had enough please do not hesitate to write to me and then we can arrange for someone else to take over. If you have any problems or anything that worries you please write. I am always willing to help.

Perhaps if you could write to Graham Tattersall at 13 Greenhead Park, Bamford, via Sheffield, S302 AS.(just in case you haven't the address anymore) and tell him your name and things, and ask for any information and pictures that he may have. He did say in his letter to me that he would be happy to assist you in any way.

Also he mentioned to me that a David Thomas of 20 East Cliff Road, Dawlish, South Devon was very interested in taking over from him, so as you are the secretary now, could you enroll David as a new member as soon as possible please. Thankyou.

Looking forward to your first enquiry!

Yours sincerely,
SARAH

And so it began. I was thirteen years old and now running the only fan organisation deemed official by the BBC. What was I going to do? I knew exactly what I was going to do. I was a huge Marvel comics fan - Stan Lee was *the* man - and I was a member of the Merry Marvel Marching Society, the fan club of the comics empire and I was going to emulate it. There would be a club badge, a membership card and a welcome letter. And a club magazine. Oh, yes, we had to have one of those. Fanzines hadn't been invented back then so I had nothing to inspire me so it was very much ground zero. I didn't even know how to print it as photocopiers or computers with printers hadn't been invented. So I needed a printer. Nowadays, you would look up eBay, but the equivalent back then was a publication called *Exchange & Mart*. It was a weekly newspaper stuffed full of any kind of crap you could think off. Perfect. I looked up "printer" and the only thing I could afford was something called a silk screen printer. This came as a kit with the "machine", ink, and something called a stencil. Fair enough, I sent off my postal order and a week later, there arrived a sizeable box, and it was the "machine". Made of wood. It was basically a wooden frame with a thin silk stretched over it. The frame then went over the stencil, which you will have typed on minus the typewriter ribbon so the keys perforated the diaphanous layer. Squidging ink onto the silk, you forced the ink through the silk and the stencil onto the paper beneath. After a great deal of experimentation, I surveyed my first print run. It was shite. But there was no other option - I was going to have to use it.

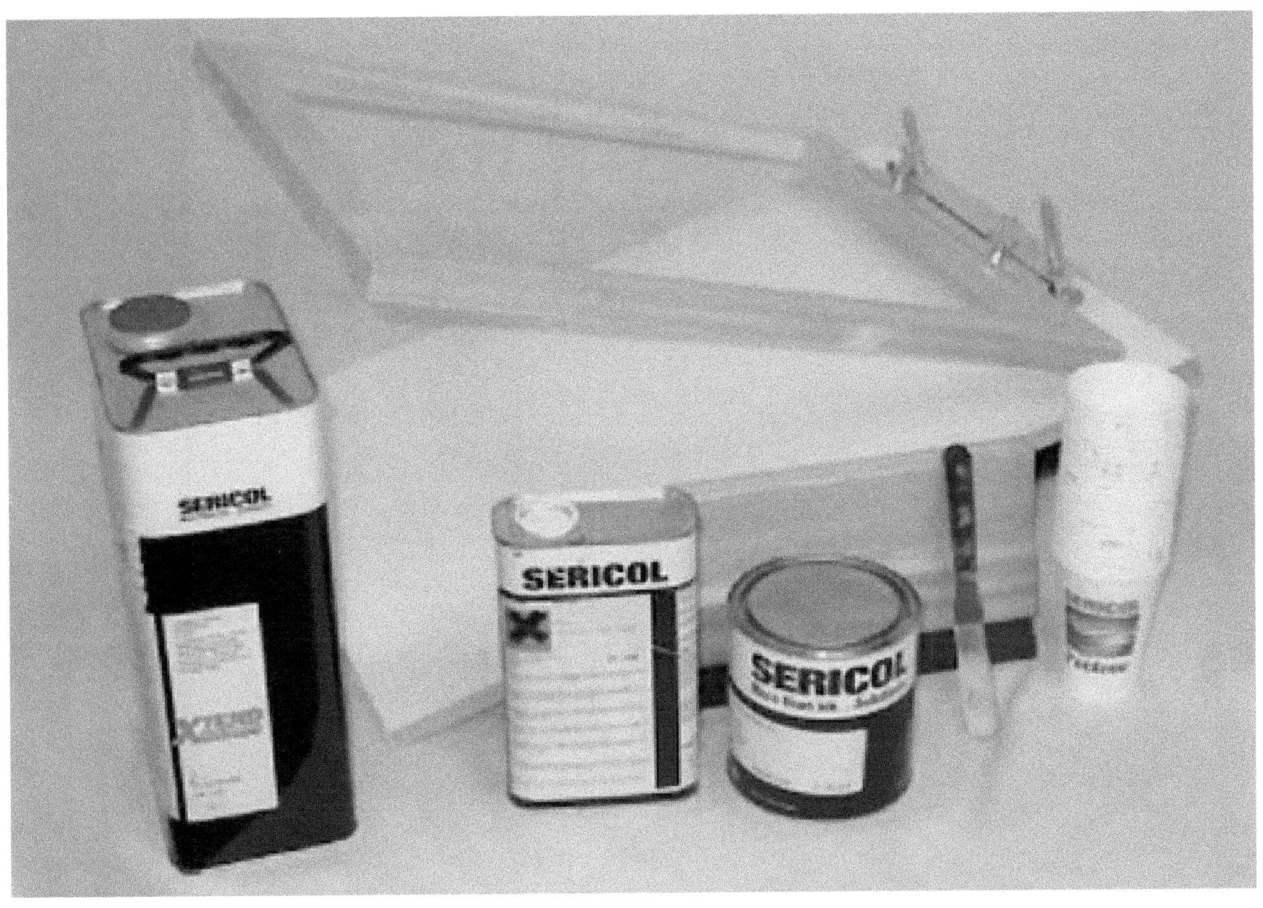

BRITISH BROADCASTING CORPORATION
TELEVISION CENTRE WOOD LANE LONDON W12 7RJ
TELEPHONE 01-743 8000 CABLES: BROADCASTS LONDON PS4
TELEGRAMS: BROADCASTS LONDON TELEX TELEX: 22182

14th January 1972

Dear Keith,

I am so glad you are happy to be the Secretary to the D.W.F.C! We are happy too!

Am digging up story synopses of old Dr.Who's for you, which I will send on as soon as poss.

I am duplicating a Dr.Who Fan Club publicity stencil which I shall send out to all the girls and boys who have written straight in to me. Also on it I shall of course mention you by name as the Sec(!) and your address. Also publicity in Radio Times is terribly expensive! So when we next have a feature in the R.T. which will be soonish I am going to get an article specially put in about the D.W.F.C. Okay? If you get too many letters send them to me and I'll help you out. This won't be til March or Something.

Now, I gather that you are wanting to come down! Super. Barry says he would love to meet you but we think it is 6 hours by train? Right? If so, Barry feels that you must stay with friends or relations for the night? Have you any relations in London? Or friends? Hope so. Then it will make it easier for you and less worry for your Mother when she knows you are travelling alone, from Scotland, and in London! So when you can sort your ~~XXXX~~ stay out, I'll let you know best dates. Okay?

Write soon and let me know.

Yours sincerely,

SARAH

(Sarah Newman)
Sec.to Barry Letts
Producer Dr.Who

K. Miller.

Sent you pictures.
Thousands of them!

Round about the same time, an even bigger box arrived from Sarah, stuffed to the gunnels (what are gunnels?) with Doctor Who goodness. I remember the smell of the contents when the box was opened. Whatever process the BBC used to print their synopses (I was obsessed by printing methods by this time), they gave off a peculiar, but not offensive, smell. The smell of Doctor Who. I had never heard the word synopses and was keen to see what they were. As I examined each stapled bundle of paper, my heart began to race. It was the History of Doctor Who. From the beginning. You have to remember, dear reader, this is way before dvds, videos or Target Books. There was nothing to remind us of the earlier adventures of the Doctor - they were gone forever after it was shown on the telly. But here, in my hands like the Dead Sea Scrolls, was something so mind-bogglingly wonderful, I felt like crying. The History of Doctor Who, episode by episode. Now I could immortalize the early stories in the club magazine! And totally piss off Jon Pertwee!

Also in the box were publicity photos - hundreds of them to be sent free of charge to those who wanted them. And brown envelopes - thousands of them with the little red BBC logo at the top. Decades later, people would tell me their little hearts leapt when they saw the brown envelope plop through their letter box - it is an integral part of their childhood.

Jon Pertwee
Dr. WHO BBC tv

I used to feel a bit sorry for our postman, Alec. He had to lug tons of mail up the four flights of stairs to our house, twice a day (there was a morning *and* an afternoon delivery in the 70's), but he never complained (well, rarely...) and frequently marvelled at the number of letters I would receive from all over the world. These all included an sae where possible, but if it was their first time of writing, then I would bundle them up into one big envelope to be franked by the BBC in London.

The newsletter too was distributed this way. Sarah from the BBC would send me, periodically, hundreds of envelopes. These had to be addressed by hand every two months, the newsletter folded and placed inside, then sealed. These were then placed into huge envelopes and wrapped with sellotape to stop them falling apart in transit. I would then place these and the letters into a huge bag and take it by bus from Moredun on the five mile journey to the BBC in Queen Street in Edinburgh.

Here, I would drop the bag off at reception, and the envelopes would enter the internal BBC mail and make their way to Sarah, who would drop them off at the BBC mailing department where they were franked, and eventually sent out. This was a long and tedious process, and even then, people complained that I wasn't answering their letters straight away. Most of the time I was - honest!

I remember the first time I dropped stuff off at BBC Edinburgh. Sarah had phoned ahead to tell them I was going to be regularly dropping stuff off to be put in the internal mail, and this news had reached the "high heid yin". The guy at reception said someone wanted to see me and he phoned upstairs. Shortly, a burly figure bounded down the internal staircase, resplendent in kilt and with a huge moustache. "So you're the Doctor Who laddie!" He grabbed my hand and shook it vigorously. "Well, done, son. It's good to bring something so high profile to Scotland." He said to drop by any time I wanted. I never knew who he was, and I never saw him again.

BRITISH BROADCASTING CORPORATION
TELEVISION CENTRE WOOD LANE LONDON W12 7RJ
TELEPHONE 01-743 8000 CABLES: BROADCASTS LONDON PS4
TELEGRAMS: BROADCASTS LONDON TELEX TELEX: 22182

18th January 1972

Dear Keith,

Before I forget. Have sent millions of letters to regular viewers (children) who write in re: Dr.Who, the piece of paper introducing you as new Secretary, so I expect you will be getting good response soonish. Now, when you have answered a good bulk of these letters don't pay the stamps yourself (only if they haven't sent you a stamped addressed envelope) send them addressed to me in a big envelope and I'll send them through BBC post, so you won't have any vast sums of your money spent on stamps. Okay? Any other things worrying you, don't be shy to ask.

Synopses I hope arriving sometime today, but I'll get this letter off first,

Incidentally, if you sometimes don't hear from me for about a week, it's because I'm either out filming or very busy, so don't despair, but whenever I can write I most surely will.

I'm awfully sorry to hear about your father. I do hope he gets better soon. I'll keep my fingers crossed. Early June is fine. The only recording dates in June are 19th/20th June. Is that okay. Could you make it on one of those? If not, come up and meet me and Barry and hope Jon Pertwee if he is around. I expect so though. You're right when the girl and sailor boy joined. Bill Hartnell now is a bit old actually. I think he has made a couple of films and things. But no television work. Michael Craze was Len Harvey in 'Crossroads'for about 8 episodes. Now making a film.

In June, I'm glad your Mother will be with you, so Barry and I shan't worry about your travelling alone when you come and see us.

Take care.

Yours sincererly,

P.T.O. Sarah Lee...

If the D.W.F.C. gets too much before your O levels please give it up for the time being. O levels are far, far, more important. Okay? Remember. There is never any rush with a club like this. People don't expect replies straight away. So please donot spend your time writing to people enquiring this and that when you are meant to be doing O level work.

POLYSTYLE PUBLICATIONS LTD., 382-386 EDGWARE ROAD, LONDON W2. TELEPHONE: 01-723 3022

20th January 1972

Keith Miller,
109 Moredun Park Rd.,
Edinburgh EH17 7HJ.

Dear Keith,

Thanks for your letter about your fan club.

I would gladly publish it in Countdown if I could be sure that you could handle the job.

Our last reader who offered to run a UFO club was inundated with replies - and remember ~~for~~ the cost of postage!

If you're still, keen please write again.

Yours sincerely,

Peter Levy

Peter Levy
Assistant Editor

P.S. I cannot guarantee to publish your letter, and if I did it would not appear for some time, as we work 6 weeks in advance.

A POLYSTYLE PUBLICATION

POLYSTYLE PUBLICATIONS LTD., 382-386 EDGWARE ROAD, LONDON W2. TELEPHONE: 01-723 3022

26th January 1972

Keith Miller,
The Dr. Who Fan Club,
c/o Keith Miller,
109 Moredun Park Road,
Edinburgh EH17 7HJ.

Dear Keith,

Thank you for your letter.

I will try and get your letter in next week's Think Tank (issue 58, March 25th, 1972).

Yours sincerely,

Peter Levy

Peter Levy
Assistant Editor

BRITISH BROADCASTING CORPORATION
TELEVISION CENTRE WOOD LANE LONDON W12 7RJ
TELEPHONE 01-743 8000 CABLES: BROADCASTS LONDON PS4
TELEGRAMS: BROADCASTS LONDON TELEX TELEX: 22182

31st January 1972

Dear Keith,

Thank you for your letter. I expect I'll be able to find some more synopsis in a couple of week time. Remind me again though, would you?

Only have photos of William Hartnell. There are'nt any others, so am afraid the fans might be a little disappointed.

'Countdown' phoned me up. So I think that's okay. I will have to check with Barry. In case it is not BBC policy to advertise? You know. Still I expect it will be okay.

No letters left of Dr.Who Fan Club. I think I may get some more run off.

William Hartnell Adress: Old Mill Cottage, Old Mill Lane, Mayfield, Sussex.

The Daleks may come back. Not sure. No further official plans yets.

Glad about 20th. Looking forward to June now. Barry will be actually directing himself in the studio at Television Centre.

Yours Sincerely

Sarah

"Hope you are happy"

BRITISH BROADCASTING CORPORATION
TELEVISION CENTRE WOOD LANE LONDON W12 7RJ
TELEPHONE 01-743 8000 CABLES: BROADCASTS LONDON PS4
TELEGRAMS: BROADCASTS LONDON TELEX TELEX: 22182

3rd February 1972

Dear Keith,

Have informed 'Countdown' that it's fine by the BBC that your letter gets published. Okay?

Hope you are happy.

Yours sincerely

SARAH
ADAM

BRITISH BROADCASTING CORPORATION
TELEVISION CENTRE WOOD LANE LONDON W12 7RJ
TELEPHONE 01-743 8000 CABLES: TELECASTS LONDONPS4
TELEGRAMS: TELECASTS LONDON TELEX TELEX: 22182

17th February

Dear Keith,

Don't bother about the T-shirt. There is a Dr.Who one anyway! Coming out shortly. Anyway, it would cost you a lot in copyright fees as you said.

Super badge and pen and card. You are so good to bother so much. We are all very pleased.

Richard Franklin is Captain Mike Yates! he has been a regular in the last season!

David Troughton is son of Patrick. Saw the comedy sketch of Dave Allen show. Very funny.

Probably 20th June will be a slightly pressurised day. Barry directing the show himself that day. So probably we shall watch him in the gallery doing camera rehearsal. Then we'll have lunch. Then I'll leave you to carry on watching while I go back to the office for a couple of hours. Actually it would be better if you came after lunch at about 2'o'clock. Okay? Nearer the time we'll arrange things more definately.

Yrs sincerely
Sarah

There now follows the first four issues of DWFC Monthly. Forgive their primitive appearance, and don't worry, things improve quickly - it was a very steep learning curve!

THE DOCTOR WHO FAN CLUB MONTHLY

YOUR KIT:YOUR KIT

I hope you recieved your badge,pen, and card okay.

I sold you the kit on a "no-profit" basis.The money you sent me is exactly how much I spent on buying the kits and so I made no profit.

Throughout your membership,new productions will be advertized in this magazine.I will either offer them to you at a no-profitprice or if there is any profits made,it will go to a Spastic charity.

Anyway,I hope you like being an official D.W.F.C. member.

''''''''''''''''''''

WELCOME

TO THE D.W.F.C. MONTHLY!!! This being the first ish of the monthly,may I take this oppertunity of welcoming you to the Dr.Who Fan Club.

Since Dr.Who began back in 1963,his fans have been scattered throughout the country,waiting forthe chance to show their admiration for the most original(and long-running) series to come out of the BBC studios,Now your chance is here!

I hope to make this the biggest thing since the eiffel tower,and with your help,we can do it8

I suppose your eagerly waiting to see whats inside so I Wont keep you.

Onward,Timelords,and spread the work and dont forget to enjoy yourselves!

Keith

NOW YOU CAN READ THE EARLIEST OF THE DOCTORS ADVENTURES

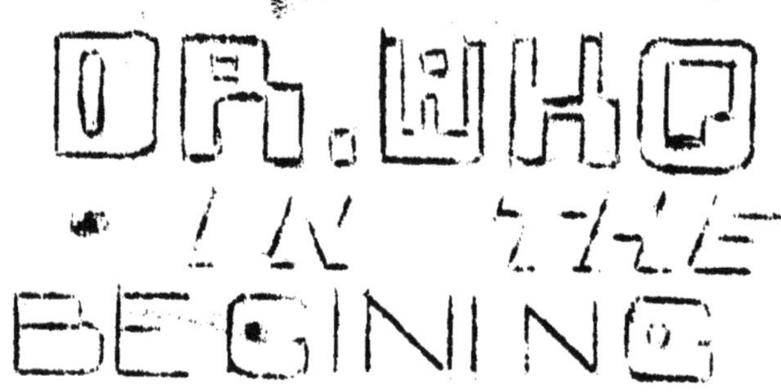

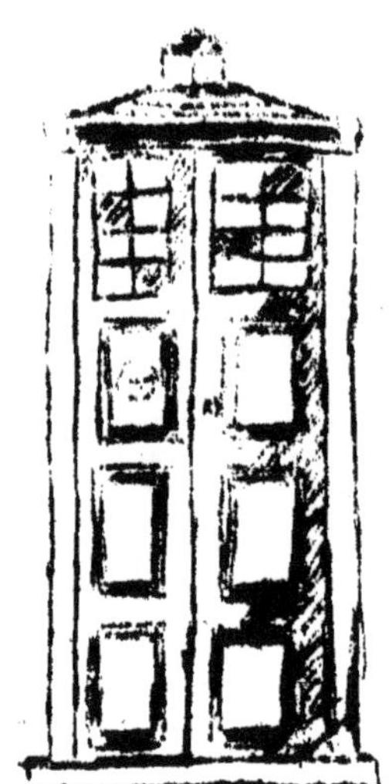

This as the title suggests, is the story from the begining. I am sure that this series will be as pop popular as the TV programme itself. So now, may I introduce the very first episode as it appeared on your TV screens, 'way back in '63.

EPISODE ONE

:starring:

William Hartnell..................Dr.Who
William russel....................Ian
Jacqueline Hill...................Barbara
and
Carol Ann Ford as Susan

....

As the clock on the school wall struck four the bell rang out it's disturbing note, much to the relief of the pupils.

The doors slammed open as the classrooms quickl emptied. Two teachers met in the corridor, all the worst for the day that had passed.

Ian Chesterton, a dark handsome man, yelled at a pupil called Jones to stop running in the corrido He turned to his associate teacher, Barbra Wright who looked absolu tly worn out.

"Everyones in a hurry these days" said Ian.

"Not quite everyone" replied Barbara, looking at a dark-haired young girl slowly walking out from her classroom.

"Problem child, eh?" asked Ian.

"No, not really. She's just...strange, thats all"

DR.WHO-IN THE BEGINING.

"What do you mean?"asked Ian.

"Well,"began Barbara"When I asked her a question today,she replied that Japan was a county in Scotland and the Spanish Armada was a castle in Greece!"

"But a twelve-year-old could answer those bett than that"

"Thats what I mean!And when I offered to take her home one night,she stopped me at a unk-yard and got out"

"Perhaps her father owns it "

"Her father is dead"said Barbara"She lives wit her grand father but I cant say where.The yard I told you about was condemned a year ago"

"Well,thres only one way to find out.Come on, my cars outside"

"You mean wre're going to follow her?"

"Thats the idea" Ian replied.

After they had locked up,and were in the car a fog developed around them and they lost sight of Susan.

"Keep going,Ian,I think I can remember the wa; Right at the next opening"

A short drive and a few wrong turnings later, they ended up at the old yard where a large noti heralding "CONDEMNED" hung loosely on the pre-fabricated wall.

Ian stopped the engine and the two sat in silence.The sky was dark and the blackness was all around them,apart from the streetlamp oppo-site the yard which cast feeble rays of light in-to the street.

"Well it's no use sitting in here"said Ian, "Lets find out whats so special about this yard"

The two stepped out of the car into the cold night air that was clouded with fog.

Ian pushed open yhee aluminium door which was unlocked,much to his surprise.Barbara followed him inside.

Around them lay all the usual objects you ex; to find in a junkyard.Then,from out of the corne of his eye,Ian saw movement in the shadows.He pushed Barbara down behind some boxes piled near-by.

THROUGHOUT THIS SERIES
Dr. Who
IS PLAYED BY:
WILLIAM HARTNELL

Before Dr.Who, William playedlots of parts in films and television, mainly the "the man you love to hate" military parts, so when Dr.Who did come along, he treated it as a real challenge.

Mr.Hartnell wasnt very interested in the science fiction part of the series but tended to go for the historical parts.

Mr.Hartnell wasnt seventeen when he started his career by touring aroung the country in Frank Bensons Shakespear Company.

Perhaps adult fans of Dr.Who will remember him IN the long-running TV series "The Army Game".

He now does a few plays and has parts in films, and may I take this occation to say thankyou to Mr.Hartnell for the good work he put into the first episodes of Dr,Who.

This section is going to be devoted entiely to YOUR letters and comments. So if YOU have anything to say concerning ANY aspect of Doctor Who, just write to me and I'll see if your letter can be fitted in.Okay?

Please address your letters to the club address which is:

TARDIS TALKBOX,
The Dr.Who Fan Club,
c/oKeith Miller,
109 Moredun Park Rd.
Edinburgh EH17 7HJ

Hope to hear from you soon,

Keith

FREE PHOTOGRAPHS!!!!!

Photographs of W.Hartnell is otainable from me.Just send an s.a.e. to the club address. Supplies are limited so it a case of first come fist served.

DR.WHO-IN THE BEGINING.

Out of a battered old police box stepped an old man with white hair, dressed as though he was in the pre-war years.

"That must be Susans grandfather"whispered Babs. "Looks a bit eccentric to me"

"Look!Its Susan!"gasped Barbara.

Around the door appeared thegirl Ian had seen earlier.She gr eted the old man in an affectionate mannerand to Ians surprise, the two of them turned round and enterd into the police box.

"He's locking her in that box!! "Ian exclaimed. "Come on,lets do the heroics"

Saying this, he jumped up and,with Barbara, and rushed through the doors.

"There he is!"shouted Ian,not noticing that the box had increased in dimensions consierably.

He pounced on the old man, pinning him to the control table in the centre of the room.The clear plastic cylinder in the centre of the table slowly began ascending and descending as the doors closed behind them.Barbara stood in astonishment at the scene that had met her eyes.

"You fool!"shouted the old man."Do you realize what you have done?"

The words did not penetrate Ians brain as he suddenly realized he was in a large room with no visible means of lighting and yet was as bright as a film studio.Deep circles were imbedded in the wall and in one of them,a TV scanner showed what was happening outside.

He could see the yard outside,but a second later it grew hazy and was finally replaced by a kaleidoscope of flashing bars of light.

"But this is impossible"said Ian slowly"We're in a police box...a five foot square police box!"

"You are in a Trans-dimensional Tardis,young man said the elderly gentleman.

"Look just who are you?"asked Ian.

"He is my gradfather and is a doctor of science answered Susan,pressing herself in a loving manne against the Doctors arm.

"Doctor Who?"

"That is of no concern of yours.You could'nt pronounce it anyway"

The Doctor walked over over to the left hand wall,opened threesof the circled partitiones in

DR. WHO-IN THE BEGINING

THE WALL AND TOOK OUT THREE stools and set them down on the steel floor.

"Be seated" ordered the Doctor.

"Look, who are you..."

"I SAID BE SEATED!!" the Doctor bellowed.

"I will now attempt an explaination as to what has happened!"

Ian looked roung to see Barbara, white and afraid. In all the con fu sion, he had forgotten all about her. He smiled, but she looked away towards the Dr. He was begining his story.

"You see, young man, my grand-daughter and I are Travellers. Not travellers as you know, but time-travellers!"

"TIME TRAVELLERS! HAH! Thats a good one!" yelled Ian. He looked at Barbara smiling. She was looking back with an expression that told Ian she Believed every word.

"You dont mean to say you believed all that? Oh, come on!"

"She is wise-She is not pigheaded, Chesterton!"

"You know my name!"

"Susan has often spoke of you!"

There was silence for a brief moment.

"Now if I maycontinue. Due to your meddling in my affairs, your are now travelling through time and space to heaven-knows-where!"

"Your a raving lunatic!" cried Ian, jumping off his stool. "Open these doors!"

"Very well. In a few minutes we will be landing, and then you shall have your proof!"

The Doctor turned his back on the party and began pressing buttons and pulling switcheson the control panel. Slowly, the cylinder sank to a halt and the Doctor anounced that they had arrived.

Outside, winds howled around the rocks and stones scattered across the barren landscape. Slowly, the shape of the police box materialized, bringing Ian and Barbara to their first adventure.

56

EPISODE TWO

THE FOURSOME EMBARK ON THEIR FIRST ADVENTURE IN THE YEAR 100,000 BC! ALL IN A BUMPER THREE EPISODE EDITION...PLUS: Some exciting news!!!!

DALEK DATA

DUE TO POPULAR DEMAND, THIS MONTHLY SERIES WILL BE DEVOTED ENTIRELY TO THE EMPIRE OF THE DALEKS

FREE PHOTOGRAPHS OF THE DALEKS!!!

If you write NOW to me , enclosing a stamped address envelope, and I'll send you a photograph. But remember, supplies are limited and so dont be too disappointed if I run out. But if you act now I'm sure you'll be seeing your photo soon.

INCIDENTAL INFORMATION

The Daleks are, at time of going to press, now battling Dr. Who in Contdown-Priced 5p.

Good luck to all the fans that entered the Dalek Competition in Radio Times. Results are to be published soon.

Did you know that Terry Nation gave the Daleks their name ater seeing the index of a Encyclopedia.-DAL-LEK.

More info next month.

The History of the Daleks
by
David Thomas.

Before the Great Explosion, a grotsque race known as the Daleks lived in peace with another strange race called the Thals.

Then, on the day of the Great Explosion, a neuclear blast sent waves of radio-activity skimming over the planets surface.

In the City, home of the Daleks, the inhabitants screamed in pain as their bodies began a process of mutillation. In haste, protective shells were built to avoid further mutilation. But by the time the creatures built these shells, all that remained was their brains.

Although all the Daleks managed to retreat into their shells, the thought of death was firmly implanted on their brains.

FOR THIS MONTH ONLY!!!A dossier on the man who plays the leading role in our fantastic TV prog.

....

Jon Pertwee stands 6ft.3 ins. tall and is the age of 51, which I may say ,he dosent look it. He Is married to a German lady whose name is Ingeborg and they have two children, Dariel and Sean.

Mr.Pertwee has a house in Barnes, Londonandnot too far away from the BBC Studios.

Mr. Pertwees hobbies are collecting, ancient souvenirs such as bows and arrows ,sculptures and other primitive works.Also he dives for treasure when on holiday in Ibiza.

On the screen, Dr. Who is always inventing new gadgets to conquer the invaders from outer space. Off screen, Jon is also one of the gadgets kings. He even peiced together a diving machine for use when on holiday.Oh yes, and the Technical talk also goes with the actions.

When out on location, people always refer to him as Doctor Who.I've often wondered if Mr.Pertwee ever gets tired of people calling him the space age doctor rather than his own name?

Mr. Pertwee is an all-round actor.He has wrked in all aspects of entertainment such as TV.radio, night clubs, films("House That Dripped Blood"), and is now making a record!!!

Jon took over the part of the Doctor from Patrick Troughton in 1970 and is in my opinion, the best Dr.Who ever, closely followed by William Hartnell .I hope Mr.Pertwee is going to carry on the good job and the programme to even greater heights than ever before.I'm sure he will.

CHAPTER ONE.

The Doctor and Jo were, as usual, in the lab trying to improve on the circutry of the Tardis.

"Doctor," asked Jo, "Why dont you just pack all th in and just settle down on Earth?"

"Never, Jo. I'm a traveller and always will be. I've never settled down and I'll never settle down as long as I have the Tardis." answered the I fixing a couple of screws with his screwdriver or the Dematerialization Circut.

"There, that should do it. Now maybye I shall be able to make a pinpoint landing in the Tardis."

He turned to the police box.

"I'm going to make a test run now. Want to come?

"As long as your sure you can get me back in on peice." answered Jo.

"I'm sure I don't know what you mean, Jo. You'd think I was frequently landing in places of dange or something." said the Doctor looking at Jo rathe ashamed.

"Oh, all right. Ltes get going then."

The duo opened the doors of the Tardis and ente ed. WellThe Doctor walked over to the conrol table and placed the circuit in its proper place.

"Now, here goes."

As the sound of some primeval beast filled the air of the lab, the Tardis left Earth once again in search of a new adventure.

THE TERROR OF TALOS

"Where are we going, Doctor?"asked Jo.

"Rigel 9.Aplanet in the second quadrent of Exilius"

"Pardon??"

"Never mind,Jo.We'll be arriving soon"

Just then,the Tardis materialized in a round roofed building made of a shiny metal similar to aluminium.A smell of static electricity hung in the air. The doors of the police box swung open and the Doctor and Jo stepped out.

"You did'nt tell me it was populated,Doctor" said Jo.

"Well...eeh.."

"You dont mean to say it isnt.Oh,Doctor,you've done it again,havent you?"

"Life could have evolved since I was here last"

"But it's highly unlikely,mm?"continued Jo.

"Mmm,I suppose it is really"answered the Doctor "But this place is strangely remeniscent of the Dalek city on Skaro"

"DALEKS!Come on Doctor.We're not staying a moment longer in this place"

"Do'nt worry,Jo"comforted the Doctor"I'm sure we're many light years away from that particular planetIn fact,this planet has probably been deserted for years!"

Behind them,a familiar shape cast a long ,evil shadow as a door opened in the wall,revealing , not the Daleks as first thought,but another of the Doctors bitter enemies.The race of Inhumans known as the Cybermen!

CHAPTER TWO NEXT MONTH!!!

FREE PHOTOGRAPHS!

Photographs of Jon Pertwee and Jo are obtainable from me.Just send a stamped address envelo to the club address(see "Tardis Talkbox") and [illegible] supplies are limited so send now!

D.W.F.C. CROSSWORD

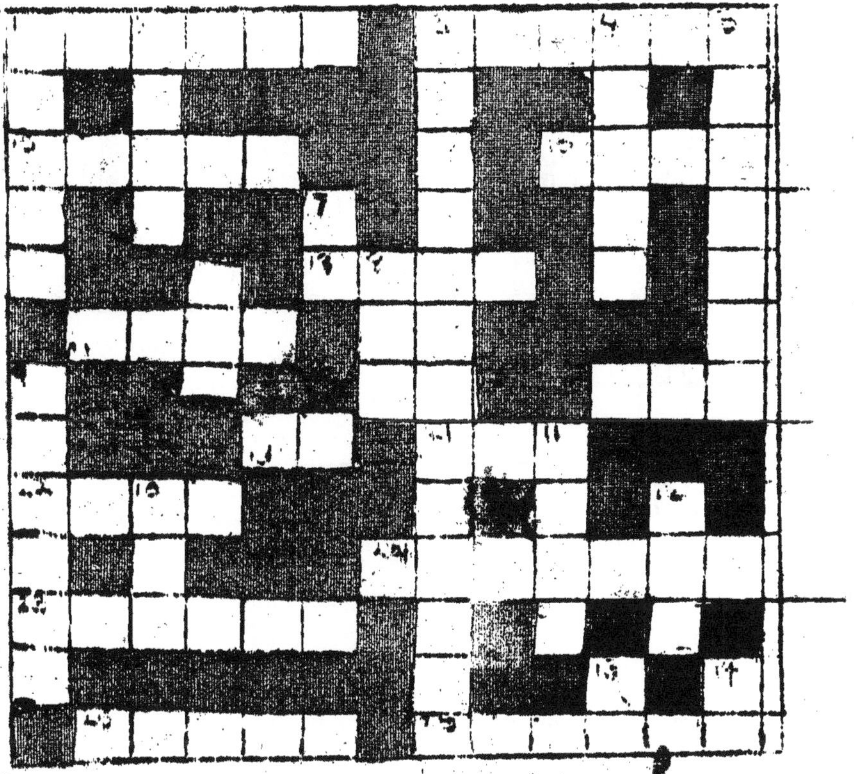

DOWN.

I."Terror of ....."
2.To get up.
3.What the Tardis does when it dissappeares.
4.Our Planet.
5.Brigadear Leth-bridge ......
6.What Benton calls his Commanding Officer.
7.All right.
8.Everything.
9.A stone from space.
IO.After April.
II.Big stone.
I2.Not to stand.
I3.An Indescribable Terror.
I4.... an alternitive.

ACROSS.

I.Doctor Who's Spaceship
8.Occupants of Skaro.
I5.Ray gun.
I6.Not true.
I7.The Brigadears army.
I8.Miss Grant.
I9.Britain.
20.Not in.
2I.Gas we breath.
22.Dr.Who travels thru' it.
23.Hydrogen plus this makes water.
24.Piece of elecrtronic
25.Shows time.
26.Who's first name.
6

Answers next month.

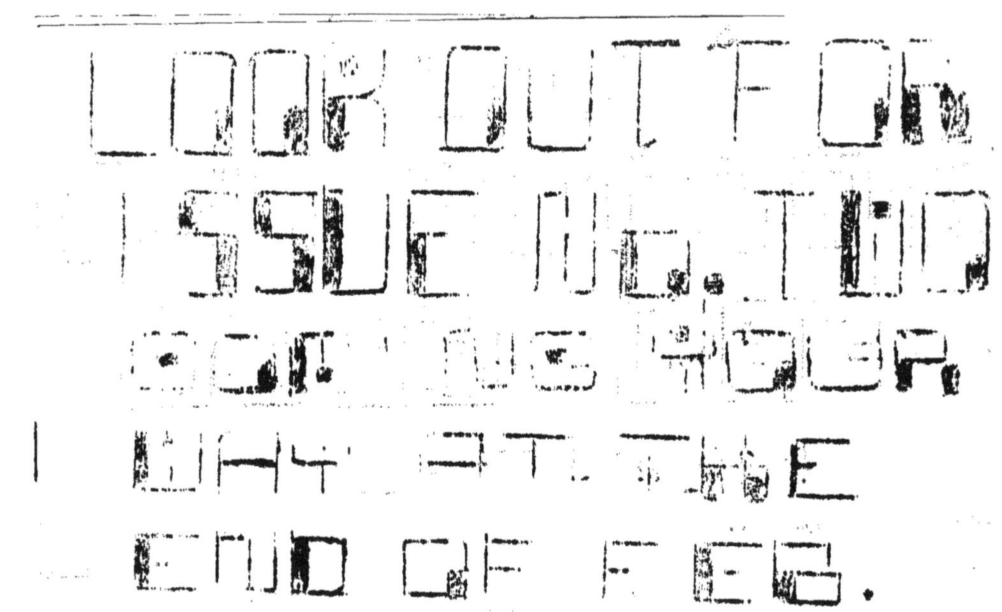
LOOK OUT FOR
ISSUE No. TWO
COMING YOUR
WAY AT THE
END OF FEB.

AND I PROMISE THE PRINTING WILL BE BETTER THAN
THIS MONTH.

IN IT WILL BE:

CHAPTER TWO OF THE TERROR OF TALOS.

EPISODES 2,3 AND 4 OF Dr.WHO-IN THE BEGINING..

PART TWO OF THE HISTORY OF THE Daleks

and

A scale map of Skaro,home of the Daleks.

plus

Some exciting news for all DALEK fans.

See you then,

Keith

BRITISH BROADCASTING CORPORATION
TELEVISION CENTRE WOOD LANE LONDON W12 7RJ
TELEPHONE 01-743 8000 CABLES: TELECASTS LONDONPS4
TELEGRAMS: TELECASTS LONDON TELEX TELEX: 22182

25th Feb.1972

Dear Keith,

Jolly good! What a super friendly newsletter. Good for you! Send the postal order back to you 'coz apparently you can cash yourself. If you have any trouble send it back to me and I'll send you the 20pence. Okay? But sure you will have no trouble. I phoned the post office myself and they said it was no trouble at all to cash these P.O.'s.

Keep well.

Yours sincerely,

Sarah

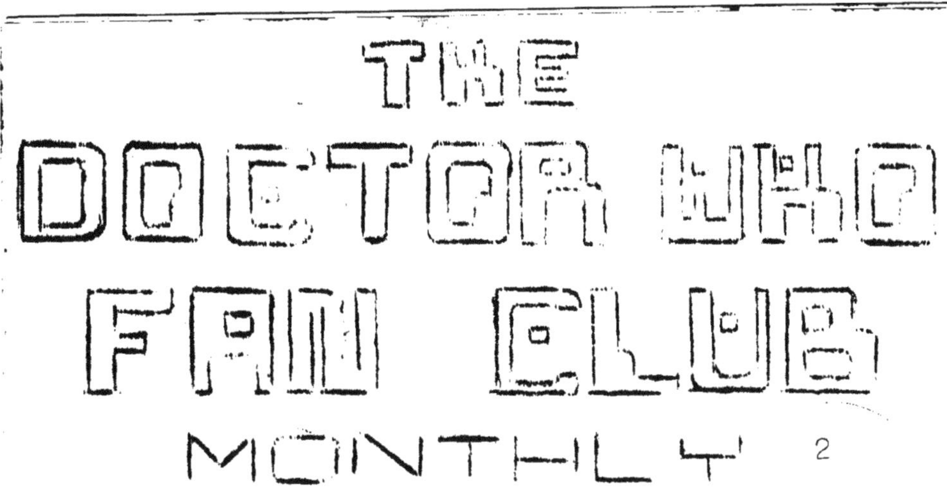

REVIEW CURSE of PELADON.

After every adventure, I shall be putting forward my views on it. You can air your views via "Tardis Talkbox".

The Curse of Peladon was exceptionally good. It brought back the Tardis for the second time since Jon Pertwee took over the part of the Doctor. By the way, David Troughton took the part of Peladon, and is the son of Patrick Troughton.

The Ice Warriors were always at the back of my mind as the sabateours. Surprisingly, it was the delagate called Arcturus.

I think the friendship between Jo and Peladon could have been developed into something more than was seen. Either Jo and Paladon gets married or Peladon joins the Doctor and Jo on their travells. It would have been rather amusing to see Peladon trying to adapt to Earths way of lif

Thats my view, Whats yours? If you disaree or agree with me, Just write to "Tardis Talkbox"

Next Review I'll be loking back at the "SEA DEVILS"

DR. WHO - IN THE BEGINING

EPISODE TWO.

"Open the doors"yelled Ian"Iwant to get back to my digs.My landlady will be throwing fits"

"Cheston,"said the Doctor"Dont you realise that we are probably in another time in your distant future or past"

"Rubbish!"exclaimed Ian"NOW OPEN THE DOORS!!!"

The Doctor shook his head in despair and pressed a row of black buttons on the control table. Ian took a step back as doors slowly swung open. Ian stood speachless at the sight that met his eyes.Barbara came to his side.

"I knew he was telling the truth"she said.

The Doctor and Susan joined them at the doors.

"I know it's hard for you to understand what has happened.I'm sorry,Chesterton"

The Doctor eased past them out of thTardis and out into the Strange landscape. Ian and the two girls followed.Ian stopped and looked back at the police box.

"Five foot police box.."he mumbled.

"Come on,Chesterton,"said the Doctor"Lets investigate.Are you coming along?"

He turned to Barbara and Susan. They looked at each other with a doubtfull expresion.They returned their eyes to the Doctorand for the first time since they left the school,Barbara smiled at Ian.

"We'll come with you"replied Susan.

"Theres some caves over there,"Said the Doctor, "Lets look"

They clammerd over the stones until they reached thecaves.

"Shall we go inside?"asked Ian.

"Okay,but I think your lady associatte had better stay out here.All right,my dear?"said the Doctor.He turned round."Chesterton!Its Barbara! Shes gone!!!

EPISODE THREE.

"Where could she have gone?"asked the Doctor.
"Well thats a stupid question,"said Ian."She's been taken somewhere by somebody!Look Doctor. Just where are we?"
"As far as I can tell,We're in the year 100,000 B.C."
"100,000 BC!Thats incredible!Did life exist then?"
"I do not wish to worry you ,Chesterton but I happen to know that Barbara ,if she has been taken by the human occupants of this age,she is in terrible danger!"
In the time that the Doctor andIan had been talking,Susan had been exploring the caves and found that the cave continued deep into the hill.
"Grand-father!"called Susan"There are footprints leading into the hill!"
Susan was quickly joined by the Doctor and Ian They followed the footprints down into a huge cavern where Cavemen danced like huge apes around a platform where Barbara was strapped and abov e her lomed a bed of sharpened Stag-mites.

EPISODE FOUR.

Acaveman was just about to cut the rope that held up the death-trap when Ian jumped out of the shadows.Everything fell silent for one fatal moment.All eyes were on Ian.Suddenly, Ian sprung on the platform,pulled of thr straps and pushed Barbara out of the way,not a moment t too late as the stalagmites smashed onto the hard stone.The cavemen were running riot.
"Get back to the ship!"said Ian,"I'll hold them off."
"But..."
"Go on!!!"yelled Ian.
The trio turned and back towards the Tardis. They reached it and went inside.Five minutes passed with no sign of Ian.Barbara watched eagerly at the screen.
"Whats keeping hi..Doctor!!Look! "
Barbara had spotted Ian stumbling across the screen.Eventually,Ian Burst in through the doors and the Doctor operated the controols.

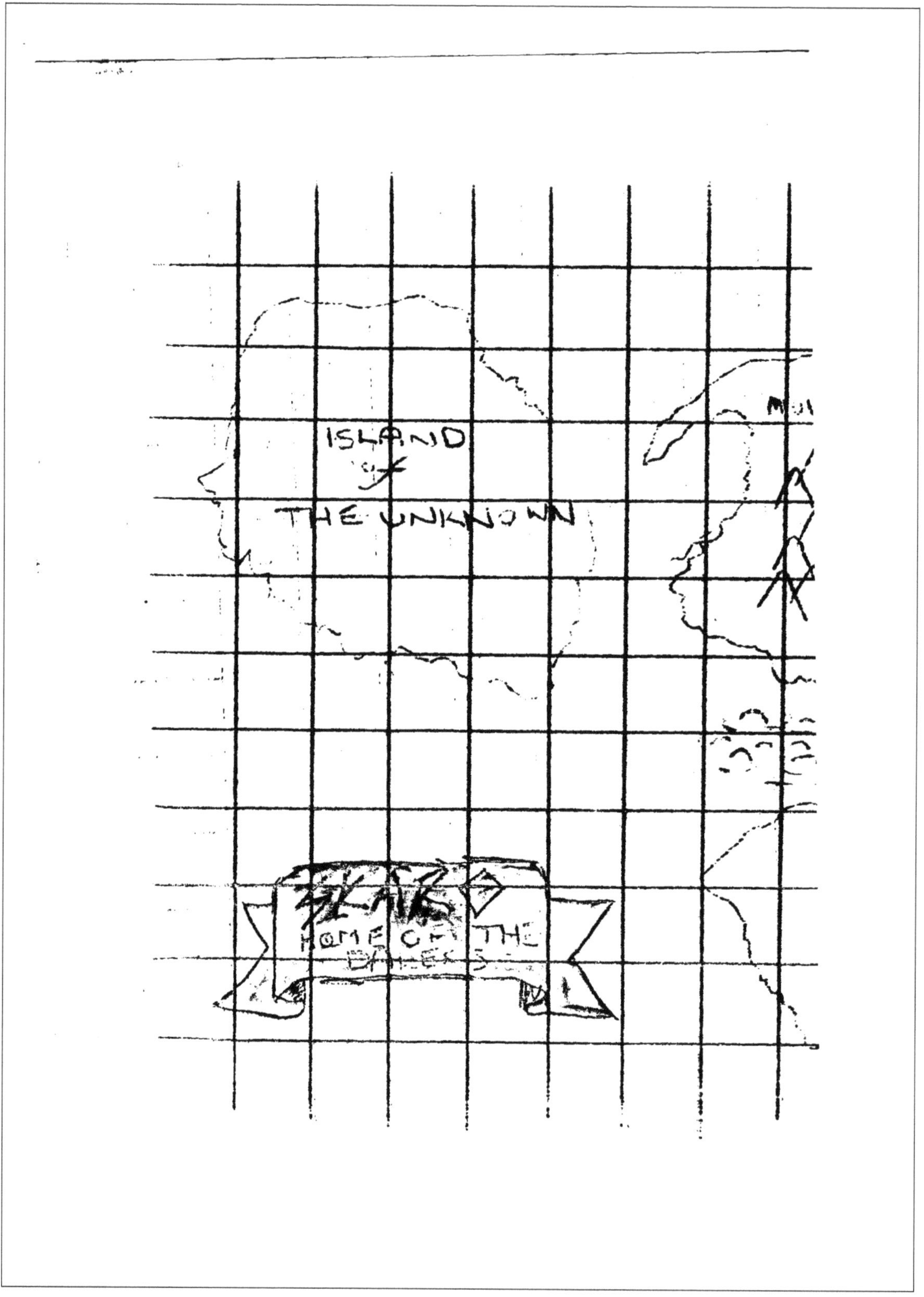
ISLAND
of
THE UNKNOWN
HOME OF THE

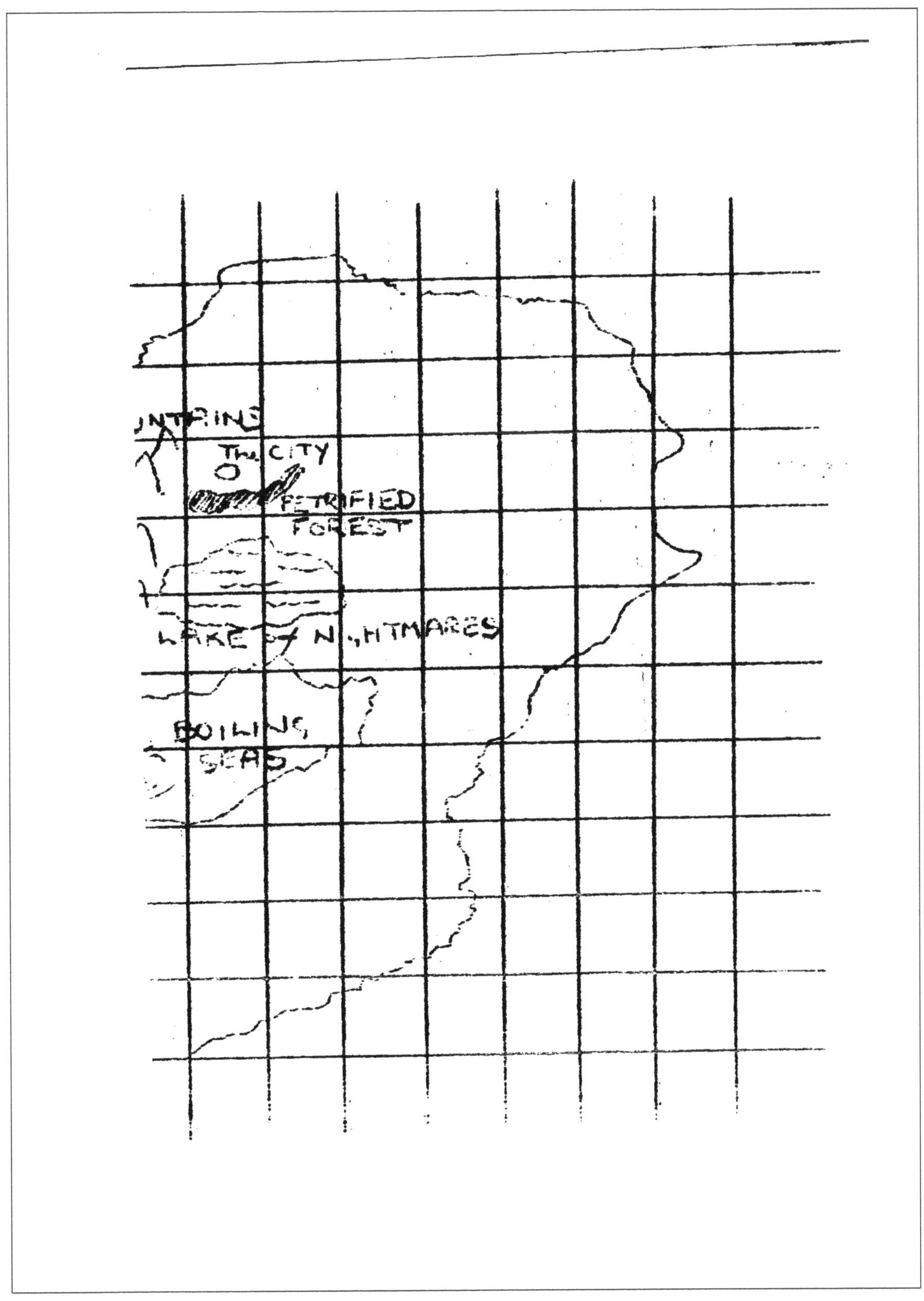
THE CITY
O
PETRIFIED
FOREST
LAKE OF NIGHTMARES
BOILING
SEAS

CHAPTER TWO.

As you will remember, last issue we left the Doctor and Jo in the hands of the Cyberman.

....

The Cyberman put a cold, steel hand on Jo's shoulder. Jo jumped and spun round.
"Doctor. We have company" she said.
"Have we? Oh, thats goo...oh, no..." the Doctor said as he saw who the company was. The The Cyberman gestured for them to walk outside. They obeyed.
"They don't seem very friendly" said Jo. She looke at the Doctor.
"No, they arent. I'm afraid weVve stumbled onto some, more of my..ahem..friends, Jo"
"Not again! First the Daleks. Then the Ice Warrior and now thw these...things"
"Cyberman, Jo"
They stepped outside the domed building and found that the structure was in fact a cell in a huge honeycomb.
"Were on Talos, Jo. The original home of the Cyber men. I visited here once before. I was slightly different then"
"You mean you were the Doctor MarkOne?"
"Mark two, Jo" answered the Doctor.
Suddenly, the Cyberman grabbed JO and placed a flat square object on her forehead.
"Jo! What have you done to her?"
The Cyberman then produced another square and, after a struggle, fixed it firmly to the Doctors forehead.
"Doctor" said Jo, "I can here what he's thinking"
"These must be some kind of thought wave exch- changer"
"Be silent" hissed the Cyberm an "And walk. I will give you the directions"
After a long journey through endless and twist- ing corridors, they arrived at a huge hall.
"Hello, Doctor," Said a voice. The Doctor turned to come face to face with the Master.

DALEK DATA

AS YOU WILL HAVE SEEN THERE IS A SPECIAL MAP INCLUDED IN THIS MONTHS ISSUE. HOPE YOU LIKE IT.

HISTORY OF THE DALEKS.

Chapter Two.

Meanwhile, the Thals were in their primitive homes when the wave of radiation hit them. Their features changed from a grotesque animal into a humans face.

Their minds, like the Daleks, changed, but went towards peace and not violence like their one time associattes.

The Daleks fitted weapons onto their shells and rejected the Thals from the City.

The Daleks then made plans for a universal master scheme to be foiled many times by one man.

The Plan: The Domination of the Universe.

The Man: Doctor Who.

A BIGGER AND MORE DETAILED VERSION OF THE DALEK HISTORY WILL BE PRODUCED IN THE VERY NEAR FUTURE.

CONGRATULATIONS!!

May I offer my congratulations to the winners of the Dalek Competion in Radio Times Under 10 Winners were Class 1M of Balgowan Primary School, Beckenham in Kent.

The over 10 winner was Peter Klosin, Brixham, South Devon.

INCIDENTAL INFORMATION

To all those of you who have written asking about the Mini Album produced by 21st Century Records, I'm sorry to dissappiont you but I'm afraid that the company has closed down.

The Daleks have been featured in two films. "Dr. Who and the Daleks" and "The Daleks in 2064" (or a title to that effect)

MORE INFO NEXT MONTH.

SUPER NEWS!!!

IN NEXT MONTHS ISSUE!!!! THE STORY OF "Dr. Who and the Daleks" AS IT WAS SEEN ON YOUR TELE-VISION SCREENS NINE YEARS AGO.

TARDIS TALKBOX!!

Send your letters to:
TARDIS TALKBOX,
DOCTOR WHO FAN CLUB,
c/oKEITH MILLER,
109 MOREDUN PARK RD.,
EDINBURGH EH17 7HJ.

I'm starting the column off with some letters from fans who asked questions with their appication letters.

Dear Sir,
Why are the Daleks on T.V. different to those in the film's?
Adrian Burch,
Middlesex.

The Daleks were different simply TO BE just that. Different!

A Drawing by Christopher Lynch.

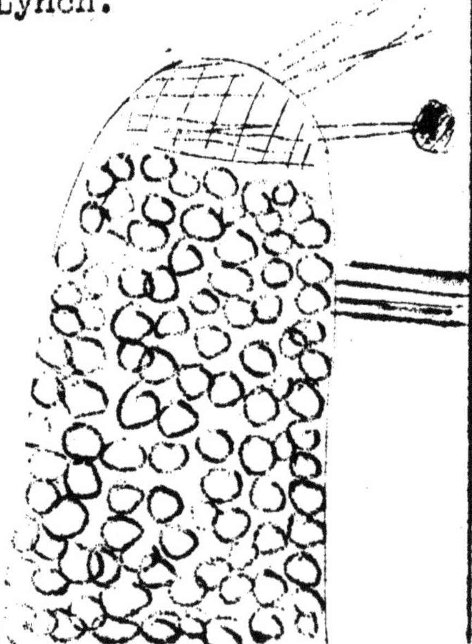

NEXT ISSUE

"THE DEAD PLANET"

EPISODES 1 of the first adventure of Dr. Who introducing the DALEKS!

"The TERROR OF TALOS"

CHAPTER THREE OF THE SERIAL!!

AND LOTS MORE

CROSSWORD.

ACROSS.

1.Tardis 3.Daleks 15. Laser 16.True 17.UNIT 18.Katy 19.UK.20.Out 21.Air 22Time 23Oxygen 24.Circuit Clock 26 Doctor.

DOWN.

1.Talos 2.Rise 3.Dematerialized 4.Earth 5.Stewart 6.Sir 7.OK 8.All 9.Meteor 10.May 11.Rock 12.Sit 13.It 14.So

BRITISH BROADCASTING CORPORATION
TELEVISION CENTRE WOOD LANE LONDON W12
TELEPHONE 01-743 8000 CABLES: BROADCASTS LONDON PS4
TELEGRAMS: BROADCASTS LONDON TELEX TELEX: 22182

7th March 1972

Dear Keith,

Before I answer your questions, do you think you could in future, wrap up your Newsletters when you send them to me a little more tightly, coz they keep falling out! The BBC postroom keeps phoning me up to complain, so do you think you could devise some other method for their dispatch? Sorry about this, but BBC is very touchy how things go out, especially as it says 'Dr.Who ' on the back, people know that is the BBC.

Dr.Who Annual '72 is in the making now. Roughly due out in September. The old Annuals I've never even seen. I doubt if there will be any spare ones, but I'll check up and see.

Doesn't matter when you get the Newsletter out at all. Your exams come first, blow the club. They'll understand, if you mention it in your last newsletter before your exams and say that there will be a period when you won't be able to answer letters quite so quickly. Okay? The first recordings of Dr.Who are all wiped, tape that is, they may exist on film which enterprises use for selling abroad. But usually, video tapes of old Dr.Who's are wiped after roughly three/four years, but there is always a copy of it on film, as Enterprises have a fantastic library. * Of course, the very first Dr.Who's probably don't exist now. I should think they are very scratchy!

Keep well and happy yourself. Haven't got a picture, but we'll be seeing you shortly anyway! 3 months!

Sincerely

SARAH

* All Jon Pertwee's Dr. Who's exist on tape. That is from 'Spearhead from Space' which

Multi-Millionaire Earth

Q *How old is the Earth and how can its age be determined?*

Leonard Walters, London SE26

A It is difficult to say exactly how old the Earth is. Clocks are an Earth invention and the age of the solar system could seem quite small when viewed from another galaxy. However, scientists now believe that the Earth, and the other bodies of the solar system, are roughly the same age—about 4500 million years old.

This figure was arrived at by the use of a similar process to that which is used to determine the age of archeological objects. It works like this: radioactive elements, such as uranium, can be studied to find out the rate at which they have decayed over the centuries. A sample, such as a piece of rock or a specimen of deep-sea sediment, will contain traces of these elements. By testing the sample with an instrument called a mass spectrograph, the scientist can determine the length of time for which the decay has been taking place. This figure is then compared to a reading from a meteorite—a body which lacks these decaying elements.

The result of this comparison enables the scientist to date the specimen fairly accurately. In the case of the age of the Earth, this is to within only a few thousand million years!

Dr. Who Fan Club

Dear Editor,

As you publish stories on the adventures of Dr. Who, perhaps readers would be interested in the Dr. Who Fan Club. All they have to do is to send a stamped addressed envelope to my address and details will be forwarded.

Keith Miller,
109 Moredun Park Road,
Edinburgh EH17 7HJ

Each week on this page I'll print letters, news items, puzzles, and pictures. Write in with your questions on any subject, scientific or mechanical—I'll try to answer the best ones and will pay £1 for each letter printed.

Moondust Discovery

DUST samples brought back from the Moon by the American Apollo 11 astronauts and the Russian unmanned probe, Luna 16, have been studied by Soviet scientists.

Some surprising discoveries have been made by experts in geochemistry (the study of the chemical composition of soil). Analysis of the Moondust under an electronic x-ray spectroscope has revealed that iron in the samples is more resistant to oxygen than iron on the Earth.

This is a very important discovery, for it means that Lunar iron has a much greater resistance to corrosion.

There's nothing new about corrosion-free metal—stainless steel has been around for a long time. But stainless steel is very expensive to produce and it lacks the strength of ordinary steel. This greatly limits its applications and emphasises the need for a cheap rustless metal.

So scientists are now trying to produce this rustless Lunar iron under artificial conditions on Earth. If they succeed, another important 'spin-off' can be added to the list of space discoveries which have benefited mankind.

Good Heavens!

THE Goodyear airship 'Europa' is now fully inflated and ready for its test flight at the end of this month. This 192-ft. long monster craft is 59 ft. high and is raised by 202,700 cubic feet of lighter-than-air, non-inflammable helium gas.

Similar craft in the United States (shown here) have made unexpected appearances at major sporting events, causing widespread wonder at the impressive sight.

A practical application for the craft could be to relay messages over cities. In New York, Goodyear's Mayflower airship is equipped with a 'Skytacular' night sign, which has 3080 coloured lights presenting a panorama of messages and animation. During a recent drought, messages flashed to New Yorkers warned of the importance of saving water.

If you've never seen an airship, then you could have a chance very soon. For the giant 'Europa' is ahead of schedule and no one can be sure when or where this aerial ambassador will be seen.

● ● ● ●

Soviet astrophysicists have calculated that comets in outer space throw off up to 2000 million tons of solid particles a year.

THE DOCTOR WHO FAN CLUB MONTHLY

REVIEW THE SEA DEVILS

The second in my reviews concerns the monsters from the deep, the Sea Devils. This adventure saw the return of the Doctors arch-enemy - The Master. The plot was godd (as all Dr. Who stories are) and was exciting from the first episode to the last.

The Sea Devils may possibly be a serious rival in popularity for Daleks.

The best episode, undoubte dly, was the last one. The boat race was great and the use of the hover-craft was cleverly done, although I doubt Jo would have been able to operate such a comkicated form of transport.

The Master, as always, managed to escape, but with the impession they gave in the Radio Times Ithought the Master was going to be eliminated once and for all!

Still, the programme would'nt be the same now without knowing that the Master would be popping up again sometime in the future.

Thats my opinion, whats yours? Write and tell me, care off Tardis Talkbox. Next month: "The Mutants".

SPECIAL DALEK ISSUE

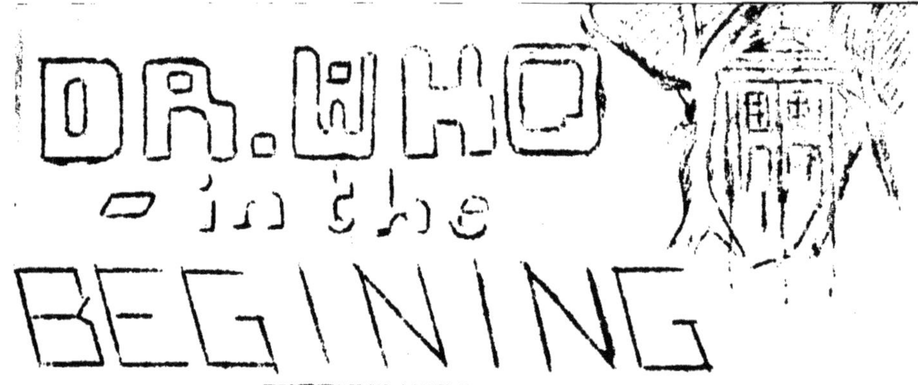

THE MUTANTS
EPISODE ONE.
starring

William Hartnell....................Dr.Who
illiam Russel.......................Ian
Jaqueline Hill ....Barbara
Carol Ann Ford......................Susan

Ian sat down on one of the stools situated y the control console.The Doctor looked up.

"Feeling better?"he asked.

"Yes..But it's no joke having a tirbe of blood hirsty cavemen charging after you."

"Never mind",said Susan,"Youll feel better after ou've eaten".

Susan then walked over to a large machine covred on one side with pushbuttons and small bulbs, he called it the food machine.

"What would you like?"she asked.

"Bacon and eggs,if you have them".

Susan pressed a few buttons.After a few seconds here was a loud buzz and a bar of some kind of hite substance dropped down onto a paper plate.

"This is bacon and eggs?!Looks more like a sick ars Bar"Ian exclaimed.

Gingerly,Ian bit a piece off the corner.

"Eggs!"he whispered,"And bacon!"

After they had eaten,the Doctor again returned o the control table and began pushing buttons and pulling levers.Lights flickered in the transarent column as it slowly sank down into the onsole.

"Weve landed",announced the Doctor,turning on the scanner.

DR.WHO-IN THE BEGINING.

Outside was a a dark grey world of ash-coloure trees and blue-black skies which could just be seen through the spaces at the top of the trees.

"Is it safe to go outside?"asked Barbara.

"Yes...yes I think so,"answered the Doctor. "Check the air content meter,Susan".

Silently,she crossed over to the side of the control console nearest the doors.

"Everything normal,Grandfather".

"Well,it seems weve made our second succesfull landing".

He opened the doors and stepped outside.His foot sank into the ground with a hollow crunch. Ian followed him with Susan and Barbara.

"Looks as if there's been some huge forest fire.What do you think,Doctor?"asked Ian.

Suddenly,someone to Ians right screamed.He spun round on one heel to find Barbara gone. He then sped into the forest,smashing into branches which disintegrated into dust.He stopped Suddenly when he broke through into a clearing where he found Barbara standing,terrified, staring at an alien beast which lay behind some underbrush.Just then,The Doctor and Susan appeared beside him.Barbara slowly made her way towards the trio.The object did'nt move.

"I think it's dead "said Susan.

She was right.Like all the other things on the planet,it was lifeless.Ian pushed back some branches and exclaimed

"Doctor.Look!"

What he saw was a massive city,made entirely out of metal that reflected the light of the planets above them.

"Can't see any sign of life",said the Doctor, "Come on,Chesterton,lets investigate."

Ian grabbed the Doctors arm.

"OOh,no,"he said"not again.The last time we "went investigating" we ended up being chased by a group of howling savages.Come on ,Doctor, back to the ship".

They journyed back and closed the doors.The

Dr.Who-In The Beginning.

Doctor then proceeded to dematerialise but instead of the smooth up and down movement of the central cylinder, it jerked erratically in its movements. The Doctor flipped a switch and all was quiet. He bent down and lifted one of the panels beneath the console.

"Oh, dear", said the Dr., "One of the fluid links have fractured and I havent any Mercury to fill it up again."

"So?" said Ian.

"So, my dear boy, that means we are stranded on this planet!"

EPISODE 2NEXT MONTH!!!!!

COMING SOON!

THE D.W.F.C. SUMMER SPECTACULAR

FEATURING "THE STORY OF THE DALEKS"

SEE SPECIAL AD NEXT MONTH!

TARDIS TALKBOX

All letters intended for publication should be sent to:
Tardis Talkbox,
D.W.F.C.,
c/o K.Miller,
109 Moredun Park Rd.
Edinburgh EH17 7HJ

Dear Keith,

Will you be doing a review on "The Day of the Daleks"?

Sean Gibbons,
Co.Donegal.

DearSean,

There will be a review on that particular adventure in the "D.W.F.C. Summer Spectacular" (see ad on this page)

Drawing by Andrew Veasey.

DALEK DATA

[illegible]

"DR.WHO AND THE DALEKS"

and

"THE DALEK INVASION:2[illegible]"

The two Dalek films made by Regal Films have been re-released and are at present touring the country. If you havent already seen them,I advise you to go. I've seen them three times and each time has been just as enjoyable.

The D.W.F.C. Summer Spectacular will feature "The Story of the Daleks!"Out soon!

The Daleks are still featured in Countdown(Now T.V.Action) Priced 5p.

MORE INFO NEXT MONTH!!!!!

DRAWINGS WANTED:

Seeing that all you fans are Leonardo Di Vinci's and some drawings have been coming into Tardis T[illegible] and so there is going to be a special section devoted to your drawings.AND THEY DON'T HAVE TO BE OF DALEKS.Most of the drawings I have are of Daleks.If you draw something different you'll have a better chance of having it published.

FILM PHOTOGRAPHS........

There are still some(not many,photo's of the Daleks still available.S.A.E. please.

If you think the Daleks in a special edition of the newsletter is a good idea, look out in this column for some more great news in a couple of months time.

The story in "Dr.Who-In The Begining" is the story on which the film"Dr.Who and the Daleks" was based.

If on this page you would like to see a serial story, just write to me and tell me what kind of stories you would like to read.(e.g. The Daleks invading London or the Daleks verses the Arcturans or something completly different,

IMPORTANT ANNOUNCEMENT!!!

During the next few weeks, I won't be able to answer your letters as quickly as I usually do,but do not fret ,all letters will be answered.

ANOTHER [illegible] DALEK ISSUE [illegible] WITH THE [illegible] OF THE [illegible],AND SPECIAL ANNOUNCEMENT ABOUT THE D.W.F.C. S.S.See you then!

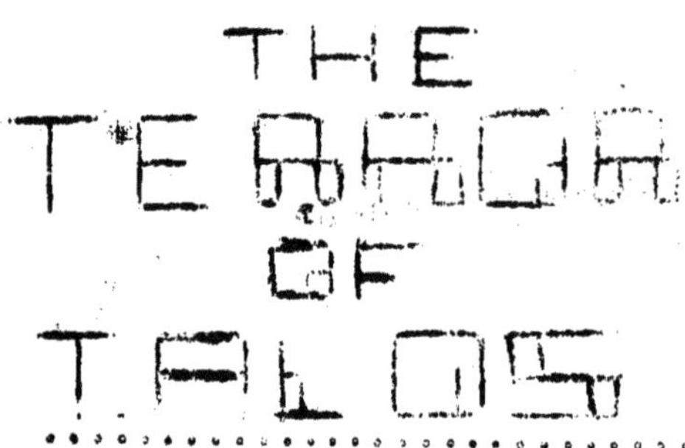

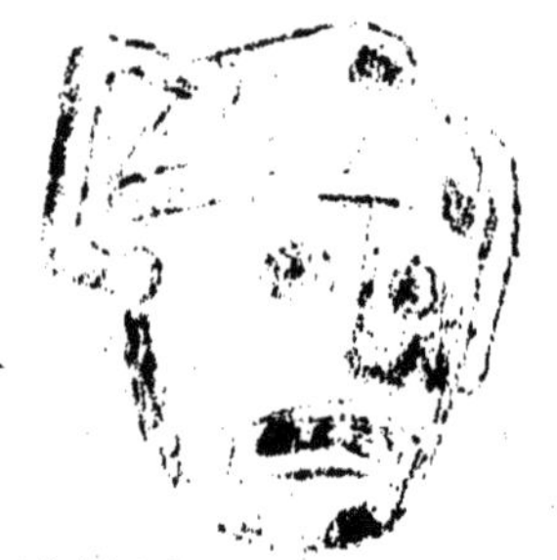

The Doctor has met two of his old enemies on Talos; the Cybermen and the Master!!

"I might have known I'd bump into you. What are you? Some kind of magnet?" asked the Doctor.

"Very humourous, Doctor. I see my friends have been taking care of you!"

The Doctor shot a quick glance at the Cyberman behind him.

"I suppose you're their leader now?"

"However did you guess? Take them away! I shall dispose of them later. But now... it's time to contact the [illegible] force..."

The Doctor and Jo were then pushed out of the main chamber along a short tunnel, and were then pushed out of the winding corridor and then into one of the prison cells. Jo gave a weary sigh and sat down on one the metal boxes, placed at random in the room.

"Oh, Doctor. Why can't we land somewhere peaceful and as far away from another living creature as possible?"

"One day, Jo... one day... Meanwhile, lets find out what the Master is up to this time."

Saying this, he took out his sonic screwdriver and began to unscrew a metal plaque, behind which operated the mechanism that kept the door firmly shut.

Suddenly, a searing dart of pain shot up his arm; the [illegible] against any who meddle with the mechanism. He collapsed in a heap onto the floor.

"Doctor!" gaped Jo, "Doctor, are you alright?"

"Yes... yes, Jo... I'm fine... fine..." answered the Doctor cradling his arm.

"But how are we going to get out of here if we can't [illegible] that metal plate off the wall!"

Already the Doctor's brain was calculating forces and electronic figures.

"That's it!" he exclaimed, after five minutes of silence. "Jo, over here, quickly!"

THE TERROR OF TALOS.

She knelt down beside himas he took from his pocket a long piece of copper wire.

"When I give the word,press the exposed head of the wire against the door."

Jo agreed and the Doctor then proceeded to twist the other end of the wire around his srewdriver.

"All right,Jo?"

She nodded.

"NOW!"he exclaimed,pressing the blade of the instrument firmly into the srewhead.

There was a flash ,then an explosion and Jo was thrown clear to the other side of the room.

"I'm sorry,my dear,"said the Doctor,"but it worked.Look,"he pointed to the door ,in the middle of which was blown a large hole.

"Luckily,there was no guard left behind,"continued the Doctor,"they are all probably in the Main hall.Come on,Jo, it's time we met the Master and his collegues for the last time."

The Doctor helped Jo up and they both stepped through the hole into the empty corridor.Suddenly,the squares on their foreheads began to howl.

"Doctor!The..The noise is deafening!"

Jo pushed her hands tightly over her ears to try and block out the high-pitched whine which echoed down the corridor.

"They must have built in some kind of alarm system,"screamed the Doctor."Hold still,Jo."

The Doctor grabbed the square on Jo's head and pulled sharply downwards.It ripped off with a squeal as its powerpack was jarred from it's socket.

Meanwhile,The Master was about to make contact with the Cybermen Task Force when the alarm siren filled the air.

"Just what I need!"snarrled the Master,"You!Take over from me while I attend to this matter.I'll make sure this never happens again."

The corridor plunged into silenceas the Doctor managed to rip off his own square.He grabbed Jo by the Arm.

"Come on,Jo,"he said,"This place is going to be swarming with Cybermen."

"I'm afraid you're too late,Doctor!"

The Doctor turned round to face the Master and ten of the Cybermen.He held a gun and the trigger was pressed, sending a laser beam towards the Doctor.He collapsed onto the floor."

"Dont bother to lift him up,my dear.He's dead!"

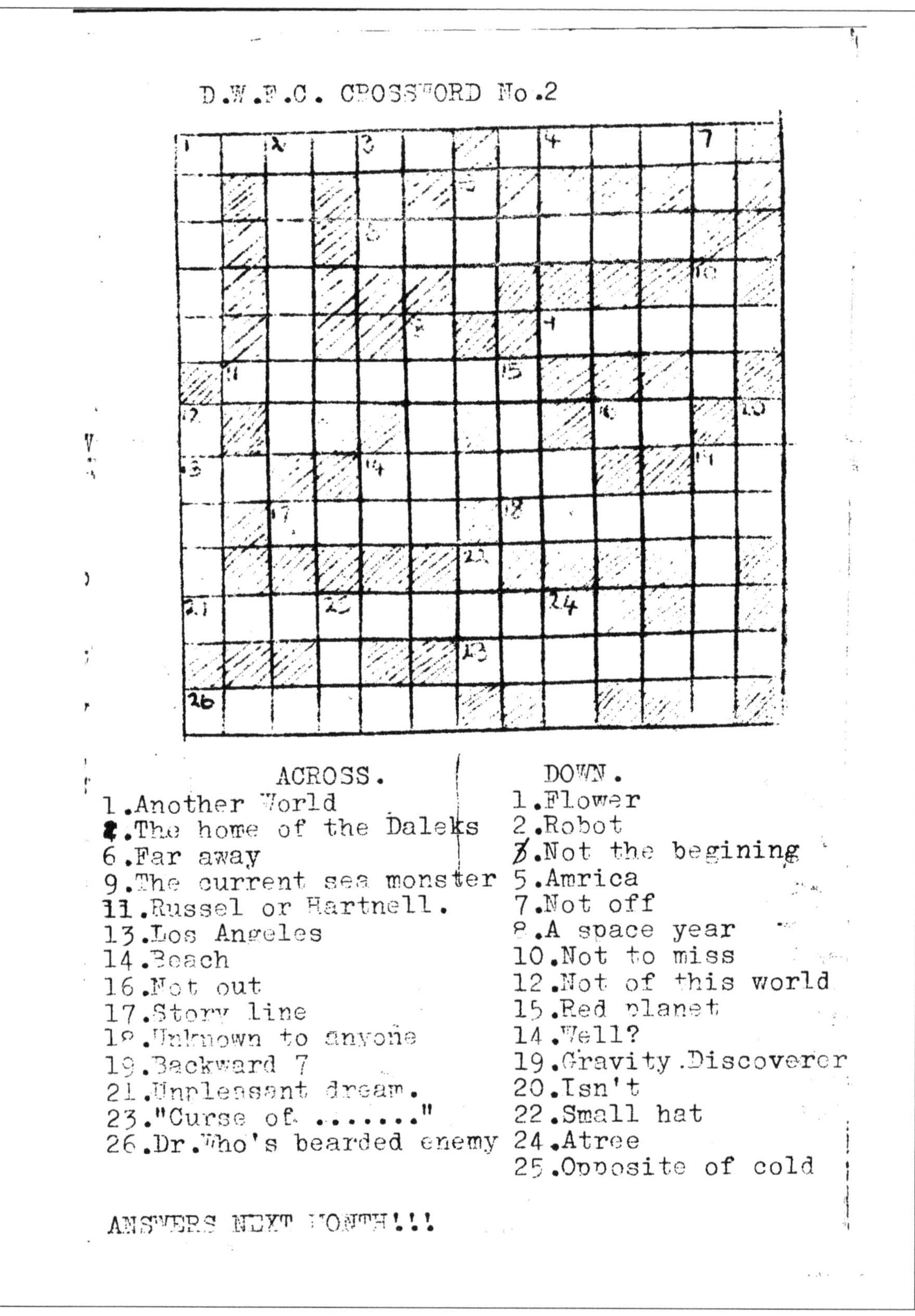

D.W.F.C. CROSSWORD No.2

ACROSS.

1. Another World
4. The home of the Daleks
6. Far away
9. The current sea monster
11. Russel or Hartnell.
13. Los Angeles
14. Beach
16. Not out
17. Story line
18. Unknown to anyone
19. Backward 7
21. Unpleasant dream.
23. "Curse of......."
26. Dr.Who's bearded enemy

DOWN.

1. Flower
2. Robot
3. Not the begining
5. Amrica
7. Not off
8. A space year
10. Not to miss
12. Not of this world
15. Red planet
14. Well?
19. Gravity Discoverer
20. Isn't
22. Small hat
24. Atree
25. Opposite of cold

ANSWERS NEXT MONTH!!!

Pan Books Limited, 33 Tothill Street, London SW1
Telephone: 01-222 7090 Cables: Pandition London SW1

Mr Keith Miller
Dr Who Fan Club
109 Moredun Park Road
Edinburgh 9

7th April 1972

Dear Mr Miller

Thank you for your letter about our book THE MAKING OF DOCTOR WHO.

We were interested to read that the BBC have appointed you to run the Dr Who Fan Club, although surprisingly enough Malcolm Hulke, the scriptwriter of the series, has never heard of it! However, I have pleasure in enclosing a copy of the book, and we should be very grateful if you could send us a copy or two of your magazine when it comes out.

Yours sincerely

Elizabeth Chadwick

Elizabeth Chadwick

BRITISH BROADCASTING CORPORATION
TELEVISION CENTRE WOOD LANE LONDON W12 7RJ
TELEPHONE 01-743 8000 CABLES: TELECASTS LONDONPS4
TELEGRAMS: TELECASTS LONDON TELEX TELEX: 22182

19th April 1972

Dear Keith,

I wonder if you would do something for me. I have received few letters from a Stuart Money and John Hudson and always on the envelope there is 'Dr.Who Official Fan Club'. Now I've told them once that you are the Fan Club official. They don't seem to take any notice. Will you write to them and tell them that you are Okay? Thanks. Enclose Envelope to show you.

Sarah

Their address ...

The Birth of Politics Within Fandom

And so was born political intrigue and skulduggery within Doctor Who fandom. Sigh. Stuart Money and John Hudson were desperate to oust me from the fan club and make it there own. At first, they were very amicable people. They didn't stay a million miles from Edinburgh, so I inivited them up and I showed them the delights of Moredun. They ventured up by train from Newcastle and we spent an afternoon getting to know each other. It soon became apparent that they were truly fanatical, which was to be made evident as they tried time and again to get me sacked as club runner in later years. But I thought they were nice guys. Then. However, it soon became clear that as far as they were concerned, I had no place being in an elevated position in new Who fandom, and slowly, and surely, they drew their plans against me...

And with alarming regularity I would receive reports that they were calling themselves the official Doctor Who fan organisation, and it was with great dismay I heard Jon Pertwee had taken them under his wing as he liked their sycophantic hero-worship. They shall be popping up regularly during this book. Unfortunately.

But then, suddenly and without warning, something happened to knock everything into perspective. My Dad died.

BRITISH BROADCASTING CORPORATION
TELEVISION CENTRE WOOD LANE LONDON W12 7RJ
TELEPHONE 01-743 8000 CABLES: TELECASTS LONDONPS4
TELEGRAMS: TELECASTS LONDON TELEX TELEX: 22182

27th April 1972

Dear Keith,

I am sorry about your father and so is everyone here. Actually my father died at roughly the same age as you are, so I know what it's like. However, I found if I was with people the whole time you tend to stop feeling so miserable.

I'll send details of your visit to London nearer the time. For me it's still way in the future, although it's not. I'll be getting you tickets in the evening but we do record in the evening on the 20th so are you in London the 21st or 19th? I can't remember I'm sure you've told me before. The recording on 20th goes on till 10.30 in the evening, and I'm sure you'll want to see that. However, your visit to the film library. Firstly, that is quite a way out of London and secondly they only have bits of films of each programme because most of the programmes are done on tape as you know. So really I don't think it will be much good. However, what I suggest is that you come to my office at about midday and then we'll have lunch in the canteen. Then I'll leave you in the studio till about four o'clock. Then I come up again for a run with the script editor. Then you will meet Barry who in fact is directing, and Jon Pertwee and Katy Manning probably. Jowever, let's leave it till later on. Okay?

Take care, and love to your Mum.

yours sincerely,

[signature]

I clean forgot to answer your questions.
No, I'm no relation to Sydney Newman, thank God!
Also, I'll find out about Jon's new L.P. No photos of sea devils or Mutants. I can't send them out coz they cost the progamme, and Barry perfers I didn't.

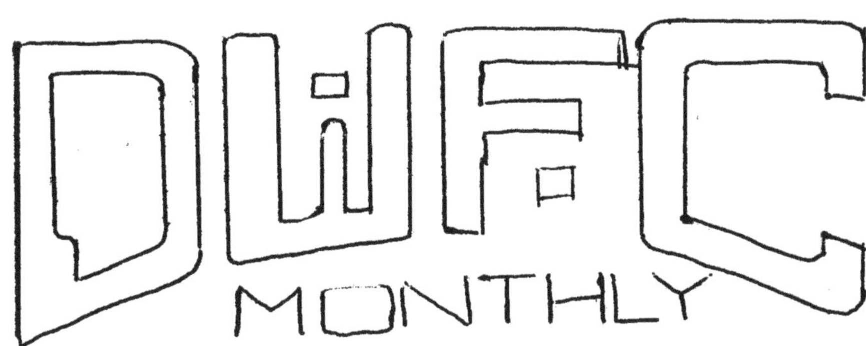

MAY EDITION..................ISSUE No.4

THE DOCTOR WHO FAN CLUB SUMMER SPECTACULAR!

....

As I said last issue, this month will see the debut of the DWFC Summer Spectacular. It's sort of a giant edition of the monthly and contains stories, special features, drawings, crosswords, reviews and a lot, lot more.

If this special edittion is a success, then you can look forward to more giant issues in the future.

Now this special will be on sale from next month and will be pricedaat 5p. Place your order now by sending a 5p PO to the club address(see Tardis Talkbox).

Hope to hear from you!

REVIEW "THE MUTANTS"

O Oddly enough, this adventure has the same title as the current story in "Dr.Who-in the Begining".

By the impression the first episode gave me, I thought that this was going to be one of the biggest failures in the history of the programme. I was soon to be proved wrong.

Special effects department must have had a ball with this escaped.

Interest boomed when the wall of the Skybase was blasted into oblivion and the crew were being sucked out into outer space. I thought that this was going to be where the Marshall would be killed. Again I was proved wrong. This adventure was to be full ofsurprises.

Back to the special effects. The boys in this dept. deserve a hearty pat on the back for the work they put into this particular production(Especially the changing of Ky)Thats my view, whats yours?

"THE MUTANTS"
Episode 2

"Stranded!"cried Ian,"You mean forever?"

"If I can't find any Mercury for the fluid links,yes-forever!"

"Haven't you any anywhere on the ship,Doctor?"asked Barbara.

"No,my dear.I was going to.."

"Oh,yes!You were going to get some more.But did you?NO and because of you we're stuck in this pit for life!"

"Kindly lower your voice when you're talking to me!!If you hadn't intefered when I wasn't fully loaded,we would have enough Mercury to get us out of here.So it wasn't me who put you in this mess,young man.You did it yourselves!"

There was silence in the ship as Ian returned to his stool.After a few minutes of deadly hush,Susan suddenly exclaimed "THE CITY!"

Susan then put forward her idea that the city they had sighted earlier might contain somewhere in its buildings a quantity of Mercury.There was a loud rap from outside the ship.Everyone again fell silent.

"The scanner,Susan.Quickly!"

She flicked a switch and the gloo my world of Skaro aga filled the screen.The picture moved slowly around the landscape,showing no signs of life.The Doctor opened the doors.On the ground lay a small box of chemicals which th Doctor later discovered were medicines.

"That proves that there is life on this planet.We had better be carefull,"said the Doctor.

They then made their way across the plain between the city and the forest. At last they came to the city wh they split up to investigate. The Dr. and Susan took the left hand section of the city, Ian the middle and BARBARA

DR.WHO-IN THE BEGINING

Took the centre. [illegible]ully she pressed the control stud on the wall of the building which operated the door. It slid up and into the wall, rather like a folding fan. She stepped in and followed a corridor which led to another corridor and then another. Suddenly she came to a dead end and turned round to go back. As she was about to back through the last door, it slammed shut inches away from her.

Meanwhile, the Doctor and Susan had met up with Ian at a crossroad corridor. The Doctor was gasping for breat[h]

"Are you all right?" asked Ian.

"Yes, dear boy, I'm fine. But not as young as I used to be."

"Don't feel too good myself...."

They rounded a corner and stepped into a large hall, where machinery on the far whirred and blinked its light

"Some kind of control room."

"Think you'll find any mercury here, Doctor?" asked Ian.

"Oh, yes. But there's plenty of time for that."

"Look, Doctor. I want to get out of here as quickly as possible. Understand?"

"DO NOT MOVE!" said a voice behind them. The most momentuos occasion in the history of the programme. They spun round to facetheDälek s.

Suddenly, Ian darted towards the doors but was stopped when aDälek fired its radiation gun at him. He fell, skidding across the metal floor. As he skimmed along a flash of light sparked between him and the floor.

"YOU WERE TOLD NOT TO MOVE!" the Dalek grated. It turned towards the remainder of the party. "YOU WILL HELP HIM TO THE CELLS"

The Dalek then backed down a ramp and waited for them as Ian limped past. Eventually, they reached the cell where they found Barbara shaken and white. She hurried across to Ian when she saw he was injured. The Dalek reversed out of the cell and the door glided to a close.

After a while, they started to complain about gidiness and feeling sick

"Of course," said the Doctor, "the air content meter must have been faulty. There is a large amount of radiation on this planet. These [illegible] must have been left to prevent us being [illegible]!"

Little did they know that the Daleks were watching their every move and listening to their every word.

[illegible]

DR. WHO-THE [illegible] NG

said the [illegible] "THE YOUNG ONE [illegible] HEALTH YEST. TELL HER [illegible] AND COLLECT THEM"

And so, Susan made her way back to the Tardis and on h her way back she was confronted by a Thal, the other inhabitants of the planet. He introduced himself as Alydon, leader of his race. Susan introduced herself and explained that the Daleks were holding her friends prisoner and that she had to get back to the city before they died. The Thal then said that the Daleks would probably take the drugs for themselves and gve her another case of the chemicals.

She then made her way back [illegible] the Daleks did take the drugs from her.

As soon as she was returnedto the cell, she explained to the party about Alydon and passed round the spare package of drugs which she had hidden beneath her cloak which the Thal had given her together with the drugs.

One Dalek entered. It was carrying a tray of food.

"TAKE THE TRAY" it said, "YOU" it said waving its sucker at Susan, "YOU WILL COME WITH ME"

She was then taken to the main control room where she was held at gun point and forced to write a letter to her friend, Alydon.

"ANBD WHEN THEY COME, WE WILL AMBUSH AND EXTERMINATE!"

TARDIS TALKBOX

Please address all letters intended for publication Keith Miller, 109 Moredun Park Road, Edinburgh EH17 7HJ

....

CROSSWORD. Across

1. Planet 4. Skaro 6. Distant 9. Devil 11. William 13. LA 14. Shore 16. In 17. Plot 18. Secret 19. No 21. Nightmare 23. Peladon 26. Master

....

Down (cont. from Page 5) 19. Newton 20. Not 22. Cap 24. Elm 25. Hot.

....

Got to appologise about the above. Running short of space

....

A Drawing by Sean Gibbons.

....

STARTS NEXT MONTH: "THE DR'S DRAWING BOARD!" Hurry and sen in YOUR drawings!

DALEK DATA

Sorry about the shrinking of the column, but there's so much to say and so littl space to say it in!

Did you know that:
A Dalek record called "The Landing of The Daleks" was made a couple of years ago? It was all instrumental but was very futuristic.

Remember to send in your ideas about a serial story about the Daleks, won't you?

There is a special chapter devoted to the Daleks in "The Making of Doctor Who"

NEXT MONTH!!!!
AS PROMISED IN ISSUE No.2, THERE IS GOING TO BE A DETAILED ACCOUNT ON THE ORIGIN OF THE DALEKS FROM THE VERY BEGINING. LOOK OUT FOR THE FIRST EPISODE OF THE ORIGIN OF THE DALEKS by DAVID THOMAS-Next Month!

EXCITING THINGS COMING FROM THE DOMAIN OF THE DALEKS! WATCH THIS SPACE!

CROSSWORD.
Down
1.Planet 2.Android 3.End 5.USA 7.On 8.Light 10.Hit 11. 12.Alien 15.Mars 14.So
Continued on Page4.

BOOK REVIEW:BOOK REVIEW:BOOK REVIEW BOOK REVIEW:BOOK REVI

"THE MAKING OF DOCTOR WHO"

PUBLISHED BY PICCOLO BOOKS.at 25p

An additional review, but this review is one with a difference. It is looking over tha fantastic book named above.

The book is simply fantastic with the centre packed with photographs from the programme, ranging from the very fist episodes to the present. And, I really mean this it is the best piece of literature I have ever read. It is worth much more than 25p.

It gives you the story of Dr.Who right from the begin-ing to the Sea Devils! If you want to see what's coming in "Dr.Who-In the Begining", turn to page43 or 65 and you can see lists and a quick summary of all the Doctors adventures.

The second half of the book tells you how a programme is made, and a special explanation of how the Tardis could exist.

May I take this oppertunity to thank Malcolme Hulke and Terrance Dicks for writing such a brilliant piece of work. If you haven't already read it, get it now!

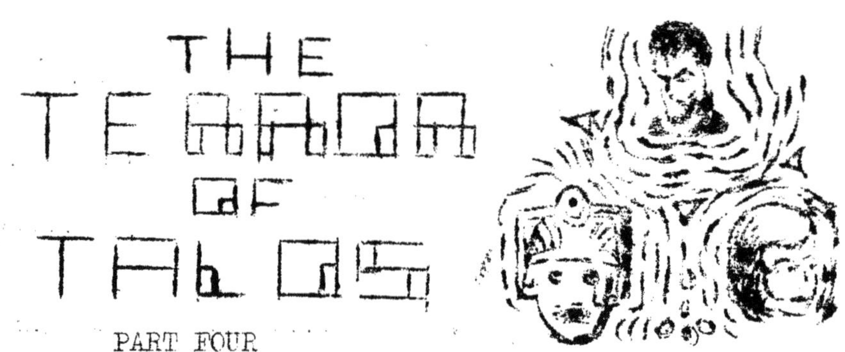

PART FOUR

"You murderer!Youve killed the Doctor in cold blood!You didn't even give him a chance to defend himself!"cried JO.

"Why should I?The Doctor has been nothing but trouble since ...well when the Doctor and I disagreed on a subject!" The Master looked away.

"Take him to cell 26.The disposing of him shall be taken care of later!"

He turned to Jo.

"Now,what shall I do with you my dear?I can't return you to Earth as in five hours time...that particular planet will be blasted into oblivion!!!Take her to cell 25."

The Master then returned to the Main Communications Room where the attack on Earth was being prepared.The Master took up his position at the transciever.

Jo was pushed into the cell where she wept for her dead companion.Silence ruled in her tiny prison.She leaned against the cell wall as the temperature in the cell cell was increasing.Smoke began to stream from the black spot which had appeared in the wall a few seconds before.The wall began tomelt and Jo turned white as the face of her "departed" friend appered.

"Hallucinations!It must be the shock.....!"she gasped.

"Thank-you,my dear,for such acompliement.I never knew you saw me like something out of your worst nightmare!"

The Doctor gave a broad grin as Jo leapt through the hole in the wall and hugged the Doc lovingly.

"Why,Jo,I never knew you cared.But come on we've got to get out!"

"But,Doctor.How come you're still alive?The laser made a direct hit!"

"For once,my dear,I've no idea!"

Jo saw the copper wire on the floor and figured that

TERROR OF TALOS
He must have used it to melt the wall.The Doctor walked over to the door and to Jo's amazment,it opened.

"But how..."

"No-one expects a dead man to walk.."

They stepped out into the corridor where Jo explained that the Master planned to blow up the Earth.The Doctor then led Jo to the Communications Room where the Master and the Cybermen were assembled together,as the final minutes ticked away towards the destruction of Earth.The The air suddenly smelt of burning rubber and the Doctor looked round to see that the copper wire burn hole had set the whole cell on fire and it was quickly spreading.

"Come on,Jo.We've got to stop the Master before this whole building becomes a blazing inferno"

They eased into the hall unnoticed,and made their way towards the large screen that displayed the progression of the Task Force.

"From up here",said the Doctor,"We should be able to see the whole of the control console"

The Doctor looked down and started studying the buttons and switches below him.As pr ecious seconds tick away, he at last found the destruct switch for the T.F. space ship and also the abort switch for the bomb.

"There,Jo!Do you think you could get to that blue switch over there?"

She nodded and climbed down from her observation point and made her way stealthily towards her objective.The Doctor also made his way to the destruct switch.Jo reached the switch and gave a thumbs up sign to the Doctor on the other side of the room.

The Doctor whispered "Good girl" to himself and returned the gesture.Jo pressed hard downwards on the switch as a red light flashed on the lighted screen.All eyes turned towards Jo.The Doctor then operated his control.The screen burst with light as the spaceship exploded.A fire alarm rang.The Doctor smiled and Jo smiled back.Then a new and teriffiing thought struck them.If the majn corridor was set alight,how were they going to get out?The Master began to panic.The Cybermen too began to panic as flames leapt towards the hall.Jo ran towards the Doctor.

"Well done,Jo.I'm proud of you"

"But how are we going to get out?"

The Doctor pointed towards the Master.He passed his hand over a section of rock. It slid upwards revealing a

TERROR OF TALOS

Corridor which led down into the storage buildings.

"I spotted the Masters Tardis down in the open section," said the Doctor."If we follow him we might just catch him."

They hurried over toethe wall.Before they could get through,it began to slide back down.The Doctor threw himself under the advancing door and the Doctorpressed his shoulder hard against it.

"Hurry,Jo.I can't hold...it..for long,"gasped the Dr.

Jo slid under the door and the Doctor let it slam to the floor.

"The Master will be well away by now",said Jo,running down the steps."By the way,just how did you escape the Masters laser?Any idea yet?"

"A fault in the gun,Jo.On the other hand perhaps the Master wanted me to..."

Jo looked at the Doctor solomly.

"No...No perhaps not."

They reached the bottom of the staircase and freedom. The Doctor looked back.The entire honeycombe was on fire.

"Life taken so quickly.."said the Doctor,entering the metal building where the Tardis was hidden.

"So quickly.."he repeated as he pened the police box doors and made their way back to Earth.

THE END

BRITISH BROADCASTING CORPORATION
TELEVISION CENTRE WOOD LANE LONDON W12 7RJ
TELEPHONE 01-743 8000 CABLES: TELECASTS LONDONPS4
TELEGRAMS: TELECASTS LONDON TELEX TELEX: 22182

10th May 1972

Dear Keith,

On the 20th June, if you would come to Reception Threshold House, which is the BBC (part of it) at the bottom of Shepherd's Bush Green at 1215 hrs. See the office meet me etc. Then we'll go to the Television Centre which is five minute walk and have lunch and meet Jon Pertwee. Then either you can come back withme and spend the afternoon in the office or stay in the studio and watch camera rehearsal, which I think would be prefereable. Then we have a producer's run at 1600 hrs till 1800 hrs. Then dinner. Then the recording which ends at 2200 hrs. Okay? An interesting day for you? Receiving parcels from you the whole time and they are sent off soon as possible. Tell me, are you keeping up with all the letters? Especially after the ad. in 'Countdown'? You can take pictures in the car park and I expect the Canteen but we'll see to that at the time. Threshold House is easy to get to. If you come by tube, take central line to Shepherds Bush. Turn right out of the station and walk down to the end of the green. Then you'll see the BBC Theatre and post Office and we are on the right of those buildings etc. Anyone will know as long as you say Threshold House or Union House (Two buildings in one!)

Sincerely, SARAH

BRITISH BROADCASTING CORPORATION
TELEVISION CENTRE WOOD LANE LONDON W12 7RJ
TELEPHONE 01-743 8000 CABLES: TELECASTS LONDONPS4
TELEGRAMS: TELECASTS LONDON TELEX TELEX: 22182

12th May

Dear Keith,

I suggest this: I enclose some stencils. Type on this, using the stencil cutter on your typewriter. Then send finished article to me to run off and then I'll send it back to you. If you haven't got a type writer or haven't got a stencil cutter , I just don't know. I think you'll have to give up because I can't honestly afford the time to do it for you I'm afraid. Still Let me know as soon as possible about the stencil and tell me if you can type it like this.

Sinerely

SARAH

BRITISH BROADCASTING CORPORATION
TELEVISION CENTRE WOOD LANE LONDON W12 7RJ
TELEPHONE 01-743 8000 CABLES: TELECASTS LONDONPS4
TELEGRAMS: TELECASTS LONDON TELEX TELEX: 22182

18th May 1972

Dear Keith,

I think you have misunderstood me. What I want you to do is to type on the stencil in the ordinary way,i.e. stencil enclosed,for referennd, then when you have finished newsletter send stencil to me I'll have it run off and send it back to you. The thing you'll have to type it having the layout in a ordinary fashion, i.e. top to bottom. I can have it done on coloured paper etc. Okay? I hope this is clear now and that the system will work.

Love

SARAH

Shock, horror! Three people have complained about the fan club - that'll be Stu Money, John Hudson and Peter Bleedin' Capaldi, then...

BRITISH BROADCASTING CORPORATION
TELEVISION CENTRE WOOD LANE LONDON W12 7RJ
TELEPHONE 01-743 8000 CABLES: TELECASTS LONDONPS4
TELEGRAMS: TELECASTS LONDON TELEX TELEX: 22182

25th May 1972

Dear Keith,

I'm afraid 'Countdown' and the BBC Publicity Officer have been onto our office about people complaining that they sent you postal orders for badges, pencils etc. in fact whatever you advertised in 'Countdown' and three people have complained that they haven't heard anything from you. Now, it's getting a bit touchy. If you think that in fact it has got out of hand, we'll send another advert in 'Countdown' explaining that the club only does Newsletters or something. I think the business of money being sent to you is really rubbing some people up the wrong way! However, if you could write to me and let me know, what your reaction is to this. I know that you send great batches of letters to me and I s end them off straight away. Are you behind in your mail? If so perhaps you ~~ougth~~XXX outght to send letters saying that you are behind but they will in fact be answered soon. I think perhaps we ought to have a real chat about this when you come down. In the meantime, perhaps you would send people letters if you are behind just to warn them so that 'Countdown' won't complain to Barry anymore. I'm sorry about this, but perhaps we had better re-think the Club out again. I enclose a letter sent to me from Countdown. I would be grateful for a very quick answer, so that I can give explantions to worried BBC publictiy men. I'm sorry about this Keith. When the first complaint came in I was not going to say anything, Barry agreed. But now that more have come we think we really aught to do something about it.

Love

Sarah

P.S. Could you answer the letter enclosed as soon as poss.
P.P.S. We still think you are best best fan club sec. to date.
P.P.P.S. I wasn't given the other names of peoples ~~xxxxxxxxx xxxxxxxxxxxxxxxxxx~~ who complained. So unfortunately you won't be able to know if you yourself remembered sending them something or not.

BRITISH BROADCASTING CORPORATION

TELEVISION CENTRE WOOD LANE LONDON W12 7RJ

TELEPHONE 01-743 8000 CABLES: BROADCASTS LONDON PS4

TELEGRAMS: BROADCASTS LONDON TELEX TELEX: 22182

30th May 1972

Dear Keith,

Good, I'm glad you sent a nice letter! I was expecting you to be upset. I think perhaps we should send a letter typed on one of my stencils leaving the top blank where you address a person and leaving space for your signature at the bottom and space for the address saying that in future there will not be kits for sale and the Club will only consist of Newsletters and photos? What about that? I think personally it will saye you a lot of trouble and let you get on with your own life a bit. Sell off the ones you have left but don't order anymore. And anymore complaints let them know as soon as possible that either you 've sent them one or else it's on its way. I'm sre you have managed it very well in fact I know you have but I think perhaps we are better with just Newsletters and keep to the arrangement we have at the moment of my sending you stencils, you typing them , me running off, you sending out! Plus all fan letters sent through the BBC. Okay? Looking forward to seeing you on 20th at 1215, at BBC Union House, Bottom Shepherd's Bush Green, W.12! Are you coming alone then? Remember our particular office isNot at the the Television Centre as stated above but not far from it, Five minute walk. So come to Union House. I don't know if I have told you before, but I was unable to get you tickets for the 20th for you and your Mum. But if ever you are in London again I will try again and get some. But I'm very cross with them 'coz I phoned them ages ago and now they say hey haven't any. If you have any other dates you are in London please let me know as sonn as poss.

See you soon,

SARAH

Pan Books Limited, 33 Tothill Street, London SW1
Telephone: 01-222 7090 Cables: Pandition London SW1

Mr Keith Miller
The Doctor Who Fan Club
109 Moredun Park Road
Edinburgh EH17 7HJ

31st May 1972

Dear Mr Miller

Thank you very much for your letter and for sending me the literature relating to The Doctor Who Fan Club, which I was extremely interested to read. It certainly seems a thriving little magazine!

I was very pleased that you like our book, and you certainly gave it a glowing review. I have sent a copy of your magazine to the authors, so that they can read it, too.

We don't at the moment have any plans for publishing another Dr Who book, but we will bear your suggestion in mind.

Yours sincerely

Elizabeth Chadwick

Elizabeth Chadwick

BRITISH BROADCASTING CORPORATION

TELEVISION CENTRE WOOD LANE LONDON W12 7RJ

TELEPHONE 01-743 8000 CABLES: TELECASTS LONDONPS4

TELEGRAMS: TELECASTS LONDON TELEX TELEX: 22182

2nd June 1972

Dear Keith,

Forget about all the little things that mean money please. I think if you re-organise the club which involves only newsletter extra then I think we shall be on the safe side. I can't do this 16 page Summer thing I'm afraid. I think you had better cut it down to the usual, one or two pages. Sorry but we really don't want to go into extremes now do we? Looking forward to seeing your Mum too. When bits of Dr.Who are shown on other programmes we are not always asked if this is okay which is real y what should happen. However, If I ever hear of interviews with the stars etc. I'll try and let you know.

Sincerely

SARAH

Keith,
Please in future leave
more space at the
top + bottom. Enclose
in another envelope stencils
I'd rather you use: Layout
the same. Also, I'm afraid
you'll have to collate them
as duplicating downstairs
won't do as it isn't official
BBC business! Don't worry though,
hope you can do it
Love Sarah

And so a new regime was in place. Sarah had access to proper Roneo machines that would run off the required amounts of DWFC Monthly, she would send them to me, I would address and fill the envelopes she provided, and these would be returned to Sarah via BBC Edinburgh, where she would send them out.

The quality improved as I got used to the new size, and I became a dab hand with a pin, scratching through the stencils and using pinpricks as shadowing. However, you would have thought someone would've pointed out to me there was three n's in "beginning"...

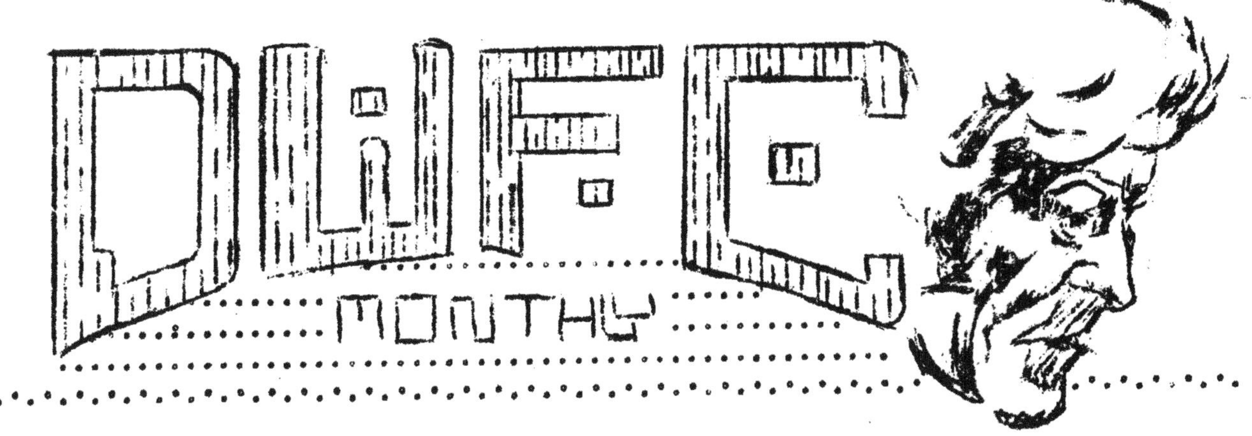

Number 5 June Edition D.W.F.C.

THE NEW LOOK NEWSLETTER!

Exciting things have been happening up here at the DWFC, so much so that I've had to enlarge the size of the monthly. How do you like it?

I'm afraid that the DWFC Summer Spectacular is going to be delayed a month, but don't worry if you've sent in your money already, it is well worth waitnig for!

I've postponed the Review for "The Time Monster" 'till next month, because it's a six part adventure and it dosent finish until the middle of the month.

This month sees the debut of David Thomas. He begins his monthly column "Origin of the Daleks" this month.

Also begining this month is the "Doctors Drawing Board!" where all you budding artists are able to display your work.

Well, I'll stop yakking now and let you get your teeth into your new, home knitted, up-to-date antique edition of this months letter.

Don't forget to enjoy yourselves!

All the best,

Keith

TARDIS TALKBOX

If you have anything to say concerning any aspect of the club or programme, please write to me and I'll try to print your query and answer. Any letters intended for publication should be addressed to-

"Tardis Talkbox",
The Doctor Who Fan Club,
c/o Keith Miller,
109 Moredun Park Road,
Edinburgh EH17 7HJ

I'll be watching my letter-box for a letter from you!

DR. WHO IN THE BEGINING

EPISODE 3
"THE MUTANTS"
starring

William Hartnell..............Dr. Who
William Russel.......Ian Chesterton.
Jaqueline Hill.......Barbara Wright.
Carol Ann Ford.......Susan Foreman.

in "The Escape"

"How are you now, Doctor?" asked Ian.

"Better, dear boy. It seems that Susan has arrived just in time!"

At that moment, the door to their prison slid open revealing Susan with a Dalek. She ran over and hugged the Doctor

"Are you all right, my child?"

The Dalek left the cell.

"What did they do to you Susan?" enquired Ian.

"They forced me to write a letter to Alydon. You remember-the Thal I met in the forest. Well, they told me to write that the Daleks are willing to give the Thals food if they meet them in the city. And once I'd finished, they said they would ambush and kill them. Oh, Grandfather; what have I done?"

She burst into tears and hugged the Doctor tightly. Ian stood up. The drugs had helped him enormously, giving him additional power in his legs. The Doctor looked up.

"Chesterton...do you remember when you were fired at?"

"Only too well!"

"What happened?"

"Well you WERE there..!"

"Do not argue with me, young man! It is vital you tell me EXACTLY what happened!"

DR.WHO-IN THE BEGINING(continued)

"As far as I remember,I made a dash for theddor and the Daleks shot their pop guns at me.I fell and skimmed across the floor.Then you.."

"No,Chesterton,There is something else.Think,man.Think!"

"How can I?I'M still trying to recover from the paralyisis in my legs! All that happened is I skimmed along the floor and....wait a minute.As I flew across the floor,I saw a flash and felt a tiny electric shock in my neck."

"EXACTLY!That is how the Daleks draw their power!They absorb it from the floor!Now if we are to escape and warn the Thals of the ambush,we must cut off this power!"

"But how,Doctor?"asked Barbara.

"Susan.Bring your cloak over here!"

The Doctor spread the material over the metalic floor.

"Now here is what we do....."

....

The Dalek glided into the cell with another tray of food.Ian slid his lighter in the corner of the door as the Dalek began to back out of the cell after Barbara had taken the tray from it.As the door began to close, Barbara took a handfull of the mushy paste the Daleks called food.The door screeched as it tried to close completely, obstuckted by the lighter The Dalek re-entered the cell.

It turned to Ian,it's back to Barbara.

"REMOVE THE OBJECT!MOVE!"

"NOW!"called the Doctor.

Barbara slapped the paste onto the eye-stick.

"UNDER ATTACK.EXTERMINATE!"

The Doctor and Ian grabbed hold of the Daleks sucker and gun and pulled it onto the cloak.

"EXTERmin...."

The Dalek was dead.The doctor lifted the head and scooped out the tiny creature inside,which was the true Dalek,with Ian's jacket and throws it into the corner.

"In you get,Chesterton" said the Doctor.

"What?You mean in there?You must be joking!"he replied.

"This is no time for jokes!Now get in!"ordered the Doctor.

Reluctantly,Ian sqeezes inside and they leave the cell.Ian manages to control the Dalek with a little from the Doctor.They pass many Daleks on the way and Ian says that he is taking them to the main control room.

When they reach the ground level, Ian discardes the Dalek and sees from a window,the Thals entering the city!

DOCTOR WHO FAN CLUB EXCLUSIVE!
STARTS THIS MONTH: by DAVID THOMAS.....

"THE ORIGIN OF THE DALEKS!"

PART ONE

Chapter One:-"The Begining"

The life of the planet Skaro began in much the same way as did that of our own planet,Earth.

In the year0 ,two suns collide resulting in a cosmic cataclysm.Matter in the form of swirling incandescent gases combine together to form a new planet.

Gradually,the gases began to cool,forming a nebula,the outer edges solidifying first,forming a crust.By the end of the genisis,there was a barren,white hot, volcanic world devoid of life.The planet -although moten-contained the ninety two elements and other substances necessary for the life which was to come.

....

Chapter Two

The Eras of Skaro

For 100 million years,the great rains washed down on the planet,cooling the land masses and forming the seas and an atmosphere.The first primitive plant life came into being,a fungi which covere the land with a blood red carpet.

Between the years 2,000 and 6000 years the life forms on the planets surface we were forming in the single cell stage, they changed shape and became more complex.Finally,a tiny snake-like shape crawled onto the land and gulped air into its lungs.This was the end of thelast phase in the Planestavian age and the begining of the age of the reptiles!

....

More next month!

....

Just a wee note to thank all of you for your your drawings,ideas and other contributions.Thanks to you next month sees the start of a new feature,

"THE DALEK DOMINATORS!"

This will be a series of stories based on the ideas you sent in.Who says I don't care about my members? Well,I'm off now so tara!

yours sincerely
Keith

JO + PELADON in PLANET OF FEAR

Part One

Jo rushed into the Tardis, looking all around for her friend.

"Doctor? Are you in here?"

No reply. She propt herself against the control console, pressing one of the black switches by mistake. The doors glided together, un-noticed by the young girl.

"Where could you have gotten to, Doctor? The car park! He'll be working on Bessie!"

She turned to leave.

"Oh, no! How did that happen?"

Jo banged on the doors and shouted for help, but to no avail. She then returned to, the console.

"I hope this is the right one," she said, pressing down on a red lever. The floor began to vibrate violently.

"Oh, Doctor! Help me!"

She pulled down two blue levers and the cylander in the centre of the hexagon jerked up and down, making the noise of a rhino with a atthorn in it's foot. Jo's hands leapt in all directions as she tried to keep the Tardis under control. The needles on the guagges spun eratically as the Tardis left the laboratory and plunged dangerously into a time warp, somewhere in deep space.

Tears formed in Jo's eyes as she tried to gain contwol of the time and space machine. The room began to spin as Jo's mind grew more and more confused. This with the sudden shock of being ripped away from here own planet caused her to black out on top of the console.

....

Jo's head throbbedas she struggled to get up. It suddenly struck her that all was quiet in the machine, except for the whirr of machinery somewhere else in the ship.

The controls were reset. She lokked around her in bewilderment. Jo then pressed the one switch she did know about. The scanner flashed into life.

Outside was a world of fire and lava. It seemed as if whole world was coming to an end. Something else than flames moved outside. It was a figure! The figure of a man! And whats more, a man she recognised!

"PELADON!" gasped Jo. He banged on the doors on thesmall craft.

"Oh, how do you open the doors?" she sobbed. Suddenly, the black switch she had accidentally pressed a few moments before operated itself on its own accord!!

The doors opened revealing the furnace Jo had seen on the scanner. Peladon collapsed on the floor, his clothes scorched and torn by the world outside. Jo pressed the switch she hadseen operate itself a few seconds ago. The doors closed. She hurried over to the man lying uncon on the floor, and lifted his head up.

"It IS you! Oh, Peladon, I thought I would never see you again!"

His eyes blinked open and he stared at the person in front of him.

"P..PRINCESS JOSEPHINE! My eyes play tricks." he said reaching out for her hand. "It IS you. We must leave. We are in great peril"

"B..But Peladon, I can't leave!!!!"

Part 2-Next Month

Dr. Who by M. Guarneri : An Ogron by Simon Gee (8) : Sea Devil by? from Glasgow

BRITISH BROADCASTING CORPORATION
TELEVISION CENTRE WOOD LANE LONDON W12 7RJ
TELEPHONE 01-743 8000 CABLES: TELECASTS LONDONPS4
TELEGRAMS: TELECASTS LONDON TELEX TELEX: 22182

20th June 1972

Dear Peter,

Thank you for your letter. Firstly, the pictures aren't ready yet, and secondly I'm afraid we have an official Dr.Who Fan Club secretary. I am passing your letter onto him and I expect he will send you a newsletter himself.

Yours sincerely,

(Sarah Newman)
Dr.Who Office

P. Capaldi,
Bishopsbriggs,
Glasgow,
Scotland.

Ah, dear old Peter Capaldi. Star of *The Thick Of It, Local Hero, Torchwood* and, of course, *Doctor Who* - and all time pain in the butt. He haunted my time running the fan club, as he was quite indignant he wasn't considered for the post, and Sarah Newman couldn't stand him, and she made no bones about telling people! The Cloister Bell will alert us when he is in the vicinity.

"I thought you would be... taller" Carnival of Monsters Set Report

On the morning of Tuesday 19 June, 1972, my Mum and I waved goodbye to the rest of the family as we got in the taxi to take us to St Andrews Square Bus Station in the centre of Edinburgh. With my Dad having been a bus driver, we went everywhere by bus, including far-flung places like London, (my Dad used to do the London run during the summer) so we boarded the coach and started the nine hour drive, pulling in eventually to Victoria Coach Station. We found a B&B nearby and settled down for a restless sleep, in anticipation of tomorrow's big day.

After breakfast, Mum decided she wanted to do a bit of shopping so we headed for Oxford Street. I remember Mum holding the door open for a very grandly dressed middle-aged lady, who simply waltzed through without a word. This irked my Mum who was big on manners, and then as were leaving, someone else in front let the door swing into my Mum's face. This made London cold and rude to my Mum, who fizzed about it for hours. I remember seeing proper African black people for the first time. We didn't have them In Edinburgh, Pakistani people being the darkest I had ever seen.

Midday was approaching so we got a taxi to take us to Shepherds Bush Green. The taxi driver didn't actually know where Union House was so he let us off in front of the BBC Theatre, famous for *Basil Brush* and *Crackerjack*. After a bit of exploration we found Threshold House, another BBC building, and Union House was just along the road. We reported to reception, who phoned Sarah to tell her we were there. Sarah appeared and the receptionist pointed to where we were sitting. As she came over, I stood up. "Keith!" she beamed, then a slight frown came over her face, "I thought you would be... taller." Later, she was to confess that even though I had told her my age right from the start, she thought from the way I wrote, I would be older. She asked my Mum if we had had a good trip down. "Yiss," replied my mother, "We hed ay verry ness joornay, thenk yu." I thought, why is she speaking in that ridiculous fashion? Turns out, it was her "telephone voice", but not being able to afford a telephone, I had never heard it before! In the lift up to the Doctor Who production office, Sarah confided, "I love your accent." I hope she was talking about mine and not the bizarre lingo Mum was spouting. "We're not allowed accents in the BBC, so it's quite refreshing."

The production office was actually a bit of a tip. There were untidy piles of paper stacked willy nilly everywhere. Photos from the present and past series plastered every inch of wall space along with newspaper clippings, one of which was an eye-catching front page headline:

"DOCTOR WHO PERFORMS ABORTIONS! Full report inside"

There was a shelf with past monster masks on it, one of

which was a Sea Devil, and another, a Mutant. Sarah passed the Sea Devil down to me. It didn't feel particularly nice, but after persuasion from my Mum, I tried it on. It smelt funny, and was quite uncomfortable. I handed it back to Sarah who put it back on the shelf, which was beside a huge white-board planner, covered in scribbled notes. And then I spotted them. Tiny photos of the Doctor, Zoe and Jamie arranged like a photo strip - loads of them. These were what was to be later called telesnaps, taken by John Cura as a photographic record of BBC productions, taken direct from a TV monitor. "Oh, we've got loads of those, "said Sarah, "I'll get you some if you like. But in the meantime, here, have one of these," and she handed me and my Mum a shooting script each, for todays episode. I got one of these each time I went down to cover filming, and at end of my seven year stint on the fan club, had quite a collection. Would be worth a fortune on eBay now, but I turfed the lot into the bin when I moved away from home. Sarah handed me a small parcel covered in tissue paper. "This is for you, Keith. For all your help." I unwrapped it, and found it to be a dark blue polyester necktie with gold embroidered police boxes all over it. "We give them to all our special people. Jon's got one!"

After making a quick phone call, Sarah said, "Right we better get down to the studio. Barry's waiting to meet you, then we'll have something to eat, then hopefully we'll get to Jon before he has to get back before the cameras. It's a short walk - we'll work up an appetite." I couldn't think about eating at all - I was far too nervous. As we made our way to the studios, I did my best in my gauche way to make conversation, but could tell Sarah, though she "loved my accent", was having a hard time understanding it! I had to repeat everything at least twice. My Mum seemed to be having better luck. "Em propah femished," she said.

There's a scene in the superb 2008 TV series Beautiful People, where the two teenage leads, Simon and Kylie run away from Reading and head into London towards the land where the Beautiful People of the title hang out - BBC TV Centre. They stumble across the building almost by accident, with an angelic choir heralding their arrival. When I saw that, I was back in 1972, being led through the BBC car park to

Reception. Sarah signed us in and she led us through the maze of USS Enterprise corridors to Studios 4 and 6, round the sets of the hold and living quarters of the SS Bernice, and the workings of the Scope. There was a small effects studio set up in the corner - merely a wooden table with a yellow table cloth, surrounded by yellow drapes, yellow being the preferred "keying" colour for CSO, (Colour Separation Overlay), or greenscreen as it's known today. On top of the table was a three-foot long Drashig. The whole studio was curiously empty. "Everyone's gone for lunch," said Sarah, "and I think we should do the same." We made our way to the exit and as we were going out, two people were coming in. Sarah introduced us to guest stars Jenny McCracken and Ian Marter. I was to meet Ian again a few years hence. And Jenny McCracken was very beautiful.

We eventually made it to the BBC Canteen (see cutaway opposite). We ate our lunch and my Mum and Sarah chatted stiltedly, but nerves were getting the better of me and I was aware my fork was shaking as I tried to get it into my mouth. I wasn't very hungry anyway, so I put the fork down and pushed my plate away.

"Okay, let's get down to the Production Suite. Barry'll be wondering where I've got to."

The Production Suite was a dark room with a wall of TV monitors, in front of which half a dozen people sat at a desk covered in buttons and switches. To one side was a small room with a large window, inside of which was a large television set and four chairs. Sarah opened the door to show us in and was surprised to see a young man lying on the floor, watching what was happening on the studio floor on the TV.

"Oh, sorry, Brian, I thought this was empty," said Sarah. "No, no, it's fine," he said, not moving, "I'm hiding. Come in, come in..."

He was a very handsome chap, with blonde hair and blouson shirt. He looked like he should've been part of

The BBC Canteen. The place to be for star spotting. Over the years, I shared the lavish (!) menu with the likes of Bert Foord, the weatherman; Donald Eccles (Krasis from *the Time Monster*): and Neil McCarthy (Barnham from *Mind of Evil*). I stood beside Christopher Casenove (*Dynasty*) as he deliberated the merits of the Dish of the Day - Shepherd's Pie. I watch as Ronnie's Barker and Corbert brought their trays to their table, then, aware all eyes were on them, do an obviously well-rehearsed comedy skit where when one sat down, the other stood up. I stood at the next urinal to newsreader Richard Baker. He was a very small man. In height.

Relaxing with Sarah and a cup of coffee, I watched as Annette Crosby, fresh from overnight success as Catherine of Aragon in *The Six Wives of Henry VIII*, strode regally into the canteen, surrounded by a gaggle of very camp men, all wearing cravats and Chanel No 5. "Her entourage," explained Sarah, "Dress designers from the fourth floor. Don't ever get out at the fourth floor by accident, Keith. They'll have you for breakfast." They adored the very ground Annette walked.

One time, I had my tray of whatever, but couldn't find any place to sit, the place was heaving. I then saw someone waving and gesticulating to me to come and sit down. I made way to the table. I knew the actors' face but didn't know his name, but I did know he had been in *I'm Alright Jack* with Peter Sellers. I later found out his name was John Comer.

"Sit down here, lad," he said, "Bit busy today inntit? Heaven knows why, have you seen that menu?" His whole face wobbled in a jolly fashion when he laughed. He extended his hand. "John". I shook it. "Keith." "You in something?" "Nope, I'm covering the making of *Doctor Who*." He smiled. "You look a bit young for a journo." "I'm not, I'm a fan. Are you filming today?" "Yes, I'm in this cracking new thing called *Last of the Summer Wine*. We film the interior scenes down here in front of an audience - they're really enjoying it - but we film the exteriors up north. Is that a Scottish accent then?" "Edinburgh," I replied. I ate my lunch as John regaled me with tales of his travels through Scotland and beyond, and of his prized possession, his caravan. I instantly took to this man and I realized quickly why. He was working class. He wasn't like all the other actors I had met to this point who made me feel shy and inferior, he was an ordinary bloke who was interested in what you had to tell him. John Comer made the role of Sid in LOTSW his own, and sadly it was to be his final role. I really liked him.

Mary Shelley's group with Lord Byron. Sarah introduced him as Brian Hodgson, and he himself summed up what he did as "making noises". I hadn't a clue who he was and was to ask Sarah weeks later who he was. You see in those days, production people weren't revered as they are today. You studied the end titles to see who starred as who, then the rest were obviously too far down the importance scale to bother about.

But unbeknown to me, this was the man who invented *the most beautiful sound in the universe*, with a key and a piano string - the Tardis. With the brakes on. He was very pleasant, but had an air of melancholy about him as we made idle chitchat. Suddenly, be became animated, as if he had just remembered something. He got up and went outside to the production desk and talked to someone, pointing to us through the window. The person nodded and Brian came back. "Can you come outside for a second" he said to us, "I want to show you something." We piled outside, but just then we were joined by someone else, a balding man with a kind face. "You made it , then," he said, beaming and shaking our hands. My Mum was grinning from ear to ear - she recognised him straight away from his acting days, "You're Barry Letts - The Silver Blade" Barry beamed even wider and was obviously chuffed that Mum had recognised him, as it had been some time since he'd given up acting. "I'm going to play them the Delaware, Barry, "said Brian, "We can get the person on the streets point of view." "Good idea,"said Barry turning to us, "Could you listen to this and tell us what you think?" Barry nodded to the guy behind the desk and he rolled the VT. The opening titles began as normal, but with a curious *boing-boingy* version of the theme tune.

"Well, what did you think," asked Barry. Mum looked at me. So did the others. "It was okay," I lied. Barry leant forward. "Okay?" "Well..." "Be honest," laughed Brian. "It was awful." I admitted. Brians' smile totally disappeared and Barry placed a hand on his shoulder. "Sorry, kiddo, but that about wraps it up. Its a no-goer."

Turns out Brian had arranged the new version of the theme on a new BBC acquisition, the Synthia 100 Delaware. And I had shot it down. I felt a total heel. Brian, of course, did loads of Doctor Who, but it wasn't until some years later, I was in the cinema, reading the opening credits to a film called The Legend of Hell House, that his name appeared as the sound architect. "That's that guy!" I remember exclaiming, which meant nothing to the person I was with...

Barry sat with us back in the Producer's Box, and we had a long chat about the history of the show and I said I wanted to document that history so it

wasn't forgotten. "Good for you, "said Barry, "but don't forget what's happening here and now, will you?" Someone chapped on the window and Barry made his exit. Rehearsals were in full swing now, and Jon and Katy and the rest of the cast were all on set in their everyday clothes, solving the mystery of the SS Bernice.

Rehearsals eventually came to their conclusion and everyone broke for dinner and to prepare for recording. Barry was in full flow with my Mum as he reminisced about his film career, including Boy, Girl and a Bike and The Cruel Sea, and I swore I saw her flutter her eyelashes at him as we entered the BBC bar. We were introduced to three men propping up the bar, one with a beard smoking a pipe, one a jolly plump man smoking a ciggy, and the final man sporting a full moustache.

"This is Robert Holmes, " said Barry as I shook hands with the bearded man, "He's the writer of today's story. And this is Terrance Dicks, our script editor..." He was the plump one. "He oversees all the stories in production. And this is Dudley Simpson." "The music man!" I exclaimed, happy at last to get someones occupation! "Helloy!" he said in his heavy Australian accent. Dudley spoke at great length about composing for Doctor Who, after all, he had been doing it since 1964. "Can I get you a drink, Jean?" Barry asked my Mum. She giggled coquettishly. "Ay'll hev a whet wine, thenk yu." Good grief, my Mum only drank at Christmas! She was throwing herself into the showbiz lifestyle big time. The shocks were to continue. Someone produced a box of Sobranie - black ciggies with a gold filter tip - and asked if anybody wanted one. "Ay don't mend if I do." said my Mum, and sparked up! I was gob-smacked. Mum never smoked and had been constantly on at my Dad to give up the dreaded weed. Who was this woman and what had she done with my Mum?!

Sarah suddenly reappeared, asking if anyone had seen Jon. "He's getting ready in his dressing room, I think" said Barry. "Come on,"said Sarah to Mum and I, "We've been missing him all day." She ushered us out of the bar and down into the bowels of the BBC, where a tiny person canonballed into me from one of the dressing rooms. "Sorry!" she bawled, clearly used to this kind of situation, "Blind as bat. Sorry." Katy Manning. Lovely little person, mad as a brush, bless. She adjusted her bottle-end glasses with fingers covered in silver rings. "Are you the fan club guy?" I'm sure she wanted me to say something to give her some kind of clue where I was. It was then I discovered that feeling that is quite widely reported now, when you meet one of your heroes, and all you want is for the ground to swallow you up as you can't think of a thing to say.

Then Jon Pertwee poked his head round the door of his dressing room to see what all the commotion was about. "Keith! I was expecting you at lunch!" And there he was. The tall lightbulb, my hero, the Doctor - standing there beaming from ear to ear. Naked.

Well, he had a towel on, but that was all. I had never seen white chest hair before and was quite mesmerised by it. Amongst it were gold chains, medallions and assorted bling. He shook my hand and I noticed the huge ring he was sporting as he ushered us into his dressing room. Thankfully, Jon never shut up - he could talk for Britain if he had an audience of one or more - and he explained in great detail the filming schedule for that evening and the storyline. He mentioned the DWFC Mag and how it was shaping up nicely, but he did express concern about the coverage of past stories. "I'm the Doctor now, after all. Not Bill Hartnell." I suddenly felt very small, but piped up that I had already said to Barry that there was a danger these stories could be lost forever. "Well,

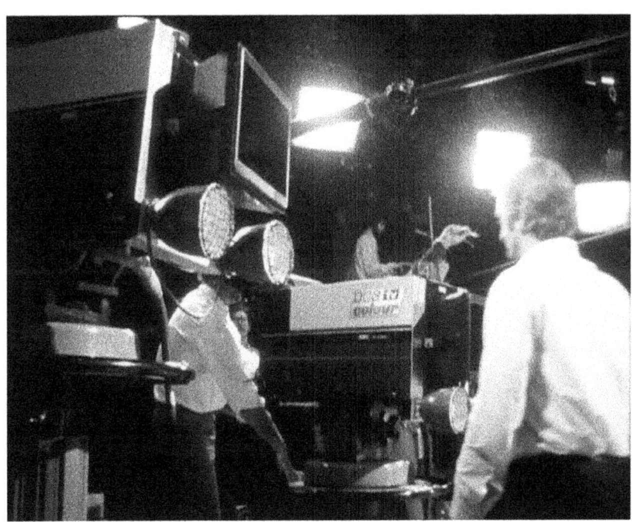

I'll let you know if I think it's getting out of hand," Jon said. And he certainly did.

Charles, Jons' dresser came in with the Doctors' velvet jacket. "Got to get ready," said Jon, stubbing out his fag. "Are you staying for the recording?" Mum said we would stay for a short while, but we really should think about getting back. "Okay, well keep in touch. Perhaps next time we could get together for lunch. Let me know when you're down again." Again? Again! I thought this a one off! I could come again? My heart soared.

We made our way back to the Producers Box and we watched as Katy and Jon, now the Doctor and Jo, dashed through the inner workings of the Scope, trying to find the way out. All the sets were quite small, but this set could be filmed from various angles making it look quite big. They were running to avoid the Drashigs, but Jon's boot skidded on the shiny floor and went A over T into the plastic tubes lining the walkway. Mum guffawed (I think the "whet wine" was kicking in), but he was fine. Katy fussed over him for a bit. I think he liked that.

Barry reappeared and Mum said we really should be going. "Well, thank you for coming to see us. Hope you enjoyed your day..." He trailed off and I could see he was watching the TV monitor over my shoulder. It was the scene where the Drashig reared up through the hull of the ship and into the forward hold. There had been some trouble from executive-types earlier (I suspect the Indian extras didn't have Equity cards, but don't quote me on that...) and Barry wanted to keep an eye on them. They were tooled up now with rifles. The rifles fired blanks, but even blanks could be dangerous. They were firing at the monster, but the smallest of the group was waving the gun around in an alarming fashion. "Oh, My Lord, "said Barry rising quickly from his chair, "The little man's gone loco!" Barry hurried to his mike and halted the production. The little man was led away, still jumping up and down.

Mum and I made our way to reception where they got us a taxi to take us back to the B&B. In the taxi, Mum, who thankfully had returned to her normal accent, sighed and said, "Well, that was a grand day out, wasn't it, son?" "Well, you certainly enjoyed yourself, " I said with more than a hint of indignance, "You practically threw yourself at Barry Letts." Mum waved a hand in the air and looked at me as if to say, "Don't be so silly."

BRITISH BROADCASTING CORPORATION

TELEVISION CENTRE WOOD LANE LONDON W12 7RJ

TELEPHONE 01-743 8000 CABLES: TELECASTS LONDONPS4

TELEGRAMS: TELECASTS LONDON TELEX TELEX: 22182

27th June 1972

Dear Keith and Mrs. Miller,

I took yesterday off, and came in today to find a telegram from you both for my birxthday. I was so thrilled that I ran and showed everyone! Thanks so very mudh for remembering me. I really am very gxxteful. As you can see I am not really in the mood for typing! Anyway, I hope you enjoyed your trip to the BBC and enjoyed the journey back. We all thought how lucky we were to have someone like you doing the fan club. We are really most grateful.

Yours sincerely,

SARAH

BY APPOINTMENT
PURVEYORS OF CONDENSED MILK TO THE LATE KING GEORGE VI

THE NESTLÉ COMPANY LTD.

(CONFECTIONERY DIVISION)

ST. GEORGE'S HOUSE CROYDON SURREY CR9 1NR

TELEPHONE: 01-686 3333 CABLES & TELEGRAMS: NESTLE CROYDON TELEX. TELEX 23117

YOUR REF. OUR REF. 1616/RHS/EMM DATE 27th June 1972

Mr.K.Miller,
109, Moredun Park Road,
Edinburgh,
EH17 7HJ.

Dear Keith,

Thank you for your recent letter concerning our "Doctor Who" Milk Chocolate. We were interested to learn that you run the fan club and publish the D W.F.C. monthly magazine.

I am arranging to send you some specimens of the display material we use to advertise this Chocolate Bar, together with one or two samples of the bar, and the packing case. We hope, in the near future, to produce a collection card that the wrapper pictures may be affixed to.

You may by all means mention our product in your magazine, and we would be interested at some time to receive a copy.

Yours sincerely,
THE NESTLE COMPANY LTD.
Marketing Dept.

R.H. STARLING
Executive

BRITISH BROADCASTING CORPORATION
TELEVISION CENTRE WOOD LANE LONDON W12 7RJ
TELEPHONE 01-743 8000 CABLES: TELECASTS LONDONPS4
TELEGRAMS: TELECASTS LONDON TELEX TELEX: 22182

28th June 1972

Dear Keith,

Thank you for your letter. Brian Hodgeson is the chap responsible for our radio phonic soudns from the Radiophonic Workshop. His credit appears every week after Dr.Who. Also, I don't think you enclosed the letters regarding the new Newsletter and the letter from Peter Capaldi? Did you firget to put them in? I don't think at the moment it would be very wise if you write to Dudley for the new music. We reaaly have to keep it in the BBC until it is transmitted once, and then I 'll send you a copy. Send you pictures of Jon and Bill Hartnell. None of Pat Troughton. I think about phoning me you better keave a while. I'll try and make enquiries here. We have a copy of Countdown thanks. Te rrance very upset by his pictures! He thinks it doesn't do him justice! The costumes in Scotland have left now, although they haven't come back to my office. All I can do about getting you in the BBC is for you to decide what dept you are interested in in Edinburgh. XXXXS Whether Radio or Television. Then write to me and I'll try and find names of people you should write to, but first let me know exactly what you want to do. You won't get a fantstic job to start withm but if you can get a job in the right department where eventually you will do whzt you want, it will be a help.

love

Shaun

love to your mother

BRITISH BROADCASTING CORPORATION
TELEVISION CENTRE WOOD LANE LONDON W12 7RJ
TELEPHONE 01-743 8000 CABLES: TELECASTS LONDONPS4
TELEGRAMS: TELECASTS LONDON TELEX TELEX: 22182

7th July 1972

Dear Keith,

How are you? Enclose envelopes. Haven't done stencils yet. Haven't had time. Hope to do them perhaps tomorrow. No photos of Nic Courtney at the moment . Hope to get more soon. Don't know about the second Dr.Who fillm. We didn't even know about the first one! Good for you about your prize! What a clever boy! We don't really have advertising in the BBC. Enterprises are the closest thing to it. They don't have an office up where you are. You could design promotion sheets (brochures that go over seas about programmes that we want to sell). When you have made up your mind a little more I'll get in touch with the Appointments Officer for the right sort of thing you want to do and get you to fill in an application form. I think you ought to be a little older though. Perhaps you should go and see the world before you really get down to work, becox you have to work all your life and its good to see other places and countries before you get tied down!

All my love to you both. Keep merry and fit. Barry is very flattered to think your Mum likes him!
P.S. Katy is very well!

Yours sincerely,

Sarah

Number 6 July Edition D.W.F.C.

AN APOLOGY.

To all of you who have written in to me with Postal Orders for 5p,who expected to get a copy of the DWFC Summer Spectacular in return,may I say that I am sorry that it has had to be cancelled.

As I said in my letter, I only hope you are not too dissappointed by this lightning cancellation.

I only hope that I can make up for it by making the monthly beter than ever!

Your reaction to the changing of the monthly seems to be one of approval.If you have any suggestions as to how I can improve the monthly,jot down your suggestion and post it off to me.I'm always glad to hear from you!

Some of you may have noticed that the article "Dr. Who-In the Begining" stopped rather abruptly last issue.This was mainly because some issues were printed without page 2 in it,so misising out 2 articles.Sorry about that!

The second part of "The Origin of the Daleks"is inside,together with the begining of yet another new serial- "THE DALEK DOMINATORS"!

Well,thats about all for now,Time Lords so I'll take my leave and wish you happiness 'till next we meet.'Bye!

Keith

A SENSORITE by J.Connors.

REVIEW "The TIME MONSTER"

Well,here I am for the last Review of year,apart from special articles,such as next month when I review the film recently shown as one of the "HIGH ADVENTURE" series-"DR.WHO AND THE DALEKS".

Anyway,this adventure was bound to please all Tardis fans as the Doctor and Jo chased the Master to and from Atlantis.The destruction of Atlantis was a good ending to a great story.

One thing did pluzzle me,though.Lets take a flashback to "The Deamons"Remember when the Master summoned Azal?And Azal warned the Master what would happen if he summoned him again?Azal said,

"I SHALL APPEAR BUT ONCE MORE,BUT BE WARNED......REMEMBER ATLANTIS !"

Now this sounds to me as if Azal caused the destruction of the underwater city, not Kronos!

In the last episode,the dual between the Doctor and the Guardian was abit daft,dont you think?You know,the Doctor doing the bullfighter bit.

This was one adventure worthy of six episodes and I wish to convey my thanks to Robert Sloman for writing such a great script.

The part of Dr. Ruth Ingram was overplayed a little with the womans lib.Otherwise the actors played their part beutifully.

Well,thats my view,whats yours? I'm always glad to hear your views of the programme,so get writing,hear?

DR.WHO IN THE BEGINING

EPISODE FOUR
"THE MUTANTS"

Starring
William Hartnell............Dr.Who
William Russel....Ian Chesterton.
Jaqueline Hill....Barbara Wright.
Carol Ann Ford.......Susan Foreman
in "The Expedition"

"Doctor,LOOK!"cried Ian pointing towards the window,"The Thals will be massacred!"

"You're right,Chesterton.We must warn them off the danger at once.."

Telling the trio to follow him,the Doctor made his way through the corridors to the outside buildings.There they see the Thals,and Ian rushes forward to warn them.

"LOOK OUT!IT'S AN AMBUSH.RUN FOR YOUR LIVES!"

The bewildered Thals begin to panic as the Daleks close in around them.

"EXTERMINATE!"chant the machines as they kill the Thals with with their deadly blast guns.However,thanks to Ians warning,many of the Thals are saved,but their leader is killed.The Doctor and Ian guide Susan and Barbara down out of the city and to the safety of the forest.

After introductions and thanks from the Thals,the Doctor asks

"Tell me,young man.Do you have any maps or plans of the area around here?"

"Yes"answers Alydon and produces a rolled up piece of canvas skin.

"Just what the Doctor ordered!Heh,heh heh.."joked Ian.Everyone gave him an anoyed glance.

The Doctor unrolled the map and studied it carefully.After a few minutes,he l looked up.

"There is another way into the city" he anounced."But the route is a dangerous one.I suggest that Chesterton, Barbara,Alydon and Kristas plus another couple of Thals journey to the mountains and in to the caves to the Dalek city!"

A few hours later,after they had made adequate precautions and preperations,the party say their goodbyes to the Doctor and their fellow Thals.

So the journey begins.Ian,Barbara and the Thals made their way to the back of the forest and entered the region of Skaro known as The Swamps.

As they made their way through the murk, one of the Thals stopped tofill his water skin.As he puts his hand into the pool,a tentacle splashes upward,slithers round the Thals neck,and pulls him down into the liquid mud.The party could do nothing to save him.They continued the expedition.

After a long trek through the Lake of Mutations,they at last came to the mountains where they started a perilous climb to the top.On their way up,one of them spots a network of pipes running up the slope.These are the pipes that carry water to the Dalek city from the lakes.This was to be their guide lines into the city of the Daleks!

At long last,they reached the ledge where the pipes ran into the caves.

Having heard nothing from the party,the Doctor and Susan enter the city by the front entrance..only to be imprisoned by the Daleks!

DALEK DATA

PART ONE:Chapter Three
"Evolution"

The Thalistunian age lasted up to the year 100,000 million.It is also known as "The Age of Monsters" due to the fact that hundreds of creatures of different species fighting and killing for food,rampaged th through the swamps and jungles of Skaro. Another form of life was developing.It was smaller and weaker than the others.This was a human being.

During the Sparasusian age,the mighty rep+iles bacame extinct,the other life form developed.They eventually formed two distinct tribes-the Dals and the Thals. The two tribes constantly warred eith each other.Tha Thals were a primitive people. They were short,ugly but a powerfull tribe who were great swordsmen.The Dals,however, were great teachers and philosophers.

Chapter Four next month!

INCIDENTAL INFORMATION

Alot of you have been aking me about the record-"THE LANDING OF THE DALEKS" Sorry!But its not available in the shops. The record was made quite a few years ago now and it's stopped being issued.

Next month the Dalek adventure comes to an end because the last TWO episodes will

DALEK DATA(continued)
be featured in "Dr.Who-In the Begining"

....

ANOTHER D.W.F.C. FIRST! THANKS TO YOUR LETTERS,THERE STARTS THIS MONTH A NEW SERIAL,STARRING NONE OTHER THAN
"THE DALEK DOMINATORS!"

"BATTLE ON ARCTURUS!"

The spaceship silently sped its way through deep space,shining like a silver bullet,fired from a gun.It too was an instrument of death,for on board was a task force of the most evil,heartless creatures in the cosmos.The scourge known throughout the universe as The Daleks!

On board,the crew were hovering back and forth from huge pieces of electrical equipment.Suddenly,there was a loud scream as the motors slowed down until they came to a full stop.All Daleks then left the control room in silence, to reassemble in a large hall which the Daleks use as sort of a briefing room.All Daleks knew their own position in the hall,and in few minutes,the Dalek force was stationary and facing a panel, which a few minutes later slid up and into the wall.The Black Dalek glided in. He moved onto a raised platform in the hall and began to speak.

"ALL IS READY.THE ANNIHILATION OF ARCTURUS MUST PROCEED!WE WILL EXTERMINATE!"

JO GRANT AND KING PELADON in

"B..But,Peladon.Whats impossible!We Can't leave!"

"Can't Leave.."whispered the young king"But we must!We are in terrible danger!This planet is about to explode!"

"Wait a minute.I've heard the Doctor say something about a time-warp.If you'll help me,perhaps we can escape"

The Tardis shook violently.

"Hurry,Princess!The planet is disintegrating!"

Jo helped her companion over to the control console.She gave him instructions on what she wanted him to do.The shaking increased.

"Oh,I do hope this is the right one" said Jo,pulling a large red lever slowly down.The cylinder began to rise and descend.The shaking stopped abruptly.

"Press the two buttons,Peladon"

He did so and the scene on the scanner grew hazy and started to change.All chances of seeing what was happening outside were lost.

"Not a bad take-off"said Jo."For a beginer anyway"

"Princess.."

"I told you before,Peladon.I'm not a.."

Suddenly,the controls on the console began to change.Levrs began easing themselves down and buttons were being pressed,as if by some invisible hands.The Time Warp control eased to the 0 mark and the time rotor, the clear plastic cylinder in the centre of the console,slid to a halt.

"Princess.What is happening?"

"I...I don't know.It was the same earlier on!"

(Drawing by Brian Kerr)

Five black buttons were pressed down and the doors swung open.Outside was awworld of fertile valleys and towering mountains.A cool breeze blew into the space-craft.Jo and Peladon stepped outside.

"This must be that planet you were on, a few million years in its past!Groovy,isn't it?"

"All this is very confusing.." said the king.

Sunlight filtered through the trees that grew nearby and towered high above their heads.Jo closed the blue door behind her, leaving a small gap so they could get back in.They climbed a hill and looked over the landscape.It seemed like a tropical paradise. On the horizon,a black cloud of smoke filled the skies.The sound of crashing trees was heard somewhere in the distance.

"How did you get here in the first place, Peladon?"

"I was makinga royal tour of all the planets in the Federation when my spaceship crash landed onto this planet.All the crew were killed.I was the only one to survive."

The crashing of trees was coming nearer. In a few seconds it was deafning.

"Peladon..The haet.."

"We must return to the box,lady."

As Peladon said this,trees crashed apart to reveal the legendary Fire Monster!

BRITISH LION FILMS LTD

YOUR REF.
OUR REF.

BROADWICK HOUSE BROADWICK STREET
LONDON W1V 2AH
TELEPHONE 01-437 8676
TELEGRAMS BRILIONFIL LONDON W1

14th July, 1972.

Mr. K. Miller,
109 Moredun Park Road,
EDINBURGH EH17 7HJ.

Dear Mr. Miller,

Replying to your letter regarding "DR. WHO AND THE DALEKS" and "DALEK INVASION EARTH", I enclose a campaign book on each and a few stills.

These are for personal use only and must not be sold.

Posters for these two films are available from National Screen Service, 15 Wadsworth Road, Perivale, Greenford, Mddsx, to whom you should apply - whether they will supply you or not I do not know, as originally they are produced for cinema use only.

We would prefer you not to mention stills are available in your club magazine as we cannot supply - we do not pay purchase tax on these stills so cannot sell them to the public. Stills photographs are taken for film promotion only.

Yours sincerely

BRITISH LION FILMS LTD.

BRITISH BROADCASTING CORPORATION
TELEVISION CENTRE WOOD LANE LONDON W12 7RJ
TELEPHONE 01-743 8000 CABLES: BROADCASTS LONDON PS4
TELEGRAMS: BROADCASTS LONDON TELEX TELEX: 22182

15th July 1972

Dear Keith,

CLEVER BOY! Intelligent lad I always knew! I shall either send you super portrait of J.P. or keep it myself.I would in the usual way throw darts at it but as you did it I shan't. Sweet memory of you too! Sending some more envelopes. These ones are actually for J.P. and his own fan mail but I shall send some more little ones later. Yes I did mean really go and live abroad for 3 months or more!But as you say you have done lots and lots and I must admit I think your Mum would miss you tremedously.(Missed the 'n') The new theme tune is fantastic. Much better. No need for you to worry about sending post down to me. Just go into BBC and say you are Dr.Who fan club secretary and address your post to me at 505 Union House, Shepherd's Bush Green. If you like I will address a letter in this one to them in case there is any trouble then you can show it to reptionist or anything. Please do phone me and reverse the charges to BBC. Ask for me and they get through to me and ask me whether I know you and that the BBC can accept charges okay? Barry does it all the time when he's outside the BBC, so please do it yourself. It would be really fun to talk to you! Number is above using extension 4111. If any spare posters come to me I shall send them to you ok? I think as an after thought I shall hang it on our office wall (your protrait) I think it's excellente! Send all my love, to you and Mum. By the way you didn't enclose the'action' letter you said you were going to. I think I ought to see it, are they being cheeky? It's none of their business. Still let me see it. Thanks. I shall send your tender love to Katy as always but sadly for you she isn't with us till September but I won't forget. You may see her in another play for the other side quite soon. Not sure what though.

Love

Sarah

It's Good To Talk

That was exciting - a direct phone line to the Doctor Who production office. Well, it was until I remembered we didn't actually have a telephone. Hey, come on, my dad was a bus driver who took early retirement due to ill health and my mum cleaned offices in Edinburgh. There wasn't a lot of money around. Luckily, Sarah told me to reverse the charges from a local phone box. Thing is, the local riff-raff took great delight in destroying phone boxes so none were ever available. But one of the shops I lived above was a baker - Mr Stevenson - who let customers use a pay-phone which was kept in a cupboard in a corner of the shop. My visits to the cupboard became local legend. A bit like the red phone box in "Local Hero" , one of my most favourite films and starring, yes you got it, Peter Bleedin' Capaldi.

As I waved to the bakers behind the counter on my way to the cupboard, they leaned over to their customers and whispered, "There goes Keith on his way to phone Doctor Who." The customers would silently "ooh..." and nod their heads, then crane their necks as they stood in the queue to try and listen in to any gossip they could hear through the door.

I had my introduction script written down to read out to the operator. I did it so many times I can repeat it verbatim even today.

"Brrr, brrr - brr, brrr -"
click
Operator: "Hello, how can I help you?"
Me: "I'd like to make a revese charge call to London, please."
Operator: "Your name?"
Me: "Keith Miller"
Operator: "And the number you're calling from?"
Me: "031 664 7980"
Operator: "And the number you're calling?"
Me: "01 743 8000"
Operator: "Hold the line please."
Sound of connecting, then ring tone
BBC: "Television Centre"
Operator: "I have a reverse charge caller, will you accept the charge?"
BBC: "What's the callers' name?"
Operator: "Keith Miller"
(Beat)
BBC: "Yes, we'll accept the call."
Operator: "Go ahead, caller." *click*
Me: "Extension 4111 please."

Then I was through to Doctor Who land!

BRITISH BROADCASTING CORPORATION

TELEVISION CENTRE WOOD LANE LONDON W12 7RJ

TELEPHONE 01-743 8000 CABLES: TELECASTS LONDONPS4

TELEGRAMS: TELECASTS LONDON TELEX TELEX: 22182

EXT:- 4111

24th July 1972

Dear Keith,

It was fun talking to you too! Please ring whenever you want. I haven't any parcels yet but they may take sometime. I don't know what's happened to them but they'll come soon. I'm sure you could come down but where would you stay?! Haven't heard much about the T Shirts. I would write direct to Decca and ask for a record there. Naughty boy about telling me you had left, I must admit I would advise you tostay on. Just another two years? What about going to a tec though and tryint them there? I'm not sure if I am in S.Money's bad books. Don't really care actually but put in a good word for me when you next write to him and tell him how super I am!!!!!!!! Nestles are making dr,who wrappers. The next Dr.Who film comes out on 19th August.on BBC-1. My holidays my holiday! Soon I hope. Haven't made any plans yet but really feel I need one. I'm actually going into a flat on 1st August and am having a lot of upsets of new life etc but hope to go on hols fairly soon.

Love

S.

From:
Room No. & Building: Tel. Ext.: date:
Subject:
To:

Keith, regarding telephone calls, try + reverse calls on public phone box as it is easier. If you ring internally it takes ages. OK?

S.

AS/20

BRITISH BROADCASTING CORPORATION
TELEVISION CENTRE WOOD LANE LONDON W12 7RJ
TELEPHONE 01-743 8000 CABLES: BROADCASTS LONDON PS4
TELEGRAMS: BROADCASTS LONDON TELEX TELEX: 22182

EXT:- 4111

1st August

Dear Keith,

I think you and I know that my memory isn't much good. .... but I don't remember Jan do da. Perhaps I wrote and told him or perhaps Barry did. That's it, I think I've cracked it. I think Barry write and told him. O.K. Sorry about my mmemory, you see I only remember the important things! Come in Octber or anytime afterwards. Recordings are 2nd/3rd October, 16th/17th XXXXXXXXXX October, 13st Oct and 1st Nov. How abotu that? Write and we'll discuss or even better discuss on 'phone! So glad stencils are nearlyy readdy............ Thanks for writing to S. Money re: Super Sarah , sure it will help! Cybermen are not coming back, yes Daleks are, but that is more or less a secret still so we don't really wan't it prenited in the newsletter yet. I'll ask Barry to write a little letter at Xmas but please please remind me again nearer the time. Don't worry I'm only going on hols for two or three weeks. It will be in September so don't worry. I'll let you know the date nearer the time. You don't take any time up. It's not to be mentioned again. I've no idea about Katy, I thought she was romancing with you!? Naughty Keith. No, no, no youare not by any means worse than XXXX Peter C. I had a very sad letter back from him today I think I had better write and apolagise! I think he's the end and I wish the daleks or someone would exterminate him or something to that effect. So sorry about shocking typing. I'm not very good at it coz I hate it but will look forward to your call and I wish you would make a few more mistakes in you r typing because then I don't feel so bad. So remember , next letter, deliberate mistakes please!

Love

S

During the next phone call to Sarah, I asked how things were going with Peter Capaldi. "Oh, god, I wish someone would sort him out." Then she paused. "Actually he stays in Scotland too, Keith. Can't you pop over to Glasgow and sort him out for me?" I giggled nervously, quickly fnished the call and worridley headed back to the house. Was she being serious? Did she *actually* want me to go over to Glasgow and "sort him out"? Was I to become *Doctor Who's* hitman? I'd never hit anyone in my life. Well apart from Susan Stott who lived next door in our first house and she ended up kicking seven shades out of me. Seriously, I worried about this for days...

BRITISH BROADCASTING CORPORATION
TELEVISION CENTRE WOOD LANE LONDON W12 7RJ
TELEPHONE 01-743 8000 CABLES: BROADCASTS LONDON PS4
TELEGRAMS: BROADCASTS LONDON TELEX TELEX: 22182
EXT:- 4111

9th August 1972

Dear Keith,

Panic! I have thrown the stencils away for the N.W.L. What are we going to do? Fool me, but I'm sure I ran off enough perhaps the machine kept a few behind to read! Thank you for those pictures of those handsome boys. I return them to you! Glad P.C. has at last got the message. About time too! I don't believe you. The mistakes you made in your letter were NOT DELIBERATE! Sure of it. Anyway, you are very kind. Yes you are right about Ian Barbara and Susna. Quite right. Has someone said you're wrong? I think drawings are fantastic! And the N.L. Very good. The triple Doctor is going to be recorded in 27th and 28th November and 11th and 12 the December. Actually thinking about it I think that show would interest you more and be much more excitinging(?!) What about asking for that day off instead. That one will really be a super show and you'll see Pat Troughton.(Remember it is still a secret) Poster are printed by Personality Posters in London. I have seen them all over the place. No I don't really want to see the medal as long as it isn't anything naughty! No, no,no, I really don't want you to go and See P.C. Sorry If I gave you the wrong impression. Please take it all back. No need to go at all. By the way Tardis pics ready in three weeks.

Love

S.

DWFC SPECIAL COMPETITION ISSUE:DWFC SPECIAL COMPETITION ISSUE:DWFC SECIAL COMP

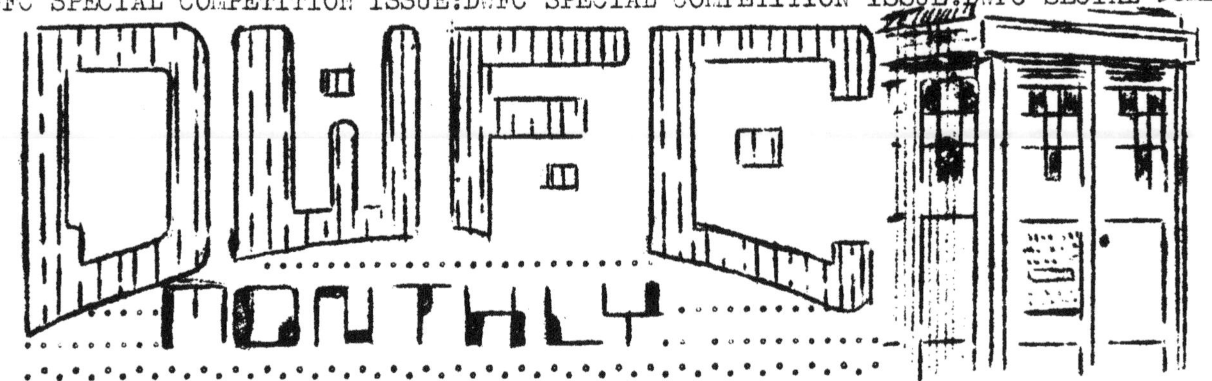

Number 7 August Edition D.W.F.C SPECIAL

THE FIRST DWFC ANNUAL COMPETITION!!!

Open to everyone in the DWFC!This competition will be held yearly and the prize is THE DWFC GOLD MEDAL!All you have to do is match the following quotations with the programme in wh which it was said.

QUOTATIONS

1."I am Alydon.I am a Thal.I tried to speak to you in the forest just now."

2."It concerns the Master.I've seen him not ten minutes ago!"said the Doctor."The Master?"gasped the Brigadier."Where?""In a dream"replied theDr.

3."Skybase one.This is Skybase one. Malfunction in storage area five.Investigation please!"

ADVENTURES

A.The film :"DR.WHO AND THE DALEKS"

B."THE MUTANTS"

C."THE TIME MONSTER"

Now,after you have matched these up, write a short story (not more than 500 words),starting with this paragraph:

"The Tardis spun through deep space as the Doctor showed Jo how to operate the simple controls.

"There,Jo,"he said,"I've shown you what to do.Now you try."

Jo looked sternly at the control panel.

"Well.You start by pressing these three buttons.Then you pull down the two blue switches.Then you..eh..then you press this!"

"NO!DON'T PRESS IT..."

But it was too late.The Tardis lurched as it was thrown into the far reaches of an unknown dimension!"

Now this is where you take over.You take the Doctor and Jo to wherever you want.

The winning entry who answers the questions correctly and writes the best story wins the DWFC 1972 Gold Medal and their story printed in the monthly.

The DOCTORS DRAWING BOARD

Zarbi by John Milburn from Hebburn.

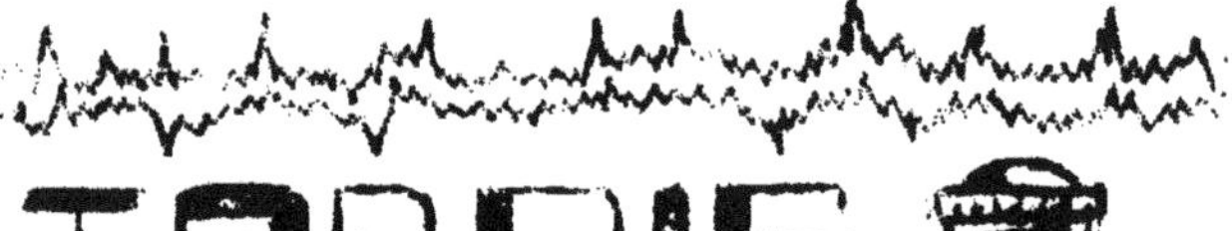

TARDIS TALKBOX

Letter intended for publication should be sent to:-
The Doctor Who Fan Club,
"Tardis Talkbow",
c/o Keith Miller,
109 Moredun Park Road,
Edinburgh EH17 7HJ.

Dear Timelord,

Since this column began,I think the question which has been asked the most is ARE THE FIRST ISSUES OF DWFC MONTHLY STILL AVAILABLE?And the answer I had to return was no. But there are some bits and peices of earlier monthlys,with the front page of issue number one etc.So if anybody wants them,they're here for the taking!

DR.WHO IN THE BEGINING

EPISODE FIVE
"THE MUTANTS"

STARRING

William Hartnell................Dr.Who
William Russel.........Ian Chesterton
Jaqueline Hill.........Barbara Wright
Carol Ann Ford.........Susan Foreman.
in "The Ordeal"

"What do want with us?"shouted the Doctor.

The Daleks ignored the question.Outside, in the forest,the Thals were debating what to do next.Alydon was speaking.

"The Doctor and his Granddaughter have been taken prisoners by the Daleks.They have helped us in the past;now we must return that help.Altough we have vowed that we must never use violence,I am cmpeled to think that it is the only way. We shall go the city of the Daleks...and we will destroy them!"

Meanwhile,the party following the pipes to find another way into the city had been walking through a network of caves which led from the cliff face.After a perilous jump over a deep crevice and another long climb,they came to a ledge and the other way into the city.But the entrance was obstructed by parralel bars of thick iron bars!

Inside the city,the Doctor had learned that the Daleks were planning to explode a neutron bomb which even the drugs of the Thals had no effect!against!The countdown had begun.......

EPISODE SIX
"The Rescue"

"What are we going to do?"asked Barbara.

"There must be a control switch somewhere"said Ian,pressing his elbow into the wall.There was a loud hum and the bars slid up into the roof.

"Well done"said Alydon"Now come on.."

They were in a brightly lit corridor on the bottom most level.As they made their way to themain control hall,they were chased by a Dalek,but they soon managed to lose it by jumping into one of the lifts.On the main control hall level, they met the other Thals who hadmanaged to get inside the city by the front entrance,left unguarded by the Daleks who were preparing to explode the bomb.The crowd made their way to the hall.Two Daleks were approaching. Ian and Alydon pressed themselves against the wall so they were out of the Daleks range of vision.When they passed them,they grabbed them from behind and swung them round to face each other as their guns shot their mist of death at each other.Their was a loud explosion,and the two Daleks were destroyed.

"COME ON!"shouted Ianwho lead the party into the hall.The Thals flooded the hall as the Daleks were caught unaware.They grabbed the Daleks andpropelled them at the machinery.

"CHESTERTON!"cried the Doctor"STOP THE COUNTDOWN!THE BOMB WILL DESTROY THE PLANET!"

Ian yelled to the Daleks and ducked as they fired their guns at the bank of machinery which controlled the bomb. There was a vast explosion as the panel disintregated in a kaleidoscope of ligh light.When the party looked up again, everything was still.Silence drooped strangely over the hall.

"They're all dead"said Barbara pushing a Dalek which glided a short way down the hall,and then stopped.

"We must have blown their entire environmental condition controls to smithereens..." said the Doctor.

Back in the forest,the Thals were waiting to say goodbye to their alien friends,who were inside the Tardis.

"You mean to tell us that there was nothing wrong with the fluid link?You wanted to explore the city and this was the only way you could do it.YOU COULD HAVE KILLED US ALL."yelled Ian.

"I have told you before,Chesterton. This is my ship and as long as you are with me,you will not take command.Out there is a world which needs rebuilding and a leader.If you don't want to come with me.."

Ian thought for a second,looked at Barbara,and said"Lets say goodbye to the Thals..."

They went outside where the Thals had gathered.

"Well,this is goodbye"said Alydon, "You have helped us in our battle against the Daleks.Please accept these." he said handing them each a cape.They said their goodbyes,and stepped once more into the Tardis.

I'm afraid the Special Annual Comp. taken up the space set aside for "DALEK DATA"but don't worry,Dalek fans it'll be back next month!

JO GRANT AND KING PELADON IN

PART THREE

Jo screamed but it could hardly be heard over the crackling of flames,the crash of falling trees and the trumpeting of the large monster.

"RUN FOR THE BOX,PRINCESS"cried the young King.

They both took to their heels and ran as fast as they could.But it was too late.The Fire Monster had seen them and giving chase.The very ground shook as the animal pounded over the plains.Tongues of fire shot at the duo, missing them only by inches.They ran into a clearing in the trees,andssaw the Tardis.But it was till some distance away.The monster was getting nearer.They flew across as fast as they could and reached the police box.

"Quickly,Josephine!Inside.The monster is nearly upon us!"

Jo pushed against the doors.

"Peladon.The doors won't open!"

She banged her fists on the box.

"Open up..PLEASE....!"she sobbed.

The monsters shadow cloaked the duo as it snarled and prepared to destroy. Peladon grabbed Jo's arm and pulled her to the left.A tongue of fire exploded against the Tardis.

"Follow me.!"panted Peladon,"Caves... on mountainside...!"

Jo shot a glance behind her.The Fire Monster was still pursuing them.They came to a slope,at the top of which was a cliff.They made their way up the slope and started to climb the cliff until they reached some caves high up the mountainside.They peered over the side.Down below them the monster gave terrific growls of anger at losing its victims.

"Well.We are safe up here!" said Peladon.

"It's turning away.It must have lost intersest..!"

"OH NO!THE MONSTER IS HEADING TO WARD THE LAKE OF LIQUID EXPLOSIVE! WE SHALL ALL BE BLOWN TO THE OTHER END OF THE COSMOS!"

THE MASTER IS ON THE LOOSE AGAIN! And you can see what what he is up to on the back of Doctor Who's own Milk Chocolate bar which is currently being made by Nestles. On the back of each bar there is a cartoon picture.When you have collected the 15 wrappers, you have the complete story of "Doctor Who Fights MasterPlan "Q""!

Later on,Nestles hope to produce a collection card for the wrappers.

D.W.F.C. CROSSWORD No.3

ACROSS

1.Inhabitant of the planet Solos.
6.Well known tree.
8.The Doctors time machine.
9.No.8 travels through this.
11."Through hill and ...."
12.The Dr.has to open this to get out of the Tardis.
14."Dr.Who Fights Master.... "Q""
17.Our Solar system is part of this.
18.The letters after 1972(or any year)
19.To materialize is to ....

DOWN

1.Another name for one across.
2.... apple
4.Small letter.
5.What you have to do to get to another planet.
7.Bearded villian.
10.Smalllife form
13.A popular Devil
14."You will ... for this,Doctor!"
15.Abbreviate "Attack,Attack,Attack8"
16.Town where we first met the Doctor.

ANSWERS NEXT MONTH!

27th and 28th

BRITISH BROADCASTING CORPORATION
TELEVISION CENTRE WOOD LANE LONDON W12
TELEPHONE 01-743 8000 CABLES: BROADCASTS LONDON PS4
TELEGRAMS: BROADCASTS LONDON TELEX TELEX: 22182

15th August

Dear Keith, I'm sorry If I sounded down yesterday but I wasn't. There were nine men sitting in my office though having a very tiring time sorting out costs for visual effects for the next story so I couldnot really be my jovial self as it would have sounded out of place. Sorry to hear about the Education place. But you being too young is what I thought would have happened. Still you must not waste your time now till you are 18. You mustn't. You must go to tec or some other form of school or even go back to school. You mustn't sit back and do nothing! I'm very serious about this, and let me know what you and your Mum decide to do. Actually reading your letter again I see that you are going back to school. Good move! Am feeling much happier now! ~~I should have read your letter properly~~!!!!!! Send you envelopes. Perhaps you could type the stencils again and I'll have more run off. Is that too much? Let me know and I'll promise I'll never throw away them again..... I know that you have have been spelling you know what' wrong but I thought It was none of my business. Chose the one with Jon and Katy for the Tardis pic....Hang on no, it was just Jon we cut Katy out. Sorry......! Send the monthly's how you like doesn't make any difference. Sorry to hear that you have competition re: the UFO club. It really aint much to do with us is it? Still I would ignore him and let him get on with it . I'm sure our club is much more efficient.... Nic Courtney wears a falsy! Take care and looking fowwrd to seeing you. So glad that you are staying on at school, and you'll be much more intelligent I'm sure by the time you get to the other place when you are 18 and beable to go straight on to their courses because I expect you are haven't got up to A levesl. I don't perhaps you have but kick me if I'm being rude! This last sentence isn't meant to be rude but reading it over it does sound a little - but please it doesn't mean any thing.

SARAH

BRITISH BROADCASTING CORPORATION

TELEVISION CENTRE WOOD LANE LONDON W12 7RJ

TELEPHONE 01-743 8000 CABLES: TELECASTS LONDONPS4

TELEGRAMS: TELECASTS LONDON TELEX TELEX: 22182

EXT:- 4111

29th August 1972

Dear Keith,

Can't I'm afraid get you the synopses you want. Sorry but they are just too old! No more news about repeats! I think the best time to phone me is during lunch times about 1300 hrs to 1400hrs if I'm not in don't worry ring next time but usually I'm here for lunches and then I can really talk to you without having to worry about people around me. Jamie I expect will be around at the date you will be down but not sure, it is too far ahead to say what recordings have been worked out. I send you Nic's pictures. I am going to France for two weeks . Can't wait. Will send you a postcard.

Love

Sarah

Interesting to note that even at this stage, Fraser Hines was expected to reprise the role of Jamie opposite Pat Throughton in The Three Doctors!

BBC
Monday.

Dear Keith,

Thank you for your very sweet letter. I really have been feeling lately that you have been neglected, but honestly I really have had so little time lately that I just don't know which way to turn sometimes. Moonbase 3 is causing a lot of work. I have been typing some of the scripts as they are needed extra quick and so it helps if I type some of them. Then there is all the owrk on that programme plus Doctor Who and thousands of letters from little people asking stupid questions that have to be answered. So you see I am busy and I haven't been ignoring you purposely. When you phone tomorrow I won't be here either becoz it is a studio day and I'll be up there instead of here.....So another wasted phone call I'm afraid. I enclose envelopes. I know they are not the right kind, but they haven't any small ones. Facotyr on strike or something. Stuart Money wrote to Jon Pertwee and asked him if he could visit studio. Jon said yes, and referred him to us. Barry had to say yes coz Jon said yes, so he is coming up in April. What's your news about? Do tell me, I love scandal. I enclose stencils too. Write to roger yourself. He isn't nearly so sticky about home address as Jon. It is 28 Park Lane, Teddington, Middx. Nice letter, you sent.

If You Build It, They Will Come

Recently, I received an e-mail from someone who used to be in the fan club. He said: "I used to think Moredun Park Road sounded so charming - a bit like Cherry Tree Lane in Mary Poppins." Crikey, if only he knew...

One thing I wasn't expecting was when members of the fan club began appearing at my front door. This used to embarrass me totally. As I've mentioned previously, I lived in one of the rougher areas in the south of Edinburgh, two stories up above a set of shops, one of which was, handily, a post office. However, the main stair to the flats was regularly used as a toilet by passing citizens, so unless my Mum was quick off the mark with her bucket of hot water and Dettol, visitors had to wade their way through oceans of urine, dodging turds on the way. The walls were covered in graffiti - my early sex eduction came from the graphic depictions scrawled at random. Smart young families on their holidays used to "drop in" on their way to their destination in Scotland. Their very accents used to make me hang my head in shame in having lured them to this dump.

But they seemed to enjoy the experience, no matter what I felt. I had painted my bedroom white, cut out roundels in Polystyrene tiles and stuck them on the wall. I built a control console where I could switch on or off any of the electrical items in the room - remote controls were very much a science fiction at this time. Mirror tiles, again with a circle motif, were on the doors, trying to give the illusion of dimensional transcendentalism. So once they were in the house, they were fine. The dads looked a bit nervous when they had to leave, mind you, probably wondering if their wheels were still intact.

Gordon had a nephew who was a Doctor Who fan and brought him round to meet me, but he was a ghastly child, determined to rubbish everything I showed him and just generally being horrid. "You've just cut holes in polystyrene tiles. I was expecting proper roundels." he grumbled.

Iain K McLaughlin was a student from St Andrews and regular visitor. I remember he used to lug around a huge briefcase, packed to the gunnels with Doctor Who paraphenalia. Iain was to go on to write audio adventures for Big Finish, and reached the upper echelons of DC Thomson, the famed comics publisher based in Dundee.

The most bizzarre visit I had was from three young kids - well two young kids and a teenager. The two young 'uns were there to support their elder chum, but their shyness made them scowl at me, in a very threatning way as they stood just behind their teenage friend. They were tiny, but I had the feeling that if I even tried to touch their pal, they would be on me in a blink of an eye. The elder, who must have been thirteen or at most fourteen, was already clearly eccentric, with nervous ticks, but with a charming smile and winning way with him. And he had the wildest sandy hair I had ever seen. It sprouted in three cones from his head, one on each side and one in the middle. He sported a high neck sweater and duffle coat, which added to his Professor Quatermass air. He had brought with him a large

rolled up poster. “Can I show you this?” he said and rolled the poster over the bedroom floor. I squinted at it. “What, em... What exactly... is it?” I asked. His smile broke a little and quickly turned into a frown. “It’s a time machine.” he replied, in an incredulous tone - how could I not know? It wasn’t a cartoon or sketch, this was a proper technical drawing of two large columns, with labelled components and detailed examples of power requirements etc. He bamboozled me with talk of tachyons (the first time I had ever heard of them), Cherenkov radiation and Fermi-Dirac statistics. But he was losing patience in me as I struggled to keep up and evetually he rolled his protoype plans up, thanked me for my time, and the three left, never to be seen again. But I like to think he built his time machine and is whirling through the Time Vortex, even as we speak.

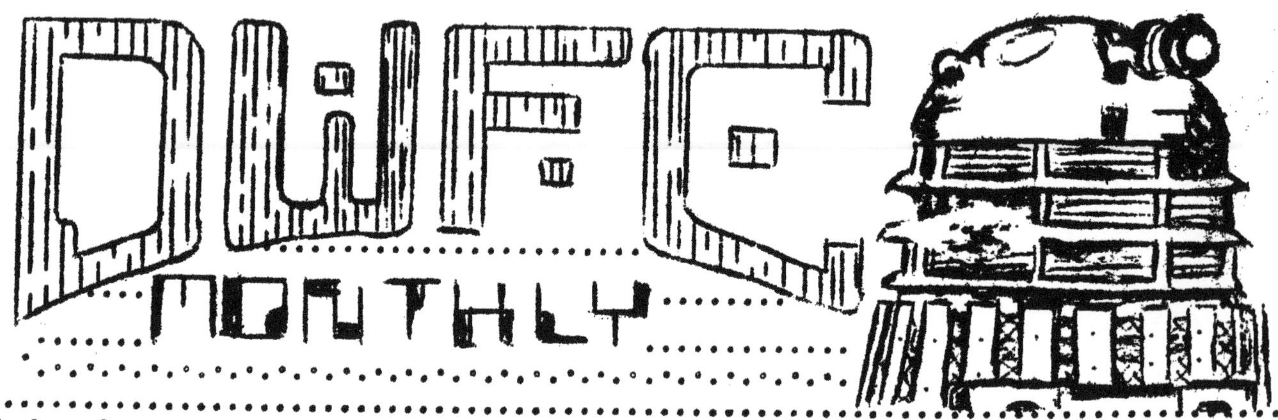

Number 8 · September Edition · D.W.F.C.

FREE PHOTOGRAPHS AND INFORMATION SHEETS

Free photographs are now available of your favourite Dr.Who stars and details are given throughout the monthly.

Free dossiers,too are available,of Jon Pertwee,Richard(Mike Yates)Franklin and Caroline(Liz Shaw)John.

For any of these free items,please write to me at The Dr.Who Fan Club,109 Moredun Park Road,Edinburgh EH17 7HJ., and don't forget to enclose a stamped addressed envelope if you want them quickly.

DOCTOR WHO FAN CLUB ANNUAL COMPETITION

Here are a couple of details I forgot to give you last month.

The competiton closes on the 1st of October,so you've got plenty of time to do it in.The winning story will be printed in the Novenber issue.Address all entryes to the club address and good luck!

DALEK DATA

"BATTLE ON ARCTURUS" part two

The Black Dalek,having finished his announcement for the conquest of Arcturus,glided back up the platform as the force of war Daleks filed out of the hall,along a short corridor,and into another huge room where large circles were painted on the floor.

Each Dalek entered its own circle and when all was still,the black circles rose up forming a scaffolding which reached up to the Daleks middle.On the front of the network was a black box with a large,round opening where the Dalek fitted his Sucker Cup.All was ready for the invasion.The Red Dalek was to act as their leader.It glided round to face the force.

"YOU HAVE BEEN INFORMED ON BATTLE PROCEEDURES"Its eye stick turned to the side of the hall where a Duty Dalek was hovering in front of a control panel.

(continued on next page)

DOCTORS DRAWING BOARD

Arcturus and Alpha Centauri by Simon Lidster.This is the last in this present series but it will return at Christmas and next year.Thanks to everyone who sent in drawings and don't give up hope!Yours could be in the Xmas issue!

TARDIS TALKBOX SPECIAL!PEN PAL SPOT!

I've had a letter from an Australian member who wants another DWFC member as a pen-pal.Apart from Dr.Who his other main interests are reading and amateur dramatics.His name is Shane Keenan and would like his pen-pal to be in the 14-15 age group.He lives in Horsham between the Grampian Mountains and the Victorian Desert.If you would like to be his pal then write a letter to him but addressed to the club then I'll pass them on to him

FROM THE BEGINNING

Transmittion date:8/2/63
Serial:C

"EDGE OF DESTRUCTION"
by David Whitaker
starring

William Hartnell...............Dr.Who
William Russel....... Ian Chesterton
Jacqueline Hill......Barbara Wright
Carole Ann Ford.........Susan Foreman

episode one

"We have now left Skaro and heading into deep space" said the Doctor as he glanced up from the control console.

"Where are heading for now?Disneyland?Or Mars perhaps?!"sneered Ian.

"Young man.I am doing my best to get you and your friend back to Earth.Now if you would kindy be quiet,perhaps I could think properly"

"look,Doctor.We're travellers with you whether we like it or not,but you must try to see it from our point of view.You've uprooted us from our way of life.Can we live here?Can you control the Ship?"

"No!The ship is incapable of making a calculated landing"

All was quiet.Barbara moved closer to Ian.

"Does that mean that we may never see Earth again?Ever?"she asked.

"I'll do my best my dear but there is something else wrong.The controls are refusing to respond"

"You mean we're out of control?" asked Susan.

"We're safe as long as we stay in the Ship.Now please let me get on with my work..."

The Doctor struggled with levers that refused to move.

"I think there is only one solution. I'll have to land..."

The Doctor managed to turn a few dials as the rotor sank.The scanner couldn't be activated so he announced that he would have to risk opening the doors.He pressed the buttons but nothing happened.

"Perhaps its the fluid links.."said Ian.

"No,no,no.They are connected to the dematerialization circutry.That kind of fault would not affect the doors.."

"Perhaps some kind of alien intelligence has taken over.."

"Don't be so silly,Susan.."replied the Doctor.

"I don't think it's silly"said Barbara, "It could well be that something invisible has taken over"

"All your explanations are highly improbable"continued the Doctor.

"Oh and I suppose you have a better one for whats going on,eh?"

"Yes,I do.I believe you have stolen a vital part of Tardis and you are going to blackmail your back to England?AM I CORRECT?"

"You old fool!Perhaps it's not a bad idea!"

"Oh,stop it!"cried Susan.

"Don't worry,Susan"said the Doctor"At our next landing place,the two of them are leaving.I will not stand for this.."

The rotor was reactivated.A short time later,the Tardis landed .

"Now.Get off my Ship!"hissed the Doctor as the doors glided open.

"Grandfather!"screamed Susan.

The Doctor spun round to see through the doors that they were suspended in space.The Tardis lurched and Susan was thrown to one side.The others clung to the console.There was a loud rumbling noise.

"DOCTOR!DO SOMETHING!"yelled Ian.

Suddenly,a blinding light filled the palatial control room.

"Now I know whats wrong"cried the Doctor"WE'RE HEADING STRAIGHT FOR THE SUN!!"

episode two next month

FREE PHOTOGRAPHS

Free photos of William Hartnell are now available

"BATTLE ON ARCTULUS"(continued)

"OPERATE THE RELEASE MECHANISM"he ordered. The Dalek obeyed.and then left the hall.A few moments later,the far wall slid open and the Daleks operated their machines.The circles rose from the floor.

"EXTERMINATE THE ARCTURANS!"chanted the force as they glided out of the ship and down onto Arcturus.

part three next month.

Due to unforseen circumstances,I'm afraid THE ORIGIN OF THE DALEKS has had to be cancelled.

FREE PHOTOGRAPHS

Free photographs of the Black Dalek and the Ogrons are now available.

JO GRANT and KING PELADON in

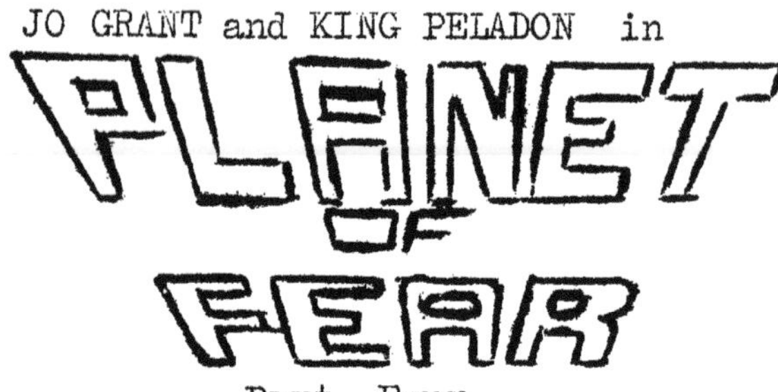

Part Four

"What will we do?"asked Jo.

"We cannot possibly stop the monster, and we cannot get back to the box"Peladon looked at Jo with sad eyes."There is nothing we can do.."

"We can't just sit here and let it happen.Look,theres obviously something wrong with the controls of the Tardis, remember how they kept operating themselves?Well,perhaps the doors are open now.."Peladon looked at Jo.

"I suppose there is a chance.."said the king,as he began to make his way back down the mountainside.

When they reached the bottom,they looked across the plain to see where the Fire Monster was.He thundered closer to the explosive lake.

"Look!I was right!The doors are open after all!"

They made their way towards the Tardis and safety.About twenty yards from the police box,the doors began to close!

"The doors are closing...RUN FOR IT PELADON!"

They both dived throught the doors and into the control room of the Ship.

"Now what?"said Jo."We could blow ourselves up if we try to get away from here!"

"We shall die anyway if we don't get off this planet"replied Peladon.

"I suppose you're right",she said,and crossing over to the control console, began the same operation of travelling through the time warp.Tears began to form in Jo's eyes as the thought of never seeing Mother Earth again struck her.

"Oh,Peladon.I'm so tired and unhappy" Silence drooped over the ship."Peladon? Why don't you answer me.."

She looked around and saw that her companion had dissapeared.The Tardis lurched as it was thrown into the Time Warp and into more unknown dangers.

LAST PART NEXT MONTH.

FREE PHOTOGRAPHS

Free photos of Katy Manning (Jo Grant) are now available.

NEW!NEW!NEW!NEW!NEW!NEW!NEW!NEW!NEW!NEW

After mountains of requests,there are now photos of the TARDIS available!

REVIEW "DR.WHO AND THE DALEKS"

This is the first special Review ofthe year.The second will be next month when I review the second Dalek film "DALEKS-INVASION EARTH:2150 AD"

This was about my fifth time of seeing this film and I found that I enjoyed it every time!Of course, I think I enjoyed it that little bit better the first time.

I would like to split the film up into two parts and look at them individually.

As a Doctor Who film,I don't think it does him justice.Peter Cushing played the part of a rather forgetfull old scientist from Earth very well,but surely it is an important point that he is an alien from some far distant planet.Not a mere scientist,but a brilliant genius!

Oh,and the inside of the Tardis.Deary me,what a mess!

Perhaps it would have been better if they stuck stricty to the TV scripts and cut out the comedy from Roy Castle who made Ian Chesterton into a clumsy clot.

Do not think that the first adventures of Dr.Who were anything like this.They were much better.

Now.As a Dalek film it was excellent. It managed to get across the cold-heart-ed ness of the metallic monsters.The motion picture Daleks are much bigger, about six foot,than the TV versions and the lights which flash when they speak and the bumper at the base was different. I'll comment more about this next month.

The ending was great with the destruction of the Daleks.No wonder it was shown again on ASK ASPEL. Well,thats my view and I would be most interested to hear <u>your</u> own view.

Another special next month with "2150 AD"

CROSSWORD No.3

Across

1.Mutant 6.Elm 8.Tardis 9.Space 11.Vale 12.Door 14.Plan 17.Galaxy 18.AD 19.Land

Down

1.Monster 2.An 4.Note 5.Travel 7.Master 10.Ant 13.Sea 14.Pay 15.AAA 16.London

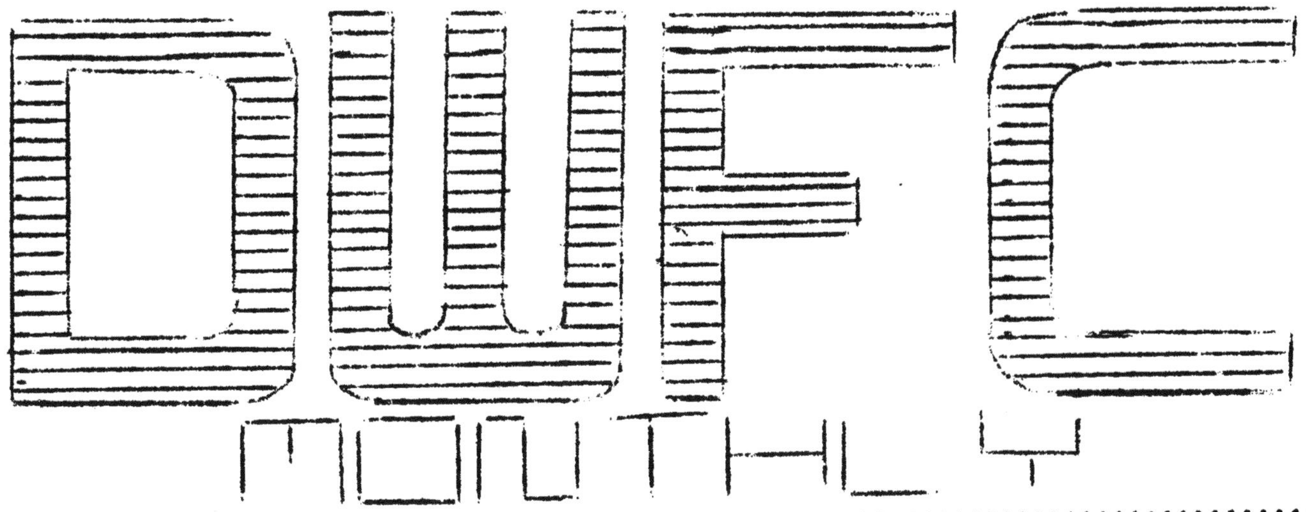

Number 9 October Edition D.W.F.C.

FINAL DETAILS FOR THE DWFC COMPETITION.

Due to the long delay of the August edition, the competition has been extended to the 31st of October. This is the final date.

ATA

"THE DALEK DOMINATORS" in
"BATTLE ON ARCTURUS"
part three

In the city below, the half robot, half creature beings known as the Arcturans had detected the oncoming fleet on their radarscopes. In their giant war hall, the top Arcturans were assembled.

"It has now been confirmned that a force of aliens known as the Daleks are planning an invasion on our planet", it squeaked, "The first fleet has handed on the outskirts of the city. A delagate has been sent to meet them, and discuss the situation...."

The delagate trundled up to the Red Dalek, who glided down a small ramp in the side of the Hovabout (the small craft they use for short air journeys)

"I have been sent from the High Council of the Arcturans. We welcolme you to our planet."

"YOU ARE AN ARCTURAN. WE PLAN TO TAKE OVER THIS PLANET. YOU ARE AN ENEMY OF THE DALEKS. YOU WILL BE EXTERMINATED!"

The defensive rings of the Arcturan began coiling from the saucer-shaped weapon on the front of its transporter but the Daleks were much quicker as their deadly radiation guns blew the Arcturan into millions of fragments of metal.

"WAR HAS BEEN DECLARED. ONWARD TO THE CITY. EXTERMINATE THE ARCTURANS!"

DALEKS - INVASION EARTH 2150 A.D.

REVIEW: REVIEW: REVIEW: REVIEW: REVIEW: REVIEW

The final Review of the year! But the series will return when the Doc comes back onto your TV screens in the new year.

This was only my second time of seeing this film and I still say that the first film was the best.

The inside of the Tardis, I'm glad to say had been tided up but no sign of the familiar sunken circles on the wall and control console, though.

Another idiot was introduced called Tom Campbell who replaced Ian Chesterton from the TV series. The dining sequence in the saucer was a nutty.

Talking about the saucer, I must congratulate the special effects department for the excellent job of the saucer in flight. Nothing fake seen at all....till the end.

The title music wasn't as good as the other film's and nethier was the incidental music. I really enjoyed the incidental music to DR WHO AND THE DALEKS when they were climbing the cliff to get to the Dalek Dalek city.

At last they replaced those gold bumpers on the Daleks with the traditional black ones.

Well, I guess thats about all for now, so it only remains for me to say that I hope you have enjoyed hearing my views and look forward to the next series of REVIEW.

JO GRANT in

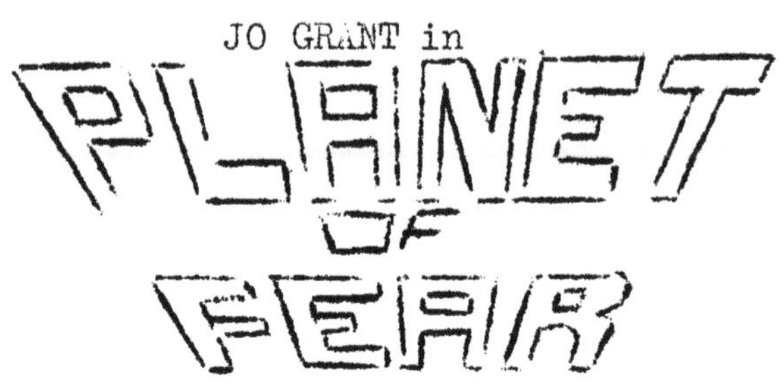

Final Episode

"PELADON WHERE ARE YOU?!"The young girl screamed but to no avail.The young king had gone.But she could not say where.

"Was he really here?"she whispered,"OR AM I GOING MAD....!"

The room spun.She found difficulty in standing.The room echoed with the bellowing of the Fire Monster and the voice of Peladon whispered "Goodbye" before she finally passed out.

When she came to,her head was neatly bandaged and a hand held her head up.Her eyes opened but were out of focus,but they soon returned to normal and defined the blurr above her as the friendly,but grimm face of the Doctor.

"Doctor,oh..I'm so glad..ohhhh...!"

"Steady,J6.You've been through a terrible ordeal,I know!"

"You..you know?"

"Yes,my dear.It happened once before a very long time ago,with a girl called Susan...!"

"But what happened.And..and wheres Peladon?Is he alright?"

"Well,lets stop talking for the moment and see if we can get you some nice,hot tea,eh?"said the Doctor,helping Jo through the doors of the Tardis.

Jo sipped at the tea,her head throbbing. She lay her head back as the empty cup was placed on the table beside the couch in the Doctors Laboratory.

"Feeling better now?"asked the Doctor.

"So many questions...but so tired... must sleep..."drowsing into a peaceful sleep with the reasurance that she was back home and with her friends.

EPILOGUE

When she had fully recovered,the Doctor sat Jo down in front of him and began to explain the nightmare which was now over.

"Fully recovered now Jo?"

"Yes,well apart from the gigantic golf ball bump I've got at the back of my head,I'm fine!"

"And so there should be.I would imagine you gave yourself a very bad bang when you collapsed!"

"Never mind that.Lets get down to the more important matters....what happened to me inside the Tardis?"

"As I said before,Jo,it happened once before,"began the Doctor,"The Tardis' telepathic sensors were faulty at the time you obviously stubled in and began to take over the running of the ship. Susan was taken to a large asteroid where large Fire Creatures dwelt..!"

"That's just like the other planet!" interupted J6,"There was fire monster there as well!"

"Yes,well this was obviously the same place.But the Tardis also brought a companion to help her as it had picked up her thought waves for help!"

"Like Peladon..."said Jo."What happened to him,Doctor?"

"Well,after you threw the Tardis into the Time Warp,the telepathis sensors began to function again and so sent Peladon back to his home planet!"

"Will he remember anything of the journey?"

"I doubt it,my dear.The Tardis probably returned him to his exact place in time Only a second at the most would have been lost.Anyway,the Tardis followed a path back to Earth where it was set for in the beginning.I doubt she'll ever do it again,will you old girl?"said the Doctor,slapping the police box's side.

"Well,it's over now,Miss Grant.Now I need some help with Bessie.I've been trying to get her in perfect order while you've been hopping around the universe like a cellestial bunny.Now come on..!"

Jo Grant smiled felt good at coming home but sad at losing Peladon.Still,perhaps some other day......

THE END

FREE PHOTOGRAPHS OF JON PERTWEE alais DR WHO are now available.Just send an sae to:- The DWFC,c/o Keith Miller,109 Moredun Park Road,Edinburgh EH17 7HJ and I'll rush one to you as fast as you can say Tardis.More details of photos on the next page!

-FROM THE BEGINNING

Transmittion date:15/2/64
Serial:C
"BRINK OF DISASTER"
by David Whitaker
starring
William Hartnell..................Dr.Who
William Russel............**Ian Chesterton**
Jaqueline Russel..........**Barbara** Wright
Carole Ann Ford............Susan Foreman
episode two

"DOCTOR,HURRY UP AND DO SOMETHING!"repeated Ian.

"I'm trying young man..."said the Doctor struggling with the door control.At last it gave way and the door glided to a close and the party released their grip on the console.Susan pulled herself to her feet.

"Are you all right,my dear?"asked the Doctor.

"Yes..yes,think so."

"So it was the controls after all,"said Barbara.

"Yes,Barbara.The controls have a defence mechanism which protects them from misuse.During our disagreement,I must have been confused and set the controls wrongly.I was sending the Tardis into the sun.However the Tardis refused to destroy itself.."

"Are we all right now?"asked Ian.

"Yes..I..eh..I think so.I'll land the ship and see if there is anything wrong in the fuel and life support system."

The dials readjusted and peace restored on the craft,it continues its journey through time and space.

The ship lands on a snowy plateu.As the party leave the ship,they notice that although there is snow and ice all around,it really isn't cold.Suddenly, Susan cries out and Ian,Barbara and the Doctor find her staring at the snow clad ground.A few yards away,was a huge foot print imbedded deep in the snow.

"Look at it.."exclaimed Barbara.

"Back to the ship,quickly"said the Doctor"There is great danger here.."

After a narrow escape from the owner of the print-a huge snow monster,fifty feet high,they reach the Tardis and enter.

"That was a narrow escape"said Ian."Is this how our lives are to be?Not knowing whether we will survive to see our own planet again?That every corner we turn, there will be a caveman,Dalek or monster lurking int the shadows?Do you call that living?"

"Don't forget you pushed your way into the ship young man,"said the Doctor"But I do simpethise with you.But you must travel with hope as well as understanding!"

The Doctor looked grave.The corners of his mouth drooped low.

"And I'm afraid that my last statement will have to be followed very carefully. Due to too many hasty dematerrializations the Tardis'electrical equipment controlling the life support system has been damaged.We need more fuel.Also,our supply of water is exhausted.If the next planet is incapable of providing these essential supplies,we won't have enough fuel to leave."O

"That means"said Barbara"we'll die!!"

....

NEXT MONTH:A complete adventure called "DR.WHO AND MARCO POLO"

....

FREE PHOTOGRAPHS:FREE PHOTOGRAPHS:FREE

The following stars and objests are now available free of charge to every member of the DWFC:-

WILLIAM HARTNELL,The BLACK DALEK and the OGRONS,KATY MANNING,and DR.WHO AND THE TARDIS CONSOLE.

More will be made available in the weeks to come.

....

LAST WORD LAST WORD LAST WORD LAST WORD

Well,here I am shifted from the first page to the last.Notice the new heading? How do you like it?Is it better than the old one?

Anyway,I suppose you've all seen the advert with JON PERTWEE in it selling a "well known gravy mixture"I've been told to say.I don't know why.Everyone knows its Bisto.....

Well,next month is the special competition story issue with news about the special Christmas issue.More about that next month.

Did you know that Nestles are running a special Dr.Who Competition?And that the Dr Who theme tune(the original that is)is on a Decca record?And that a poster has been of you know who by Personality Posters?And that Dr Who appears in the Countdown/TV Action Annual?And that the DR.WHO ANNUAL 1973 is now on sale?And that I'm running out of space.See you next month.Be happy!Bye!

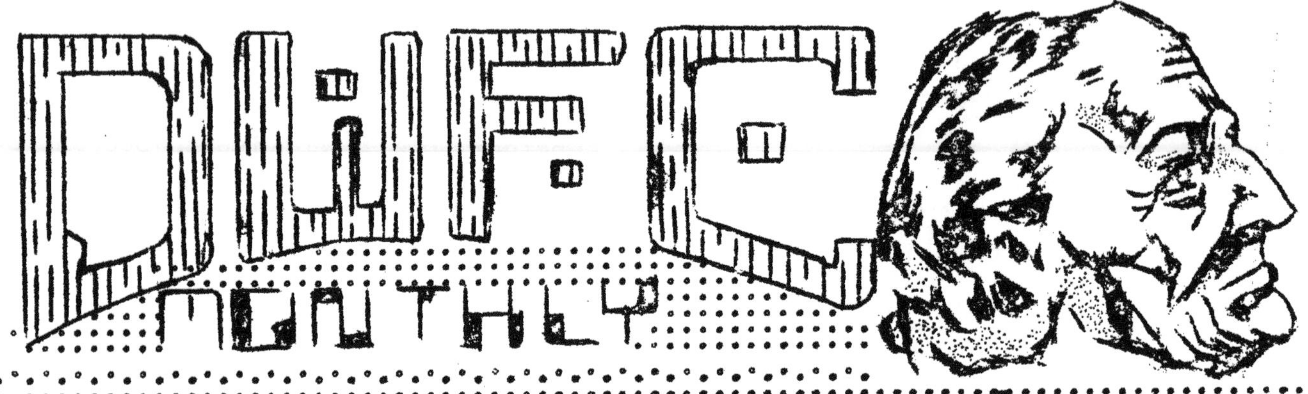

Number 10 November Edition DWFC COMPETITION SPECIAL

THE WINNER OF THE FIRST DWFC ANNUAL COMPETITION IS

GORDON BLOWS

from East Ham, London E.6

Congratulations to all who entered the first DWFC Annual Competition! You all did very well, indeed! You took the Doctor and Jo to worlds of Robots, Monsters and of Daleks and Mechanoids. But I think that this story is the most original, followed closely by the story of Stuart Moneys. Congratulations to you, Stuart on being a runner up.

The answers to the first part are as follows:

QUOTATION		ADVENTURE
1	"DR.WHO and the DALEKS"	A
2	"THE TIME MONSTER	C
3	"THE MUTANTS"	B

Now, DWFC proudly presents the winning story...

"JOURNEY INTO DANGER" by G.Blows

The Tardis spun through deep space as the Doctor showed Jo how to operate the simple controls.

"There, Jo" he said, "I've shown you what to do. Now you try."

Jo looked sternly at the control panel.

"Well. You start by pressing these three buttons. Then you pull down the two blue switches. Then you..eh..then you press this!"

"NO! DON'T PRESS IT!"

But it was too late. The Tardis lurched as it was thrown into the far reaches of an unknown dimension!

Doctor Who picked himself up from the floor. The doors of the Tardis were wide open, and a strong light filled the room. He helped Jo up.

"I wonder why the doors are open?" she asked. But her tall companion had no explanation.

"I'm going out," said the Doctor. Jo protested until the Doctor agreed to take her. They stepped out of the police box, into what? All around them was day, then night, and each seemed to flash by in a second.

"What's happened?" said Jo Nervously.

"The Tardis," frowned the scientist, "has been trapped between one second of time and another, but of course, Mother Nature cannot accept an object to be lodged in time, so her forces are trying to throw us out. Thus the visions of day and night occuring and reoccuring."

The Doctor watched fascinated. Jo gave a squeal as a form materialized by them. Dr Who Turned to see the thing appear. The form continually changed its shapedmaking Jo feel rather sick.

"Who are you?" groaned the voice. The fact that it talked, surprised the Doctor. Yet he knew it was some kind of mental telepathy.

"We are from Earth. The place that we are surrounded by but cannot enter." answered the Doctor.

"So you found out about me, that I was going to enter Earths time span and drain the peoples minds, but you will not live to tell the rest of your civilization of my existence. You will both die!"

The Doctor pushed Jo through the open doors of the police box. The creature followed them. Doctor Who rushed to the control panel as the form hovered into the transdimensional craft.

"Hold tight, Jo!" he yelled as he pushed forward a bright red lever.

The Time and Space machine spun like a top through a corridor of nuclear force. It lurched forward, sending the alien intellegence out through the doorway. Dr Who reached for the lever that would seal the doors as Jo slid dangerously towards them. His hand tugged at the control and the door closed. The Doctor operated another control and the Tardis steadied.

"Because of your mistake, Jo, Earth has been saved from something it might not have been able to cope with."

THE COMPLETE STORY OF DR.WHO AND MARCO POLO
Serial:D
Transmittion dates:(22/2/64)(29/2/64)(7/3/64)(14/3/64)(21/3/64)(28/3/64)(4/4/64)
Starring:William Hartnell as Dr Who,William Russel as Ian Chesterton,Jacqueline Hill as Barbara Wright,Carole Ann Ford as Susan Foreman,Marco Polo is played by Mark Eden and Derren Nesbitt as Tegana with Martin Miller as Kublai Khan.
Produced by Verity Lambert and Directed by Waris Hussien.

1.ROOF OF THE WORLD:The Tardis slowly materialized on the Pamir plateau in Central Asia and inside,the partywere relieved when the Doctor announced that itwas likely they would be able to pick up supplies and fuel there.The Doctor opened the doors and they met a warlord called Tegana who led them to Marco Polos camp.After a heavy meal,Polo announced that hewas taking the Tardis from the travellers and hoped to give it to Kublai Khan as payment for his journey back to Venice.The travellers persuadedPolo to let them go with him and so they set off,unaware that the water barrels had been poisoned by Tegana.

2.THE SINGING SANDS:During the journey,Susan became great friends with Ping-Cho,a teenage girl who was on her way to marry Khan,who is over 70!As they made their way through the Gobi Desert,they saw Tegana walk away from the party and they decided to follow him.The girls lost him in a sandstorm,but the three managed to make it back to the camp safley.The water useless,Polo sent Tegana ahead to fill the barrels up again.However,when Tegana reached the oasis,he drank his fill,but had no intention going back.

3.FIVE HUNDRED EYES:Back at the camp,the travellers were in dire need of water.But the Doctor discovered that the cold nights were causing condensation on the metal walls of the Tardis and he collected this water and they managed to reach the water hole.From here they made it to Tun-Huang.The Doctor managed to sneak aboard the Tardis and refill the empty water and fuel tanks.Tegana left the party and walked up to the cave of Five hundred eyes.Barbara followed him but was captured by Tegana and another man.

4.WALL OF LIES:Ian finds Barbara in the cave,but when she tried to tell Polo about his "trusted friend",Tegana said that she was lying.The Doctor whispered to the other three that the Tardis is now ready,but when they tried to board it,Tegana saw and stopped them.

5.RIDER FROM SHANG-TU:Tegana was working for the Mongols,who were planning an ambush on the party.Ian discovered a murdered sentry,and raised the alarm.The ambush is thwarted.Then a messanger from Khan arrived,telling them to leave heavy baggage behind and to get to Peking as soon as possible.The Tardis is left behind.

6.MIGHTY KUBLAI KHAN:Ping-Cho,realizing that she was near the end of her journey, could not bear to think of marrying an old man so she ran away.Ian went after her. The rest of the party are presented to Khan himself.The Doctor finds they have something in common.The aches and pains of old age!The Khan then tells Polo that the Mongols are gathering on the Cathay frontier.

7.ASSASSIN AT PEKING:Ian caught up with Ping-Cho and they were both found by Tegana who was going to kill them.But the messanger from the Khan arrived and accused them of trying to steal the Tardis and are taken to Peking under arrest.The Doctor had been playing backgammon with the Khan,and wins horses and jewels,but lost the Tardis Ian and Ping-Cho arrived at the palace,and Ian exlpained why Ping-Cho ran away.The Khan decided not to marry her after all.Ian tells the Khan about Tegana and is believed.Tegana tries to assassinate the Khan,but the invasion fleet is stopped, so Tegana kills himself.The Tardis had been moved into the throne room,and Marco Polo gave Ian the key which he had taken earlier.The Doctor placed the key in the lock and the party boarded the Tardis.The Khan saw the Tardis dematerialize and sighs."He probably would have won it back after all.."he says.

NEXT MONTH!A quick summary of serials E,F,G,H and J(this is because there are no records of these adventures)then for all those fans who missed it-the very first episode of DR WHO-IN THE BEGINNING.See ya then,Timelord!

DALEK DATA:DALEK DATA:DALEK DATA:DALEK DA

THE DALEK DOMINATORS in BATTLE ON ARCTURUS

The Daleks took to the air again, leaving behind a mass of molten metal which was once an Arcturan. They swarmed the city like a cloud of locusts ready to kill any who dare to prevent them taking over the entire planet. However, the Arcturans were not going to be taken lightly. Out of the buildings they brought their magnatrons which would atract the Daleks and their craft down to the ground and into the hands of the Arcturans. The machine was operated.

"DISPERSE" grated the Red Dalek, "REASSEMBLE" AT THE WAR HALL!"

At this command, the Fleet of Daleks began to descend. Down below them, the Arcturans fought a loosing battle against the invasion from the skies. But the Daleks soon began to feel the effects of the the magnotron. The hovabouts began to shake eractically as the machines entered the zone of magnetism. Then they spun out of control to a violent death on the ground. The Dalek force was weakening.

At the War Hall, many of the Daleks had managed to evade the magnotron and join their leader. It glided down from its machine and blasted down the door. Inside were millions of Arcturans, waiting to protect their leader, the Warlord. Behind them, the sound of war rang out its tones of death as metal crashed into fragments on the ground.

Up above, in the giant needle like space ship of the Daleks, the Gold Dalek was discussing the situation with the Black Dalek.

"THE ARCTURANS ARE PROVING TO BE BE MORE DIFFICULT THAN WE ANTICIPATED. ORDERS FROM THE DALEK SUPREME STATE THAT THE INVASION BE POSTPONED. THEY COULD BE OF USE TO US LATER!"

Back at the War Hall, the Red Dalek had recieved the message of retreat.

"ATTACK!" grated the Dalek.

"ORDER HAVE BEEN RECIEVED FROM SKARO..."

"THOSE ORDERS HAVE BEEN COUNTERMANDED! ATTACK THE ARCTURANS!"

The fleet moved forward, spraying their mist of death over the alien beings. The Arcturans returned the gesture and Daleks melted under the spiral rings of death which issued forth from the weapons of the monsters.

Somehow the Red Dalek managed to escape a afte of death and glided along a short passage towards the Grand Chamber. He blasted down the door and revealed a battered old machine surrounded by computers. The rebel Red Dalek knew that this was the Arcturan Warlord.

"You are indeed a great race.." groaned the old Arcturans, "We are a warlike race and so it is affitting end.."

But the Arcturans was doomed never to end the sentence. The renegade Dalek destroyed the Warlord and started a chain of explosions along the bank of computers. It made a hasty retreat as a giant explosion shook the giant building as it began to cruble. The Red Dalek fled to the entrance. The Arcturans were all dead. Their life support machines had been put out of action by the demolition of the main life computer. The ceiling began to crack.

"RETURN TO THE SPACESHIP. WE HAVE COMPLETED OUR MISSION. THE ARCTURANS HAVE BEEN EXTERMINATED!" chanted the Red Dalek as he mounted his hovabout. The machine gave a light whirr as the machinary began to operate. From the air, the fleet of Daleks saw the great, magnificent War Hall crumble into dust as the walls cracked and toppled. Silence now reigned on Arcturus.

THE END

Next story: Will the Red Dalek be greeted as a hero or a traitor? Find out in two months time when the DALEK DOMINATORS return to do battle with another planet!

LAST WORD

It's almost over again, sigh. Never mind, with this copy out of the way, the Christmas issue is next! And I can promise you double portions of everything as my Christmas present to you. So look out for the double issue coming next month!

And after that, the series comes back! Oh it's going to be a great year....

The offer of photos and dossiers is now closed. The responce has been tremendous. However, in next months ish, there will be a chance to get more photos of the Docs old travelling chums. You can see who they are then. But this is for one month only.

Okay, okay, okay I can take a hint! The old heading has been restored. So please, NO more letters!

I had a visit from Geoffrey Dunn from Newark in Notts. Thanks for popping up!

Well, the studios are buzzing with actio as they make the new series of Dr Who. I'll be popping down for a quick visit and you can see how I got on in the first issue of the new year. Golly, I've just thought of something. We'll be one year old then! How time flies.....

Oh, and before I forget, remember 'way back in issue no.5 when in the first edition of THE DRS DRAWING BOARD there was a drawing by ?. Well ? is now Peter Capaldi. Opps not much space left. Look forward to seeing you again next month!

BRITISH BROADCASTING CORPORATION

TELEVISION CENTRE WOOD LANE LONDON W12 7RJ

TELEPHONE 01-743 8000 CABLES: TELECASTS LONDONPS4

TELEGRAMS: TELECASTS LONDON TELEX TELEX: 22182

EXT:- 4111

5th September 1972

Dear Keith,

I'm off on hols on Friday afternnon so do hope that they stencils are with me soon. Hope you weren't too hard on Han Thingy 'coz I only mentioned in passing! We have all the scripts in for next season except for the last story, so we are pretty far ahead of our-selves. Mike Ferguson is a super person, really nice, he hasn't done a Dr.Who for us since Claws of Axos. I'll have to let you know about Peter Hawkins. In fact I have just looked him up and you are right. Clever boy! Can't wait for me hols, write to me after the 25th sometime. Ok?

Love

[signature]

BRITISH BROADCASTING CORPORATION

TELEVISION CENTRE WOOD LANE LONDON W12 7RJ

TELEPHONE 01-743 8000 CABLES: TELECASTS LONDONPS4

TELEGRAMS: TELECASTS LONDON TELEX TELEX: 22182

27th Septe.

Dear Keith,

Thank you for your letter and apologise for telephone call yesterday. I really agree with you and feel that midday isn't a good time but I can't think of any other time. I really think the best time would be about 9.15 in the morning or anytime after 1'O'Clock to 2' O'clock. I don't expect these t mes coinside with your free periods however we'll just have to see. No idea why the stencils were held up, I didn't know even that they were. Glad to hear that you are getting well at school.

Love

Sarah

BRITISH BROADCASTING CORPORATION

TELEVISION CENTRE WOOD LANE LONDON W12 7RJ

TELEPHONE 01-743 8000 CABLES: TELECASTS LONDONPS4

TELEGRAMS: TELECASTS LONDON TELEX TELEX: 22182

30th October 1972

Dear Keith,

Why do you need Terry Nation's address? Tell you why because I don't really want to give it you as he gets very angry at that sort of thing. We were filmed once sometime ago whilst doing a programme but I think that has been shown, and I gather it was for the 50 Centruy thing. By the way you forgto to enclose the DWFC medal! Ogrons are next season, Daleks and Drashigs and a few more but don't tell the fans because Barry wouldn't be very pleased if they knew exactly what was going to happen.

Short letter because am very busy at long last. It's gets busy now till the Christmas and just after.

Love

Sarah

17 NOTTINGHAM STREET, LONDON W1

7th November 1972

K. Miller,
109 Moredun Park Road,
Edinburgh,
Scotland.

Dear Keith Miller,

John Stanley has asked me to drop you a line just to give you some advance information that on this Friday, 10th November, Jon Pertwee is releasing a single record on the Purple Label No. PUR 111 called "WHO IS THE DOCTOR".

This is actually based on the Dr. Who theme music which is not going to be used in the new series; instead fresh electronic music is being recorded.

Thought it might be of some interest to your club members.

Yours sincerely,

Olive Stonehouse

"Kevin!"
The Three Doctors Set Report

After careful consideration, my Mum decided it would be okay for me to travel down to London on my own - after all, I was nearly 15 - but there would be no overnight stay. I would travel the nine hour journey down to London one night, then do the reverse trip the night after. Sounds like hell on earth to me now, but back then I was used to long distance coach travel and never gave it a second thought.

The bus rolled into a freezing cold Victoria Coach Station at 7am on Monday 27 November 1972. After a quick coffee to warm me up, I broke open the A to Z to get my bearings. I had 6 hours to waste before I was due at TV Centre, so I thought I'd do some sightseeing. I emerged onto the London streets and looked up and down Eccleston Place (timey wimey...). It was still dark and I needed to get walking to heat me up so took off down the road. Westminster, Buckingham Palace then back through St James Park to Hyde Park Corner. I then wandered aimlessly in and out of shops in Knightsbridge, before the crowds got too much for me and I escaped into a green park on the other side of the road. It was huge. And I had a curious feeling I had been here before as I skirted the huge lake at the centre of the garden. I was to find out this was Kensington Gardens, made famous by J M Barrie's Peter Pan. I adored the story as a child, and remember cutting up the Arthur Rackham colour plates from a well thumbed hardback, mounting the characters onto cardboard and placing them in a huge home made papier mache diorama of Kensington Gardens. I was delighted to happen upon a superb statue to Peter and his animal chums and spent half an hour watching the world go by from a bench not far from the statue itself. Mum had packed some sandwiches for me, so I nibbled on them, but again the nerves were beginning to get to me, and I didn't really feel very hungry. Still, I forced some down, then fed the pigeons with the rest. Deciding it was time to get to the BBC, I left the gardens and hailed a taxi which whisked me towards the hallowed Green of Shepherds Bush.

I was meeting Sarah at TV Centre this time, and felt very important as the security man peered at me in the back of the taxi from his little cubicle. After reading my letter from Sarah confirming the meeting time. The barrier was lifted and I was driven to the Reception area. I paid the driver and started towards the entrance door, when the taxi driver exploded into a rage, shouting out the cab window, calling me a "tight, little Scottish bastard!" and drove off at speed. It was then I realised London taxi drivers expected a tip.

Reception at TV Centre was a very exciting place. It was huge, with a massive mural by John Piper at one end, and was flooded with light from the huge windows which looked out onto the circular courtyard with Helios atop the massive fountain at its centre. Crossing it was Ronnie Barker with rolls of paper stuffed under his arms, dropping them one by one and stooping down to pick them up. He looked like he was in one of his Two Ronnies sketches. People were laughing, which I thought was a bit rude, as he wasn't doing it to get a laugh, but was having real trouble keeping his paperwork under control. Perhaps that was a mark of his comedy genius - even everyday actions could be made to look funny, even if he didn't intend it to be.

Sarah appeared looking terribly harassed. "Things are

in full swing, Keith," she grumbled, whatever that meant, "I'm in full blue arsed fly mode." I hadn't a clue what that meant, but I did know that she swore. There was a lot of swearing at the Beeb, which I wasn't used to, and it was quite shocking to hear the Doctor or the Brigadier use a four letter expletive, which they did frequently, sometimes to just see the look on my face, I suspect. But more of that later.

"Have you eaten?" she asked. I replied I had. "Thank God for that. I don't have time for lunch. Better get along to TC1. We're in the Tardis today, how exciting is that?" My heart leapt. The Tardis! "It is, " I agreed, "And I'm very excited William Hartnell's here." Sarah's face fell. "Oh dear. I'm afraid I've some bad news for you then..."

As we made our way along to Studio TC1, Sarah handed me the shooting script for todays filming. "We're doing most of the Tardis scenes today, everything set in UNIT and on the planet of the Time Lords." Remember, we're still many years from being told the name, Gallifrey. Pushing open the door of the Studio, Sarah showed me round the sets, but compared to last time, this was a whirlwind tour. There were a few production people around, but no cast. Sarah had just shown me the Tardis set when she spotted someone. "Hold on a second, will you? I need to get someone to sign something. Lennie!" I was left alone. In the Tardis. I was literally two steps away from the console. I had been told NEVER to TOUCH ANYTHING. But how could I resist? This was it at last. My fifteen years on this earth had been leading up to this one moment. I stepped forward and stopped. I reached out. My fingers touched the Tardis console.

"Kevin!"

I just about shat myself. It was Terrance Dicks. "You here again?" he said, "Thought we would've scared you off the last time. Better warn you - things are a bit hairy today, so you may get lost in the rush. You actually look a bit lost now, isn't Sarah with you?" "I'm here, I'm here," said Sarah returning with her signed document, "Are you going up to the box, Terry? You couldn't do me a favour and take Keith up with you?" "Who's Keith?" asked Terrance. "I am" I replied. "I thought your name was Kevin." Terrance sucked on his unlit pipe and chuckled, making me suspect he knew my name all along. Sarah bustled out of the studio. "Come on then." said Terrance, " The Bristol Boys are up in the box, I'll introduce you." As always, I hadn't a clue who he was talking about. As we entered the Production Suite, Barry Letts spotted me and waved. He came over, smiling benignly. "Hello, there. Is Jean not with you this time?" Jean? Jean?! When did my Mum suddenly become Jean?! "Not this time. Sorry." Barry almost sighed. "Probably just as well, I can't afford to chinwag today. This is a very tight shooting schedule today. Have you met the writers yet?" "Not yet," said Terrance. "Can I leave you to do that, Terrance?" Terrance sighed. "Baby-sitting isn't in my contract... he grumbled. In the Producers Box, two men watched as the studio floor was being set up for the days filming. Terrance pointed his hand at the tall, thin one. "Dave Martin." Then the shorter, broader one, "Bob Baker. Otherwise known as The Bristol Boys. This is Kevin." "It's Keith actually." Terrance chuckled again. "Sorry, sorry. KEITH! He runs the official fan club on our behalf. These chaps are the writers of todays story."

Bob Baker and Dave Martin were fairly new writers to Doctor Who. Up to that point they had had two stories broadcast, The Claws of Axos and The Mutants, both of which I had loved. I was to become a huge fan of their work and I'm proud to say that Bob quotes my reviews of his Doctor Who stories as published in the DWFC fanzine on his website www.bobbaker.tv, even today. It was always a treat to see their names in the Radio Times for upcoming stories, their style came over as fresh, new and exciting, which spilt over into their other work too, including the superb Sky. It was during the writing of the Mutants, Bob told me, they were asked to do a multi-Doctor story for the series tenth anniversary.

"It had been bandied around for ages, the idea of getting the three Doctors meeting each other. Then one day Terrance had a visit from an old geezer looking for some work. It was Bill Hartnell, so Terrance pitched the idea to Barry that now would be a good time to do it. So we finished The Mutants and headed straight into The Three Doctors. The first version of the script was sent to Bill, which his wife had opened and was horrified with what she saw. She immediately got on the phone to Terrance saying "He's an ill man! He's not up to this, he can barely remember his name, never mind lines!". So we had to drastically rewrite his part, giving lots of his lines to the other cast members - a lot of them to Sergeant Benton. Its given John Levene a chance to shine, as you'll see this evening."

Barry stuck his head round the door. "Sorry to interrupt, people, but I'll have to relocate you into the Production Suite, I need this box for a meeting." So we were shifted out into the hub of production activity, taking seats directly behind the production crew and being able to see action on the studio floor from the myriad of monitors on the wall. Standing up I could see through large windows down onto the floor itself. Rehearsals were in full swing, with Jon Pertwee and Katy Manning in their everyday clothes - Jon in black jumper and trousers, sporting a huge, silver belt buckle, and Katy in white flares and yellow top with a large question mark brooch pinned to it. This was the beginning of the Producers Run - a prerecording run through to give the Producer an idea of how the scenes will look - which is why Barry needed the telly in the Producers Box.

Sarah appeared, looking a bit more relaxed. "That's the worst bit over, I think. Come on, we'll grab some dinner in the Club, I'm starving." In the Club, Sarah and I tucked into Ploughman's Salads. "Mind if I join you?" said a voice with a particularly heavy Australian twang.
"Hulloy, Keith, howya doin'?" It was Dudley Simpson, Doctor Who music composer supremo, whom I met briefly first time I was down. "At least you got the name right," I said, "Terrance is convinced I'm called Kevin!" "Nah, good Australian name Keith Miller!" I was named after the Australian Test cricketer - I was originally going to be called Robert as my projected birth date was January 25th, birth date of Scots poet, Robert Burns, but I was a day late so my sports-mad brother Peter begged my parents to call me Keith, which they eventually agreed to. This made me alright in Dudley's eyes. "Are you staying for tonights recording?" he asked me. "Not really, I've to catch the night bus back to Edinburgh." "Crikey!" exclaimed Dudley, "Down one night and back the next! You're a glutton for punishment!" Dudley then regaled us with a story of how he had to make half a dozen trips up and down the motorway between his recording studio and the BBC and was pulled over by a police car who had been watching him yo-yo backwards and forwards. The policeman was delighted when he found out Dudley worked for Doctor Who. "Wouldn't surprise me if he's one of your members, Keith."

Dudley finished his meal and sloped off. Sarah pushed her plate away and looked at me seriously. She was looking very tired.
"Keith, Jon's been complaining about you featuring old stories in the club magazine. Barry and I don't think it's a bad idea, but Jon hates it. He really does, and I try to avoid anything that upsets him as he gives me real grief sometimes." I suddenly felt put on the spot. I didn't want to agree to drop the history of the show. I think my face went red. "Perhaps if you could think about dropping it down to half a page or something. Anything to get Jon off our backs." "Yes, of course," I said, with no intention of doing any such thing...

Back in the Production Suite it was coming up to 8pm and Lennie Mayne, Director of this story, leant forward and spoke into his microphone. "Run telecine" and the recording of the first episode of The Three Doctors commenced. A good part of the episode was already shot on film so I got to see quite a bit of it. Lennie was very proud of the flock of birds taking off from the water when the Gel "stung" Mr Ollis, Barry and Terrance were laughing at his smugness. The Gel was actually a feather boa with a bit tinsel twisted round it. Crackin' stuff.

Back in the UNIT lab, the Doctor was puzzling over the face of Mr Ollis in the "space lightning". Or rather he wasn't. "Can we make the face a bit more apparent?" asked Lennie, "The camera's aren't picking it up at all." Lighting was changed, camera's zoomed in. They rolled again. "Nope it's no good. Can we get the art guys onto it?" The transparencies were taken away and someone with a Magic Marker "coloured in" the faded features. They were hung up again. "Is that any better?"asked the art guy. "Looks like someones been at it with a Magic Marker," sighed Lennie.

Years later, I recounted the next part of the visit in an article published by my chums at TV Cream:

"Here at TV Cream's Dr Who Matrix Database, we love readers' letters as much as digital radio station disc jockeys love ideologically sound deodorant. So you can imagine our glee when Old Friend of Creamguide Keith Miller (who signs himself 'Father of Fandom' - he really does) dropped us a line this week on matrix @tvcream.co.uk. "I'm surprised no-one at the TV Cream Towers (or OG for that matter)," he begins promisingly, "has picked up on the rather jarring occasions over the past few weeks when the Doctor swore. 'Why the hell did you do that?!!' Not content with hinting that the good Doctor has had his fair share of shags, they're turning him into a potty-mouth too." Good point... although, at the moment we're more taken with the phrase "*The* TV Cream Tower*s*", which, to us, conjures up a hugely pleasing image of a trio of TVC branded nostalgia-spires. There's a campus full of busy lifts, with an unconvincing pyramid on the top and John Leeson scampering around the place, being pursued by baseball cap wearing youngsters and a man in a nasty sweater.

Er, anyway, Keith continues, "Which reminds me of a time when I was covering the filming of 'The Three Doctors'. Jon P was getting himself in a right state by cocking up his dimensionally transcendental spiel ('Well, Sergeant, aren't you going to say its bigger on the outside than the inside?') so there was a break whilst the shot was set up again. Ready to roll the floor manager asked where Katy (Manning) was. 'She's gone for a slash', JP informed him. I was gobsmacked. a) The Doctor swore and b) the companions went to the toilet. It was a defining moment for me I can tell you." And a defining moment for us too, as this is surely the best email we've ever received - bar that one from Bob Monkhouse, sent five minutes before his This Is Your Life episode went out on BBC1."

It was tea break. Everything stopped, cameras were deserted, sets abandoned as everyone crowded round the tea trolley outside the studio, manned by a proper Mrs Mop in headscarf and pinny. The Brigadier was the last one off stage, but I stared in disbelief as Nic Courtney peeled off his moustache and stuck it to the Time Rotor! I never suspected for a second the mouser was a fake! Presumably he didn't want it getting lost in his tea. After tea, Nic came back and stuck the mouser back on again, and he had to be wired up with a hand held walkie talkie, which involved getting a hole cut in his trouser pocket and a length of thick wire poked into his nether regions by a nervous wardrobe girl, as Nic bit his bottom lip and stared skywards in a very naughty fashion.

It was coming to the time when Pat Troughton was to join the action. Terrance appeared beside me, as did Dudley, who introduced me to Katy's manager. They all crowded round as Pat cheekily reappeared in the Tardis, to a giant cheer from the production crew in the gallery. I hope Jon didn't hear it.

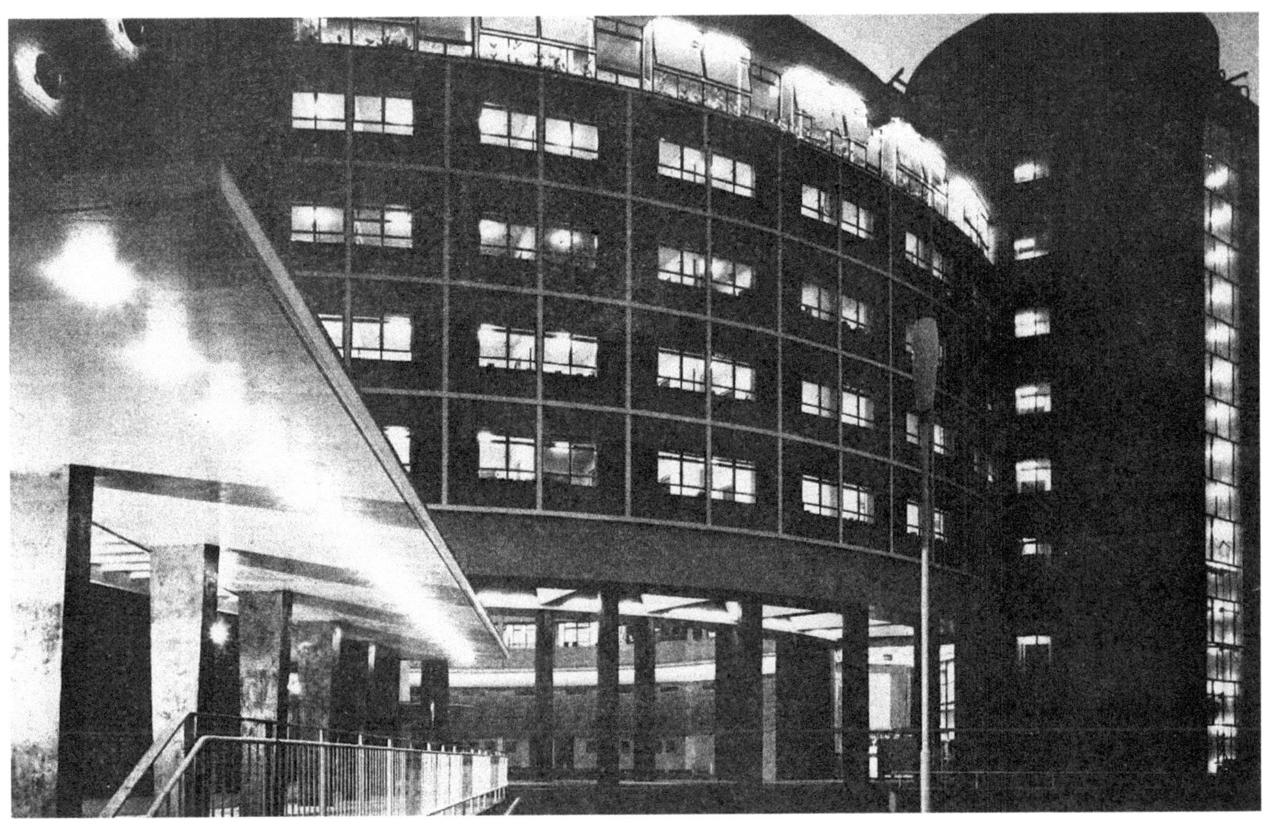

I was beginning to get agitated that I might miss my bus back to Edinburgh, so I decided to get my taxi to Victoria. "I don't know where Sarah is..." I said to Terrance. "I suppose that's you wanting me to sign you out the building?" "If you don't mind," I replied. Terrance sighed and escorted me to Reception, sucking on his unlit pipe (did he ever light it, I wondered?). It didn't take long for the taxi to arrive, and as I climbed on board and prepared to propel myself into night-time London, I heard a voice behind me shout, "See you later, Kevin!"

BRITISH LION FILMS LTD

BROADWICK HOUSE BROADWICK STREET
LONDON W1V 2AH
TELEPHONE 01-437 8676
TELEGRAMS BRILIONFIL LONDON W1

YOUR REF.
OUR REF. TC/JW

6th December 1972

Keith Miller Esq.,
The Doctor Who Fan Club,
109 Moredun Park Road,
Edinburgh EH17 7HJ

Dear Mr. Miller,

Thank you for your letter.

It is quite in order for you to reproduce the article on 'edible Daleks' in the Christmas issue of your magazine.

Yours sincerely,

p.p. J.? Williams

Ted Collins.

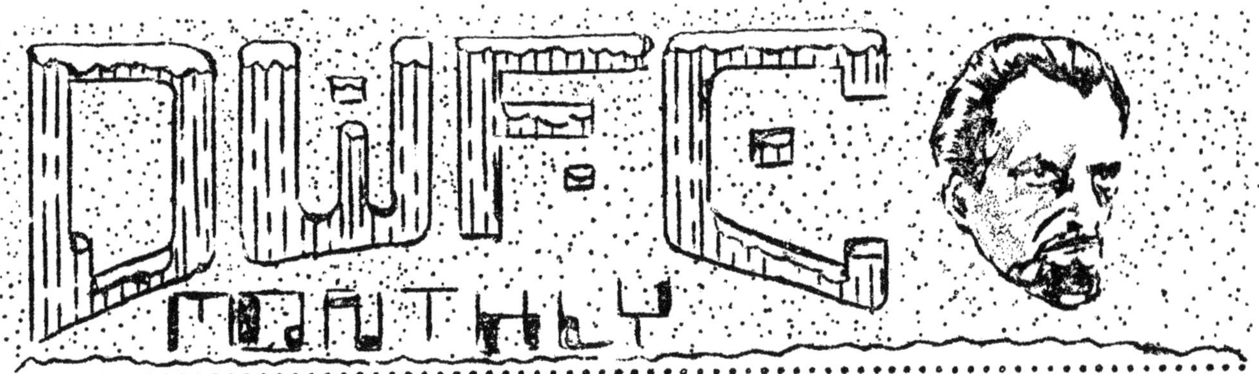

Number 11 Christmas Edition D.W.F.C.Double Special!

HERE IT IS!THE SPECIAL DOUBLE SIZE CHRISTMAS ISSUE AS OUR PRESENT TO YOU!!!! AND LETS START THE BALL ROLLING WITH A FESTIVE NOTE BY SAYING

Merry Christmas...

...and from everyone at UNIT,the BBC,and the DWFC!We all hope you have a super time this month,and as our present to you,we're giving you a double size monthly.In it are the regular articles,with lots of new ones in betw■en.

Well,after this issue,the format of the monthly is going to changed. I've tended to slip a little into the past lately,dwelling too much with past adventures.But don't worry.DR WHO-FROM THE BEGINNING will simply be changed to THE BEST OF DR WHO.

Now back to the festivitites.In afew days time,DR WHO AND SEA DEVILS will be screened again(or should I say screamed again)as a super spectacular for your delight!Then the series comes back with more threats to Earth and other planets for the Doctor and Jo to fight,including the Drashigs-huge,green dragon like monsters,on a planet many light years away...or is it?

Well,I guess I've talked enough for now,but I'll■talking to you again at the end of this extravaganza!So lets start by journeying back into time(only this once,Jon)to the very first episode of DR WHO in...

Transmittion date:23/11/63
Serial:A
"UNBORN CHILD"
Episode 1
starring

William Hartnell...............Dr.Who
William Russel.......Ian Chesterton
Jacqueline Hill........Barbara Wright
Carole Ann Ford.........Susan Foreman

....

As the clock on the school wall struck four,the bell rang out its disturbing note,much to the relief of the pupils.

The doors slammed open as the class rooms quickly emptied.Two teachers met in the corridor,all the worse for the day that had passed.

Ian Chesterton,a dark,handsome man yelled at a pupil called Jones to stop running in the corridor,then turned to his associate teacher,Barbara Wright,who looked absolutly worn out.

"Everyones in a hurry these days," said Ian.

"Not quite everyone,"replied Barbara, looking at a dark haired young girl, slowly walking out from her classroom.

"Problem Child,eh?"asked Ian.

"No,not really;she's just strange, that's all.When I asked her a question today,she replied that Japan was a county in Scotland,but she is really brilliant at science class."

"That's strange.."

"And when I offered to take her home one night,she stopped me at a junkyard and got out."

"Perhaps her father owns it."

"Her father is dead,"said Barbara,"She lives with her grandfather,but I can't say where.The yard I told you about was condemned a year ago.."

"Well there's only one way to find out.Come on,my car's outside."

"You mean we're going to follow her?"

"That's the idea.."

After they had locked up,and were in the car,a fog developed around them and they lost sight of Susan.

"Keep going,Ian,I think I can remember the way.Right at the next opening."

A short drive and a few wrong turnings later,they ended up at the old yard, where a large notice heralding

CONDEMNED

hung loosly on the prefabricated wall.

Ian stopped the engine and the two sat in silence.The sky was dark and the blackness was all around them,apart from the streetlamp opposite the yard which cast feeble rays of light into the street.

"Well,it's no use sitting in here," said Ian,"Lets find out what's so special about this yard."

The duo stepped out of the car into the cold night air which was clouded with fog.Ian pushed the aluminium door open which was unlocked,much to his surprise.Barbara followed him inside.

Around them lay all the usual things you expect to find in a junkyard.Then from out of the corner of his eye,Ian saw movement in the shadows.He pushed Barbara down behind some boxes,piled nearby.

Out of a battered old police box stepped an old man with white hair,dressed as though he was in the pre-war years.

"That must be Susans grandfather", whispered Barbara.

"Looks a bit eccentris to me."

"Look!It's Susan!"gasped Barbara.

Around the door appeared the girl Ian had seen earlier.She greeted the old man in an affectionate manner and to Ians surprise,the two of them turned around and entered the police box.

"He's locking her in that box!"exclaimed Ian,"Come on,Lets do the heroics."

Saying this,he jumped up and,with Barbara rushed through the doors.

"There he is,"shouted Ian,not noticing that the box had increased considerably in dimensions.

He pounced on the old man,pinning him to the control table in the middle of room.The clear plastic cylinder in the centre of the table began ascending and descending as the doors closed behind them.Barbara gasped in astonishment at the sight that met her eyes.

"You fool!"shouted the old man."Do you realise what you have done?!"

The words did not penetrate Ians brain as he suddenly realised that the room was very bright...and also very large.Deep circles were imbedded in the wall and in one of them,a TV scanner showed the yard outside,but a second later it grew hazy and was

DR WHO-UNBORN CHILD(cont)

finally replaced by a kaleidoscope of flashing bars of light.

"But this is impossible,"said Ian slowly,"We're in a police box...a five foot square police box!"

"You are in a Transdimensional Tardis, young man,"said the elderly gentleman.

"Look...just WHO are you?"

"He is my grandfather and a doctor of science,"answered Susan,pressing her self against the Doctors arm in a loving manner.

"Doctor Who?"

"That is of no concern of yours.You couldn't pronounce it anyway."

The Doctor walked over to the left hand wall,opened three of the circled partitions and took out three stools and set them down on the metal floor.

"Be seated,"ordered the Doctor.

"Look...who do you.."

"I SAID BE SEATED!!"the Doctor bellowed."I will now attempt an explanation as to what has happened."

Ian looked around to see Barbara, white and afraid.In all the confusion, he had forgotten all about her.He smiled,but she looked away towards the Doctor.He was beginning his story.

"You see,young man,my granddaughter and I are travellers.Not travellers as you know,...but Time travellers!"

"TIME TRAVELLERS!HAH!That's a good one!"yelled Ian,looking at Barbara Smiling but she was looking back with an expression that told him she believed every word.

"You don't mean to say you believe a all that?Oooh,come on!"

"She is wise,-she is not pig-headed, Chesterton!"

"You know my name!"

"Susan has often spoken of you!"

There was silence for a brief moment.

"Now,if I may continue.Due to your meddling in my affairs,you are now travelling through time and space to heaven-knows-where!"

"You're a raving lunatic!"cried Ian, jumping off his stool,"Open these doors!"

"Very well.In a few minutes we shall be landing;then you shall have your proof!"

The Doctor turned to the control panel where the cylinder sank to a halt.

"We have arrived,"announced the Doctor.

Outside,winds howled round the rocks and stones scattered across the barren landscape.Slowly,the shape of the police box materialized,bringing Ian and Barbara to their first adventure.

THE END

DALEKS INVADE THE CHRISTMAS DINNER TABLE!!

A Christmas Special for all Dalek fans for the Christmas table! So here is the recipe for

CHOCOLATE DALEKS

Ingredients

6oz.Chocolate Buttons
8 small digestive biscuits
2 oz. butter
2 oz. Sugar Puffs
8 marsh mallows
4 oz. icing sugar (sieved)
8 dariole moulds or small glasses
1 packet of sweet cigarettes

The Mixture

Take 6 oz. of Chocolate Buttons and after placing to one side 16 for later use as decoration melt the remaining in a bowl over hot water.Take each of the biscuits in turn and coat one side allowing to set.Stir the Sugar Puffs into the remaining chocolate mixture until well coated,then divide the mixture into 8 and put into moulds allowing to set.Cream butter and sieved icing sugar together and place in a forcing bag with a writing nozzle.Remove the mould by quickly dipping in hot water being careful not to wet the mixture. Remove carefully.Spread butter icing on chocolate side of biscuit and place body of Dalek on top.Place a marshmallow on top of head,splitting marshmallow if too big.Finish with icing "spots",Polka Dots andplace a sweet cigarette in the marshmallow for the eye stick,and "cement" one on the left of the Dalek for it's sucker and use a half cig. for the gun,using the butter icing as the adhesive.

The mixture will make 8 Daleks

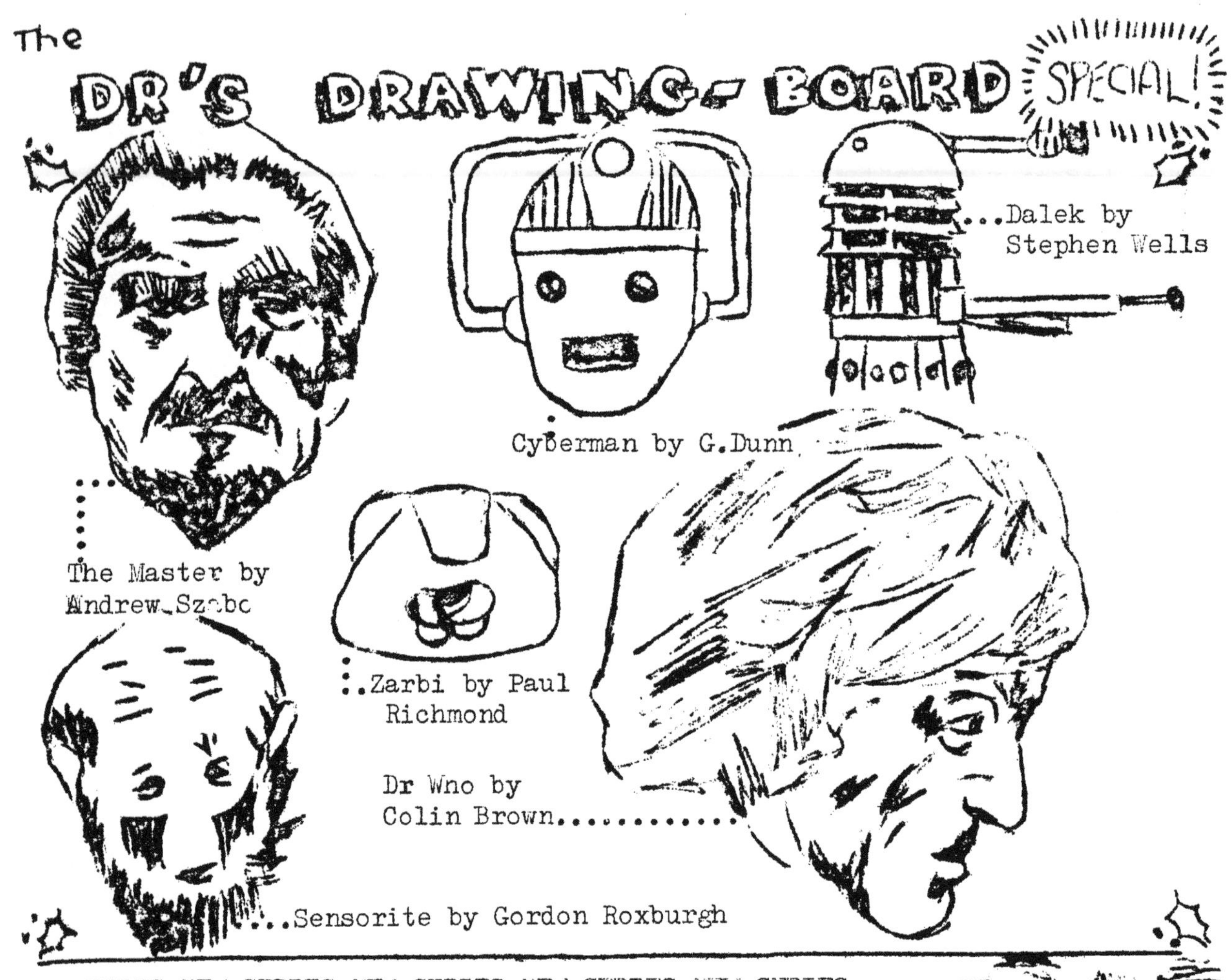

NEW SERIES:NEW SERIES:NEW SERIES:NEW SERIES:NEW SERIES

DR.WHO PEOPLE

This series will look behind the scenes at the people who work together to get the programme onto your TV screens.

No.1:JON PERTWEE/DR WHO

We'll start the series off with a look at the lives of the actors of the series.Before Dr Who,Jon Pertwee was renowned for his parts in Radio comedy programmes such as The Navy Lark, which he still provides the voices for,with Commander Weatherby and oddly enough,a character known as the Master!

He's attall man of 6 ft 3ins,and keeps in trim by indulging in his favourite hobby-diving for treasure. He loves gadgets and motor bikes and loves to fiddle with cars and engines.He's the man to have around if Bessie breaks down!

When Jon took over the part of the Doctor,he changed the part to bring it more up to date,so that instead of the slightly out of place Doctor of Patrick Troughton,we have the modern,energetic Time Lord.As Matthew Coady said in the Daily Mirror-"Jon Pertwee's Doctor is wholly acceptable-the newest recruit is suave and confident;obviously a Harley Street doctor!"

Jon is a super man to work with as Katy Manning and the rest of the cast will tell you,even though he is just a little bad tempered,which is one of his downfalls,as he said in a Radio Programme last Christmas.But he rarely flies off the handle at anyone,and is super fun to be with off screen.He has real personallity,and he wishes everyone in the fan club a fantastic Christmas and is looking forward to being in your homes when the series returns on the 30th of December.

NEXT MONTH:Katy Manning/Jo Grant.

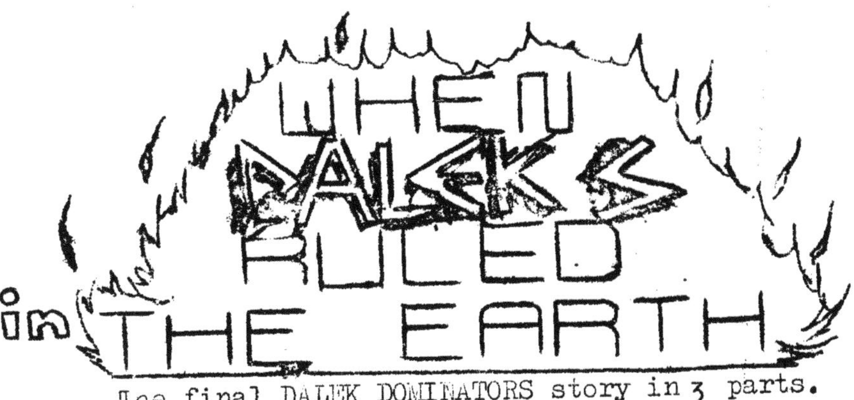

The final DALEK DOMINATORS story in 3 parts.

Episode One

The sleek,shining airliner pointed its blunt nose towards the clouds until the white fleece parted to reveal a vast expanse of blue.

On board,all was well with the crew as the captain wished his passengers welcome to his bird of travel.As time floated by,the "first time" passengers grew more relaxed,helped no doubt by the double brandies which were quickly gulped to extinguish the fire of fear burning inside them.Little did they realize that the next few days would be thrice more frighting.And it would all begin on this ill-fated plane.

In seat number fifteen,Mr R Kelad sat motionless,staring,bulging eyes behind the dark sun glasses which hid his horrific,blank stare.

Suddenly,he unfastened his seatbelt and walked quickly down the aisle,swaying just a little with the movement of the craft.He reached for the handle of the captains cabin,but his wrist was grasped by a hand from the galley.

"I'm sorry,sir,but passengers aren't allowed in the control cabin,"said the stewardess.

He raised his hand and caressed her neck.

"Yes...Go ahead."

He slid the door open,revealing the captain and co-pilot busy at the control console.

"Just put the coffee down there,Jane," said the co-pilot,pointing at a small ledge over the undercarriage controls.

The stranger pressed his two hands on the back of the necks of the pilots.The plane gave a small lurch,but continued on its way as the pilots said

"The function of the human is to obey."

Jo pushed open the doors of the Doctors lab with her elbow,due to the huge wrapped parcel she held in both hands. They glided together again silently as she made her way to the figure working at the bench beside a large blue police box,humming "Silent Night."She crept stealthly up to the Doctor and shouted MERRY CHRISTMAS as the Doctors workpeice went flying over his head and smashed into tiny peices on the other side of the room.

"What the devil do you think.."he yelled as he spun round to face a large blue and white decorated box.

"From us,to you."

"Us?"

"Everyone at UNIT.Merry Chri.."

Jo never did finish the sentence as Benton burst through the doors.

"I thought you were on leave?"said Jo.

"Been recalled,"panted the Sergeant."The Brigadier wants to see you pronto in the TV room.Been a plane hi-jacked or something.Landed off the coast of Cornwall of all places."

The airliner screeched to a halt on the end of a long-forgotten runway,built on the small island as testing grounds for prewar airplanes.The side of the cliff nearest the plane held a secret door which levered down and a conveyer slid out and attached itself to the door of the craft.The strange Mr.R Kelad led a procession of mindless zombies along the pathway into the mountain.After passing through the rock wall,they proceeded down a long corridor at the end of which was thick reinforced metal,which grinded open to reveal a huge control room which blinked red,blue and white with the light controls on the walls and the central control boxes.

The Doctor marched into the TV Room, followed by the Sergeant and Jo,saying,

"Well,Brigadier?What strange mishap has happened this time?"

"A plane crash,or hi-jack,or lost.."

"Can't you make up your mind?"asked the Doctor.

"All we know is that it cam down in an island off the coast of Cornwall... and we can't get near it because of a dome shaped force field covering the entire island."

"Oh,Isee.."

"Well,I was thinking.Now that you seem to have got that load of electronic doda working again.."

"Not quite...but I'll have try.Where is this island?"

WHEN DALEKS RULED THE EARTH(cont)

The rock door closed together with the giant metal shutters.Kelad turned to face his silent followers.He held his hand up infront of his face.

"The function of the human is to obey!" chanted the crowd in toneless voices which echoed around the gigantic control room.

Kelad turned and passed his hand in front of an electric eye,which operated a metal door in the wall which glided up and into the right hand corner of the half circle archway.Inside lay complicated machinery which hummed with activity and blinked off and on with regular pulses,and in the centre of the room...lay the empty shell of the Red Dalek.

The Doctor pushed open the doors of the lab and Jo hurried after him.

"I don't suppose you want to come,do you Jo?Being Christmas.."

"Well my parents are on some trip abroad,and if you promise to get me back for the party tonight.."

"I'll try anyway.."

"Good enough for me!"said Jo.

"Well,Doctor, Report as soon as you can"said the Brigadier, watching the Doctor enter the Tardis and saw it slowly fade.

Inside,the Doctor studied the control panel intently.

"If the Time Lords are with me,I'll try and make a pin-point landing on the landing strip on the island"said the Doctor.

"In that case,we'll probably end up somewhere in outer space!"joked Jo.

The Doctor shot a curt glance at the young girl,who smiled at her companion who quickly returned to his work.

The Tardis gave a slight lurch.

"That was the force field.."said the Doctor,"We're landing now!"

The Doctor opened the doors,to reveal not a bleak landscape,but the control room of Kelad,who was standing on the rectangle platform of the Red Dalek.A large beam of light shone down on him, as his figure shimmered,then dissolved. The light faded,then the eye stick of the Red Dalek turned to see the Tardis!

LAST WORD

Well,it's almost over for this year. But before I have a chat with you, here's a word from our sponsor...

THE FINAL FREE PHOTO OFFER!

Free photographs are now available of Ben and Polly,two of the Doctors early companions.Supplies are limited so don't be dissappointed if you're left out.Send an sae to The DWFC,109 Moredun Park Road,Edinburgh EH17 7HJ.

BACK ISSUES!

The following issues are free to all fans.Those marked LS are in short stock.

No.4 (middle pages,bad print)LS
No.5 (front page,very low stock)LS
No.6 (complete and 1st 2 pages)
No.7 (complete and last 2 pages)
No.8 (complete)
No.9 (Complete)
No.10 (complete)

Now,after that comercial break,lets have a talk about the next issue and series.

Well,time has rushed by,and the DWFC reaches it's first birthday.This year has had its ups and downs,perhaps more than any other,but things wouldn't have been the same if it hadn't been for Sarah Newman,the producers-Barry Letts-secretary.Thanks for getting me started.

The series returns on the 30th of this month,with some very special guest stars, and if you look in the Christmas issue of the Radio Times,you'll see who they are.I was there a couple of weeks ago seeing them making it.and I'll be talking about it next month in a celebration Birthday article.This is also where the Gelguards make theme debut.Watch out, world!

"Next month also sees the beginning of the end for DR WHO-IN/FROM THE BEGINNING with THE BEST OF DR WHO story-"PLANET OF DESCISION"

Then,the second of the new series- DR WHO PEOPLE features that groovy little Miss from the prog.Miss Katy Manning. And the second part of WHEN DALEKS RULED THE EARTH",the last story of the Dalek Dominators.

And of course,REVIEW will be returning soon,and a special competition with the chance to win a unique DWFC T-Shirt.

So,that's it.I hope you have enjoyed this Christmas Spectacular,and once again,have a super time on the big day, and I hope you find the Dr Who Annual in your stocking!MERRY CHRISTMAS! Keith

Keith Miller Esq.,
The Doctor Who Fan Club,
109 Moredun Park Road,
Edinburgh,
EH17 7HJ.

Ref: JFJ/JJB

Date: 20th December, 1972

Head Office: 8b Lonsdale Gardens Tunbridge Wells Kent. Tel:0892 22442 Directors: M D Farrow(Financial) J F Jones(Managing)
Design Office: 185 Westbourne Grove London W11 2SD. Tel:01-229 8241 R A Farrow (Design) E B S Farrow

Dear Mr. Miller,

Many thanks for your letter.

We would be delighted for you to publicise our Dalek Iron On transfers in the DWFC MONTHLY.

I enclose a sample and hope this will be useful to you.

The normal retail price for this item is 50p but we would in this instance be willing to offer them for sale through your magazine for 40p including packing and postage.

If you decided to handle the distribution yourself we would be prepared to supply them to you direct (in bulk quantities) for 20p each for you to forward to interested readers.

Please let us know if you would like any further information and I look forward to receiving a copy of your magazine.

Yours sincerely,
DODO DESIGNS (MFRS) LTD.

Jonathan F. Jones
Managing Director

BRITISH BROADCASTING CORPORATION

TELEVISION CENTRE WOOD LANE LONDON W12 7RJ

TELEPHONE 01-743 8000 CABLES: TELECASTS LONDONPS4

TELEGRAMS: TELECASTS LONDON TELEX TELEX: 22182

Dear Keith, Thank you very much for the super present. Really sweet of you. You shouldn't have! Jon Pertwee spoke to Barry + said that he wasn't pleased with fan club etc... So please in future, could we have more up to date stories with Jon Pertwee the main attraction. Not so much of the old stories O.K.? Thanks again

BIRTHDAY ISSUE:BIRTHDAY ISSUE:BIRTHDAY ISSUE:BIRTHDAY ISSUE:BIRTHDAY ISSUE:BIRTHDA

Number 12 January 1973 Edition 1st Anniversary Issue!

A SPECIAL ANNIVERSARY

THREE DOCTORS REPORT!

THIS IS THE YEAR OF THE DOCTOR!It will ten years in November since the prog began,and to mark this special occasion, I'm going to try to make this year extra special for all Doctor Who fans!

To begin with,I've pushed aside all the regular articles to make way for this special report on the making of THE 3 DOCTORS,possibly the most exciting story ever!

But first,a few announcments.You may remember that I said IN THE BEGINNING would be changed to THE BEST OF DR WHO? Well,I think it would be best if I left it as it was,but sadly,it can't continue So I think it was best finishing the series where it started,with the first episode printed last month.I hope you enjoyed the stories,anyway.

I'm sorry if the Christmas issue didn't reach you before the big day.Hope you enjoyed it though.And thanks to everyone who sent me Christmas cards,including Brian Smith,Andrew Veasey,Beverley Manton, Trevor and Andrew Hirst and everyone else. It was very kind of you.Thanks!

Here we are.One year old already-sigh- Seems like only yesterday that I first started answering your letters and sending out the magazine when it was pocket size and the printing was terrible.Oh, for the good ol' days...

Before I forget,there is a super new exhibtion on in London at the moment called the BBC TV SPECIAL EFFECTS EXHIBITION with Daleks,Ogrons,a Sea Devil,an Axon, the Tardis(inside and out!),the Axons space ship,Skybase,Liz 49 (from a Pat Troughton story) and lots, lots more.So if you are in London any time from now 'til the 6th of June,try and get along to see it.It's well worth it.

I think I've chatted anough now,so lets trot along to the BBC and see whats going on...

THE MAKING OF
THE

THREE DOCTORS

Sarah Newman,Barry Letts secretary,ushered me into the Producers Booth,a small room with a large window that looked out into the Control Room.I sat down in front of the TV set in the corner.Miss Newman had more work to do,so she hurried back to the DR WHO Office,leaving me in the room where I could see what was going on in the Control Room,while not missing the action on the studio floor.The actors and crew had been there from early morning,but it was now just after One as the TV Screen flickered into life,and the scene of the Doctors lab came into view.But it was still a few minutes until the Rehersals began.The control room is dimly lit,so that there isn't any bothersome reflections on the numerous TV screens collected together in front of the Control Desk,where the Director and his assistants work.Producer Barry Letts sat behind them,checking the schedule for the days recording.Then my attention was drawn back to the TV screen where the tall,familiar figure of Jon Pertwee strode through the Lab doors.

He was dressed in his own clothes -a black jumper and trousers with a giant belt buckle that glinted in the light of the studio.He was closly followed by Katy Manning,also in her personal clothes,with a large badge or brooch with a white question mark embedded on it.You may have noticed Katy wearing it before, like in her photo in the Radio Times article.I think it must be a good luck charm or something.Anyway,after a while,Nicholas Courtney and Rex Robinson (Dr Tyler) were on the scene,and the Rehersals began.

During the coffee break,I had hoped to rush down to the Dressing Rooms to have a chat with Jon,Katy and anyone else that was around,but Sarah hadn't returned so I missed them.But perhaps next time...

The coffee break lasted about ten minutes,then it was back to work.Barry retutned to his seat,and the Rehersals continued.Then Miss Newman returned and we went to the Canteen for lunch.After this was the Producers Run,so when I returned,the Producers Booth was going to be used by Barry where he tells everyone if there's going to be any changes made or bits cut out.Barry,however, had arranged for me to sit in the Control Room with Bob Baker and Dave Martin, the writers of the Three Doctors.From here,I could see at close hand,everything that was going on.Behind me,Barry was surrounded by Sound Technichans and Floor Managers and everyone else that is important in the production of the programme. Then Lennie Mayne,the Director,spoke into a microphone,"Run Telecine",and the swirling patterns of the opening titles appeared on the TV screens.The first episode of the Three Doctors was beginning it's dress rehersal.The episode ran smoothly until it came to the part in the story where the Gel started to ooze out of the orange box,this is where it became very interesting.I bet you'll never guess what the Gell is.It's a feather boa which a peice of tinsel tied around it,and if you let a colour TV camera slip out of focus...you have a Gel! Very clever!

Then it came to the time where Patrick Troughton was re-introduced as Dr Who. He made his "materialization" by spliting the TV picture into two halves,with one camera on another set of the Tardis,and another camera on the original set. Then Pat is "covered" by the blanked out area of the original then faded in by fading out the second set.This gives the appearance of Pat being zapped in.Well, I think I've given enough of the Special Effects secrets,so let's move on.

At the end of the Producers Run,Miss Newman beckoned to me to come round to the box where I met her and we had dinneraat the BBC club.Here I met for the second time(this was my second visit)Dudley Simpson,the man who composed a lot of the incidental music for many of the programmes.He was up at the Beeb to see the episode so he could decide what kind of music to put to the action.He told us:

"The other day,"he said in his native Australian tongue,"I was journeying back and forward to the BBC with music,when a police car suddenly appeared and stopped me.I stopped and got out of the car and asked what was the matter?The copper says "Do you know,Sir,that you have been past this point nearly six times.May I ask just what you are doing?"So I replied that I was working at the BBC,and that

THE MAKING OF THE THREE DOCTORS (cont.)

I composed the music for Dr Who."Oh,"he replied"You don't!That's my favourite TV programme!""Perhaps he'll be joining the Fan Club soon....

Anyway,after dinner,we went back down to the studios where I met Terrance Dicks,Script Editor for the series and writer of "THE MAKING OF DR WHO"

"How are things going?Any problems?" I asked.

"Well,everytprogramme has it's problems perhaps this one more than most 'cause of all the camera work and so on.but all things considered,things are going pretty smoothly"

Then the standby came over the loud-speaker and Terry rushed away to the Control Room.Down below us,we could see the final preperations being made on the set of the Tardis and the Time Lords scenery.Then the cast entered the studios in their assigned clothes...the Doctor in his cape,Jo in her blue dress (her question mark under the collar)and the Brigadier in his UNIT uniform.From now on it wasn't Jon,Katy and Nic,it was Doctor,Jo and the Brigadier.Again the swirling patterns appeared on the TV screens,and the programme began again. After a few minutes,Dudley rejoined us together with Katys manager.And so my day at the Beeb was almost at an end, I was rather dissappointed that I hadn't met any of the cast,but I recieved a letter a few days later from Jon,telling me that perhaps we'll meet again in the New Year,and if I do,then I hope you join me again in another report.

And so I said my goodbyes to Barry and the crew,and Miss Newman saw that I got out of the maze of corridors safley.My taxi arrived,I stepped in,said my final goodbye as the Taxi drove off and glanced back at the huge circular building of the BBC with it's lights burning brightly against the now dark skies of London.

....

LAST WORD:LAST WORD:LAST WORD:LAST WORD

THIS IS THE YEAR OF THE DOCTOR

AND THE CELEBRATIONS START NOW!But before an erthshattering announcement, remember and spread the word!THIS IS THE YEAR OF THE DOCTOR!And all fans in the DWFC will enjoy the year more than

THE DALEKS ARE BACK!FOR ALL MEMBERS OF THE DWFC,THE DODO DESIGN COMPANY ARE OFFERING THEIR

DALEK IRON-ON TRANS-FER!!

AT THE SPECIAL PRICE OF 40p.THEY ARE USUALLY 50p,but the Dodo Manufacturers have kindly dropped 10p plus the postage and packing off the orginal price,for DWFC MEMBERS ONLY!

You can iron the transfer onto Jeans, T-Shirts,Skirts,Blouses,Anoraks,Jackets, Shirts,Pants,Caps and hats so you can have a whole OUTFIT of Dalek articles!

To get your Dalek Transfer,simply write to this address:

DODO DESIGNS,
185 WESTBOURNE GROVE,
LONDON W11 2SD

stating that you would like a Dalek Transfer and that either you are a member of the DWFC,or simply give your member-ship number,but remember to put DWFC in front of it e.g.DWFC K095,and make your 40p postal order out to DODO DESIGNS LTD. Then pop it in the post box and in a few days you'll recieve your super transfer. Thanks to the Dodo Company for reducing the price for us!

I hope you have all got your copy of Jon's record WHO IS THE DOCTOR!If not, but it now!It's on the Purple Record label No.PUR 111.Send it to No.1!

NEWS FLASH!

Simon Lidster(A027) has told me that Three Daleks were stolen,yes,STOLEN!A firm was advertising WHO IS THE DOCTOR and had booked Three Daleks to be displayed in the windows.And so the work men left them in the van while they went for their dinner,and when they came back,they were gone!Perhaps they were reactivated and are now attempting another invasion!

Well,the celebrations continue next month with a special competition with a JON PERTWEE/DR WHO/DWFC T-Shirt as the prize,plus episode 2 of WHEN DALEKS RULED THE EARTH and the return of REVIEW! See you then,Timelord!

BBC

28th Feb.1973

Dear Keith,

Poor you! What a horrid little boy. If only I had known before he wrote to J.P about coming to studio I would have mentioned the matter to Barry and I'm sure Barry would have said 'no' or written to the little bugger and told him off. Never mind, he will never take over the fan club as long as I am in this seat. Never, never fear. Yes, I would rather write to you in future. Thanks. Sorfy about delays of mag, all due to me I know. Of course Jon charged Roger rent! The monthly has improved a heck of a lot but dear Keith, your spelling is fascinating! As good as mine...! I think journalism would be an <u>extremely</u>, good idea. I really do. I'm very, very glad for you. Anyway, take care, write to me when you want. I hate Stuart Money too. Reading this letter over the language is quite terrible....sorry....so would hate you to keep this one...please tear up. Thanks.

P.S. Refuse to send J.P.'s letter to Stuart. Write + tell him you've got the letter + you'll <u>be</u> keeping it yourself.

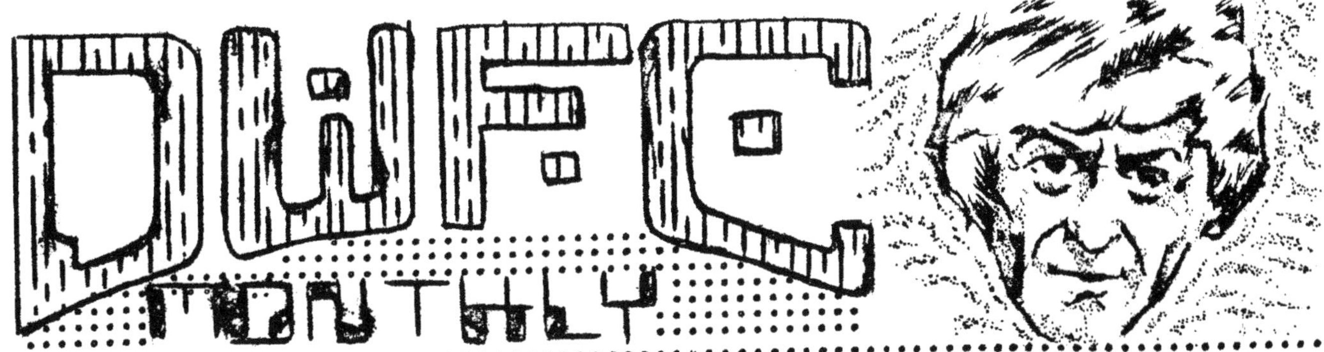

Number 13 February Edition D.W.F.C.

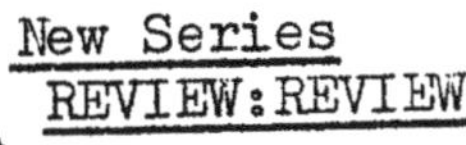

New Series
REVIEW:REVIEW

THE THREE DOCTORS

A brilliant start to what I'm sure is going to be one of the best series in the history of the programme.The story, acting,sets,music were all fantastic,the best I've seen and heard for a long time.It showed how much the Doctor has changed over the ten years he has been in our homes.

William Hartnell,the first Doctor,brought forward the hard,but lovable,nature that introduced the Timelord,all those years ago.Patrick Troughton portrayed the Doctor in his own,comical and sometimes very serious manner.And then Jon Pertwee,repeating his own inimatable style of modern looks while not abandoning the scientific wonderment which has accompanied each of the Doctors.

Omega was fantastic!He was played by actor Stephen Thorne,who also portrayed Azal in "The Deamons"His voice is as clear as James Masons'one min ute then it explodes with the fury of the devil the next.Really fantastic.

The first episode,subject of Report last month,was very good,but the second was undoubtedly better.The ring of explosions when the Gelguards arrived to meet the Doctor,Jo and Dr Tyler was very impressive indeed.The best effect was at the end when the whole of Unit HQ soared through the Black Hole into the world of Anti-matter.How the BBC got a whole building to disappear I've yet to find out! I thought Dudley Simpsons "ring-dingy" music was perfect for Bessy.Seemed to fit the car like a glove.

The Gelguards I thought were rather comical,although,of course,they weren't meant to be.Nevertheless,they did look funny hobbling around making that burping sound.

Well,I think that this adventure will go down in the annals of science fiction as the best Dr Who story to date.But I can promise you that exciting things are happening at the BBC.One of them is the Daleks!

Next issue I'll be reviewing "THE CARNIVAL OF MONSTERS" by Robert Holmes.

Drawings with the help of Brian Smith

DR.WHO PEOPLE

No.2:KATY MANNING/JO GRANT

Katy Manning otherwise know as Jo Grant,says that a lot of Katy gets mixed up with Jo.

"Jo's a scatty,slightly messy and very happy person,"she says,"And thats me."

Katy's career started with TV commercials,advertsing cheese,milk and eggs."The big three"as she puts it.From there she broke into TV plays and serials like Man at the Top and Softly,Softly then auditioned for the part of Jo Grant and got the part.

When she's off screen,Katy's always in a muddle,forgetting where she's put her scripts and so."But Jon is so stable and marvelous,he's forever finding things I've lost."

Katy's handicap is her eyes.Without her glasses she's as blind as a bat!Another habit she has,or rather had,was nail biting.Again, Jon came to her escue.Every time he saw Katy having a chew at her nails,he'd go "Tch,tch."Then every time she chewed her nails, she could imagine she could hear him!

Jo Grant first made her appearance in "Terror of the Autons" when Liz Shaw had to go back to Cambridge.Her first action was to ruin a very delecate experiment which the Doctor was conducting by attacking it with a fire hose.It was an accident,of course,but this made the Doctor very unwilling to consider her for a new assistant.But the Doctor came to like her,and she's grown very fond of him over the years.She's saved the Doctor quite a few times,too,such as their encounter with the Deamons where she saved the Earth by throwing herself in front of Azal.

Katy gets on very well with everyone,on and off the screen.I found her very nice when I met her last year.And I agree with her that a certain amount of Katy is in Jo!

Next Issue:Roger Delgado/The Master

LAST WORD:LAST WORD:LAST WORD:LAST WORD

THIS IS THE YEAR OF THE DOCTOR!And we are continuing the celebrations by this months fantastic competition with a unique

DR.WHO/JON PERTWEE

(Can only be obtained through DWFC Monthly competitions)

All you have to do is:

On the front page of this magazine, you will find a drawing from The THREE DOCTORS at the bottom of the page.State the names of each person(real and stage) IN ORDER from left to right.And that's all!All correct entries will be entered into the competition and the winning entry will be picked out the 31st of March,1973,the closing date.Address all entries to:

DR.WHO T-SHIRT COMP.,DWFC,c/o Keith Miller,109 Moredun Park Road,Edinburgh.

Now,after that exciting peice of news, on with the last section of the monthly.

I hope you like the monthly in it's "new"form.A new series of THE DR'S DRAWING BOARD will be starting this year,so drawings please to the club address.

I must apologise for the late arrival of the January edition.As you will know, the monthly has been late the past few months,so next month,I'll be putting forward a plan which could change this.

Please note that offer for Ben and Polly photos is now closed(except to overseas members)

You may notice that Brian Smith is mentioned on the cover this month.He is now DWFC Photographer,helping to carry the monthly up to greater heights!

In case you were expecting a Review on the Dr Who Annual 1973,don't hold your breath.Only one word to describe it-rubbish.

Well,that's about it again for another month,but next month,the final part of WHEN DALEKS RULED THE EARTH,Review of CARNIVAL OF MONSTERS and another competition with DR WHO Rings as prizes.See you then,Timelord!

JON PERTWEE as

in

WHEN DALEKS RULED THE EARTH

Episode Two

Jo screamed.The Doctor slammed his fist down onto the door control,shutting out the terrifying scene they had just witnessed.He streched his arms out and propped himself up against the console.

"What now,Doctor?"asked Jo.

The Doctor looked up from the control panel.

"There's only one thing I can do.."he said,"...find out what it is the Daleks want here,then destroy them."

The Doctor operated the scanner which surveyed the room outside.The Red Dalek could be seen gliding down from it's platform and hover towards a screen imbedded in the wall.It glowed with life,showing another of it's species-The Black Dalek.

"Re-port!"ordered it's superior.

"The Doc-tor has dis-covered my base of oper-a-tions.His time ma-chine is here."

"The time ma-chine can-not be de-stroy-ed.You must find some way to..."

Suddenly,the light on top of the box began to flash and the Tardis sounded it's cry of dematerialization as it slowly faded.

"The Doc-tor has e-scaped!"cried the Red Dalek.

"This will not fa-vour highly with the Dalek Su-preme.You must find the Doc-tor and destroy him...or you will not be forgiven for the in-ci-dent on Arc-tu-rus...and you will be ex-ter-min-ated!"

The screen died.The Dalek glided out of the room and rejoined his prisoners.

"You know what you must do."

The crowd remained silent,then turned and reentered their aircraft.The engines burst into life and metal bird soared into the blue,as it's passengers chatted cheerfully and the crew guided the plane towards London.

"Doctor?What's happening?"

"I don't know...the controls seem to be under Timelord control again,but I can't be sure.."

"Could it be the Daleks?"gasped the girl.

Before the Doctor could answer,the Ship came to rest in what looked like a Victorian bed chamber.The duo stepped out and Jo looked around puzzled.

"Why on earth did the Timelords bring us here?"

"Perhaps here isn't where you think it is!"said the Doctor pointing behind her.

To her amazement,there was no forth wall!Instead there was a dark hole,thru which she could just see the glint of something metallic.

"Daleks!"hissed Jo;

The Doctor walked over and guided inaa TV Camera.

"I don't think so.."he said with a grin.

"But why here?"replied Jo.

"Let's find out.."said the Doctor, making his way out of the studio and into a corridor which disappeared round in a huge arc.Above them a notice read

BBC STUDIO 4:Do not enter when light is on.

"TV Studio?"exclaimed Jo scratching her head,"This get's madder by the minute!"

The Doctor,too,was puzzled.He looked up and down the silent and empty corridor.

"Jo,there's something wrong here.These corridors should be busy.."

"Perhaps it's Sunday.."

"They make programmes every day of the week you know."

Jo shrugged her shoulders then made her way down the corridor,searching for any sign of life.She peered round a corner then slammed the Doctor and herself flat against the wall.

"What the..!"exclaimed her friend.

"Sssshhh!"hissed the young girl.

A few moments later,a Dalek glided past as Jo held her breath for fear of being heard.The Dalek turned and entered one of the Studios,leaving the duo in the corridor.

"Of course!"cried the Doctor,"We've travelled forward in time a few days, and it seems the Daleks have been once more succesful.."

"Succesful?"

"Jo,Earth has been taken over by the Daleks!"

"Oh,no.."she groaned.

The Doctor signalled to her to follow him,and they both cautiously entered the studio the Dalek had disappeared into a few minutes earlier.Darkness surrounded them,but in the gallery up stairs,they could see Daleks hovering to and fro, operating switches.Suddenly,an eye stick detected movement in the shadows below.

"AL-ERT!AL-ERT!IN-TRU-DERS IN STU-DIO 5!"it grated as the sea of lights above them burst into life,revealing the duo.

BRITISH BROADCASTING CORPORATION
TELEVISION CENTRE WOOD LANE LONDON W12 7RJ
TELEPHONE 01-743 8000 CABLES: TELECASTS LONDONPS4
TELEGRAMS: TELECASTS LONDON TELEX TELEX: 22182

7th March 1973

Dear Keith,

Thank you for your letter. There is going to be special booklet of Dr.Who this year with a document inside on how to make various monsters etc. Deadly hush though. Very good booklets. We are about to start filming again fairly shortly. Dalek story much better than other one. Let's discuss your coming down to studio at a later date. Perhaps in the Summer.

Love

Sarah

The DWFC t-shirt given as a prize in the competition in issue 13 of DWFC Monthly were screen-printed by me, using the redundant equipment used to print the first four issues of the fanzine. Two were sent to Jon, who loved them and he dressed his kids, Daryll and Sean, in them.

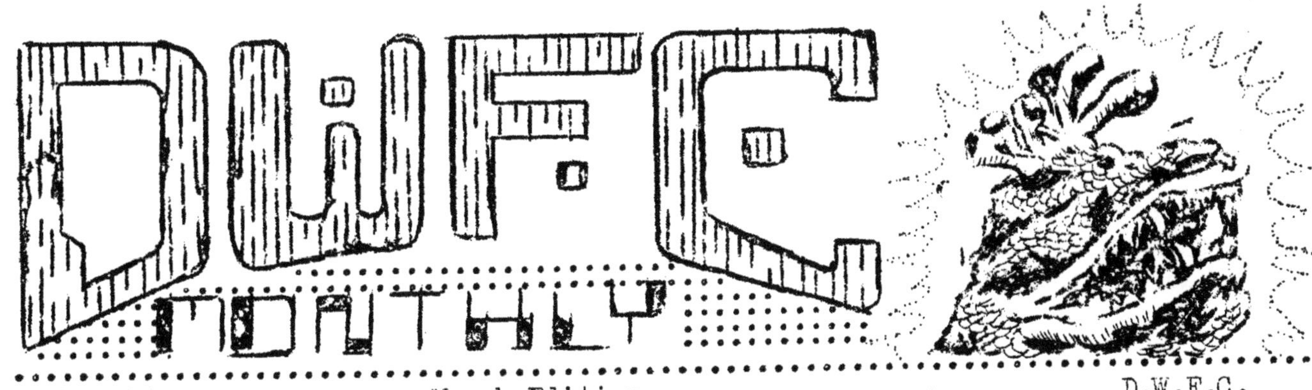

Number 14 March Edition D.W.F.C.

CARNIVAL OF MONSTERS

REPORT:REPORT:REPORT:REPORT:REPORT

In Issue 12,you will remember I told you about my second visit to the BBC to see the filming of the THREE DOCTORS.Well now the DWFC proudly presents another REPORT on THE CARNIVAL OF MONSTERS,my first visit!

I met Sarah Newman at the Dr Who Office where she had been working.answering letters and so on.The office overlooks Shepherds Bush Green and is just along from the BBC TV Theatre where Basil Brush comes from.I entered the room only to come face to face with a Sea Devil!I took a step back then saw a Mutant!I was just about to run for the hills when Miss Newman picked up the headpeices and handed one to me.It was the head of the Sea Devil.It was thick and rubbery and I pitied the actor who had to work in one of those.

But time was pressing on so we collected our things together and stepped out into the midday traffic.A short walk later,we rounded a corner and the giant, circular building of the Beeb loomed up in front of us.

We entered through a side door and started our journey through the vast network of corridors which spread out like a spiders web over the complex.Walking through the brightly lit corridors,it suddenly sprung to mind where I had seen the inside of this place before!It bore a remarkable resemblence to the interior of the Star Ship Enterprise!

At the end of the trek,Sarah pushed open the double doors of the studio and we entered.The studio was quiet,apart from some scenery workers hammering over the other side of the hall.In front of us stood the inside of the Scope,with its glowing corridors and shiny floors.Sarah guided around the studio showing first the Scope and then the hold of the ship of Major Daly and his crew.Then again I came up against another monster-a Drashig!It was standing four or five feet away, it's teeth showing a fearsome white grin.But not to worry.The Drashigs are really only three or four feet long!They're superimposed onto the main picture by a special camera process(see THE MAKING OF DR WHO).At this time,camera men began to come in and take up their positions at the back of the colour TV cameras.Miss Newman decided it was time to leave them to their preparations so she showed up to the BBC canteen where we had lunch.I looked around and saw Ronnie Barker and Ronnie Corbett sitting at the next table.Marching through the doors was the weather man Bert Foord.Behind him was Donald Eccles (Krasis from THE TIME MONSTER) and Neil McCarthy(Barnham from MIND OF EVIL).It was all very exciting but it's time to get back to the studio.We re-entered the corridors and made our way back.

REPORT:CARNIVAL OF MONSTERS(continued)

We sat in the Producers Box and watched the rehersals taking place.Shooting was out of phase at that time-that is scenes were being shot which don't follow each other on the TV screens-out of sequence,so this made the following of the story line very difficult.

But then Jon Pertwee,Katy Manning,Jenny McCraken,Tenniel Evans and the rest of the actors come onto the sets,dressed in their everyday clothes.Katy,of course had her question mark with her and it is her lucky charm.

The rehersals went pretty smoothly then we returned to the canteen for where I was introduced to Barry Letts and Terrance Dicks.Ask your Mum or Dad if they remember a TV serial called The Silver Sword.If they do,they'll probably remember Barry playing one of the leading roles in it.In fact,he's done quite a lot of acting in films like "Boy,Girl and a Bike"and numerous other TV programmes.We discussed the history of the programme like when the very first episode was repeated the second week following.How many of you remember that?

Everything is hurried in the BBC so before we knew it was time to get back and see that the final preparationswere made before filming.

We sat down again at the TV set and watched Katy and Jon,now in TV gear,hurry through the Scope trying to find the way out and escape from the Drashigs.You may remember that the Doctor and Jo rushed down a corridor with a very shiny metal floor which I mentioned earlier,with tubes of coloured plastic positioned along the sides.Well,the acting was going very well with Katy running along with Jon behind.They came to the end of the ramp and Katy quickly turned the corner and headed in a new direction,but the surface was slippery and Jon's boot skidded from beneath him sending him toppling into the tall,coloured plastic tubes.There was a terrible clatter and the screen went dead.Second passed and nothing was seen. ~~Then there~~ was a curious puffing sound and Jons head suddenly appeared on the screen.He seemed to be okay,then Katy rushed forward and helped him up.She asked if he was alright and he replied yes but his leg hurt for some time after that. But things restored,the play went ahead.

The next scene was when the Drashig reared up through the ship and into the forward hold.This called for the crew to have firearms-in this case rifles.But although they are equipped with blank bullets,the guns can still be dangerous with the empty cartridge shells flying through the air.So extra precautions have to be made to ensure complete saftey for the rest of the crew.The practise shots rang through the air,with John and the sailors firing at the monster,but there was one little chap there who was going berserk!He was firing at everyone except the monster,waving the gun about like a madman and jumping up and down like a thing possessed.Barry,who was directing this particular adventure as well as producing it,wondered what on earth this little man was up to,so they had to take him off and replace him!He was still jumping up and down when they took him away........

And so the rehersals continued until the last scene was played through-where Major Daly and Claire were saying goodnight to each other in the final episode-then there was a coffee break for 15 minutes.

Suddenly,Sarah rose to her feet."Come on,"she said,"This is our chance,"and she whisked me out of the room,down a small corridor,into a lift,down a couple of floors,then out into another corridor.I then discovered that this was the dressing room area.We walked down the long corridor and a small figure stepped out in front of me,and I nearly bumped into her.I said I was sorry and the little lady turned round.She wore a smile I had seen countless times before.It belonged to Jo Grant! "That's okay!"she said,then Miss Newman introduced us.She asked me if I was enjoying myself and I said yes,tremendously.She then said she had to see Jon about something then led me down into another dressing room where another familiar face greeted me.The face of the Doctor!He stepped forward and shook my hand.

"I thought you would have been down here at the lunch break!"he said bursting into that broad grin which makes his face so distinctive.I explained we were talking to Barry Letts then and we couldn't make it.We then went on discussing how things were going and what he had to do.But a few minutes later a message came telling him he only had a few minutes to get back on the set,so I said goodbye and he replied that he hoped one day we might get together for longer.We returned to the box,my head still in the clouds.

And so there it was.My day was almost complete and the hands on the clock told it was Ten'o clock.Sarah showed me down to the entrance where I stepped out into the cool night and into the taxi,ending a very exciting day with DOCTOR WHO.

REVIEW:REVIEW:REVIEW:REVIEW:REVIEW:REVIEW

CARNIVAL OF MONSTERS

Written by:Robert Holmes Serial:PPP

I think opening up this series of REVIEW was a bad idea because if the first two stories of this series are anything to go by,this is going to be one of the best session of programmes ever.

Speaking generally,there was one element here lacking in the past few adventures-seriousness.For once,Jo actually said "Doctor,I just can't take it in!"instead of accepting every fact that happened to come along.And no witty remarks during the exciting bits which,in my view, spoiled some parts.Don't think I'Ve no sense of humour,but I don't think one would crack jokes in the middle of a battle with terrifying aliens.True,there was some fun at the beginning and at the end,and that is how it should be.

I think the part that made the most impact,judging from most of the reactions I've heard is the end of episode one when the giant hand lifted up the Tardis.

The best part for me was when the Drashig crashed up through the roof of the ship in the last episode.

But I was rather disappointed with the beginning.Not a goodbye to Earth to be heard!I thought at least there could have been a final tara to the Brigadier or the like.But nothing.Very disappointing.

The acting is getting better by the episode.I don't know what the writers are doing to make the prog better,but whatever it is,I hope it continues!

Now for the rundown episode by episode. Episode one started off rather well and continued to get better as it went on. Episode two continued the good work with the spectacular scenes of the Doctor and Jo inside the works of the Scope.The ending,I think,was classic with the Drashig towering up out of the water and screaming so loud my telly almost had a nervous breakdown!At the beginning of episode three,it seemed there was to be no end to the brilliance of the acting and special effects when Jo was being sucked down into the swamp and the Doctor scared the monsters away with those fantastic fire explosions!Great stuff!I'll never forget that scene.Episode four proved to be a great ending to an almost classic adverture,a fantastic follow-up to the Three Doctors.In my opinion,it was a four star adventure.

Next:Frontier in Space by Malcome Hulke.

LAST WORD:LAST WORD:LAST WORD:LAST WORD

Now.A very important announcement!Next month,you will find that the magazine will have more pages than before,six to be exact,which proves that the DWFC is climbing to greater heights!But you'll understand when I tell you that this is because we're going bi-monthly - that is you'll get the mag every two months.This will prevent the monthly being late,as it has been the last few months,and it'll give me more oppertunity to introduce new items.The reason for the lateness of the monthlies was the increase in the membership numbers so this meant more envelopes for me to type out and this took up a lot of time,making the mags late.So you see,it's best if the mag is double the size and comes to you every two months.Let me hear your reactions to this idea,anyway.

THIS IS THE YEAR OF THE DOCTOR!And the year marches on and brings the second DWFC Tenth Year Competition!This time the prize is a fantastic DR WHO RING! There are two of these rings to be won and this is what you have to do.

In THE CARNIVAL OF MONSTERS,the Drashigs were finally defeated by the Eradicator.Design a weapon capable of destroying a Drashig but also small enough to be held in the hand.

Send your designs to:DWFC COMPETITION 2, c/o Keith Miller,109 Moredun Park Road, Edinburgh EH17 7HJ.

All entries must be in by the 30th of April.

Hint:Make your weapon as futuristic as you can.

So we're coming to the end of another issue.I hope you have enjoyed the Report, as I think it'll be the last one the year. Next month,it'll be the first double edition with the final part of WHEN DALEKS RULED THE EARTH,which proved to be very popular with you,a special letter from the Master himself,with a DR WHO PEOPLE report on Roger Delgado,REVIEW of FRONTIER IN SPACE,plus news and lots of info together with yet another competition for another DR WHO T-SHIRT.

I've some space left,which is unusual, so I can tell you what's coming soon.You will probably know by now that the Daleks are coming back - in April to be exact, and the Daleks you will be seeing are the the original models used in the first adventure nine years ago.You'll be meetin them again on the planet Spiridon.

Well,I guess that's it again,Timelord. Keep marching on and spread the word.Bye!

The ring given as a prize in *DWFC Monthly No 14* was made by me using a toy kit called *Plasticraft*, which became the number 1 toy of 1973. It was basically molten plastic you mixed with hardner and poured into a mould - but it produced lethal amounts of fumes! All windows had to be open whilst using it or your head began to spin. No Health and Safety in those days!

BRITISH BROADCASTING CORPORATION
TELEVISION CENTRE WOOD LANE LONDON W12 7RJ
TELEPHONE 01-743 8000 CABLES: TELECASTS LONDONPS4
TELEGRAMS: TELECASTS LONDON TELEX TELEX: 22182

26.3.73.

De r Keith,

I'd ask Jon for an interview yourself. He can only say no! I doubt if you will be able to get an interview with Verity because she is no longer with the BBC and with Thames, so you won't be able to get to her. The dates you are in London aren't recording dates unfortunately.

Sarah

Vy busy at the moment so short letter.

2.5.73.

Dear Keith

No, of course Jon's not leaving the programme. While that the 4th person from Scotland who's asked me? What is it all about?

Love

SARAH

Katy is though, but thats a secret.

And that was a bomb-shell casually thrown in at the end! My beloved Katy was leaving. I was heart-broken. Until I met Lis. I'm so fickle.

Noting that I had earlier reviewed the Doctor Who Annual as rubbish, Barry suggested I got in touch with World Distributors, enclosing sample issues of the fanzine with my stories in them, as he thought they were better written...

World Distributors *Publishers*

Head Office: P.O. Box 111, 12 Lever Street, Manchester M60 1TS
Telephone: 061-228 3841 *Telex:* 66 8609 *Cables:* Sydpem, Manchester
London Office: 36 Great Russell Street, WCIB 3PP. *Telephone:* 01-636 5544/9476

Keith Miller Esq
Dr Who Fan Club
109 Moredun Park Road
Edinburgh EH17 7HJ

22nd May 1973

Dear Mr Miller

Thank you for your recent letter, and the samples of stories from your fan club magazine.

All our annual stories are passed by the creators of the BBC television programme, and they are of course very particular about the standard. We do have one difficulty however. Due to licensing problems with the creators of the monsters, we are not allowed to use the Daleks or any of the other television monsters in our stories. This probably accounts for the discrepancies you noticed between the series and the annual stories.

If you would care to submit any original and unpublished Dr Who stories, we will of course be willing to consider them, but you must of course bear in mind the copyright point which I have mentioned. Thank you for your interest.

Yours sincerely

M Broadley

Mae Broadley BA (Mrs)
Editor

WORLD DISTRIBUTORS (Manchester) LTD. A member of the Marshall, Morgan & Scott Group
Registered in England No. 468030. Registered Office: 12 Lever Street, Manchester M60 1TS.

...and one was accepted! This became the first time a fan writer crossed over into the professional arena - take that, Russell! Got paid the princely sum of £9, but that was worth quite a lot in 1973!

The Doctor Who Fan Club,
c/o Keith Miller,
109 Moredun Park Road,
Edinburgh EH17 7HJ

Dear Mrs.Broadley,

Thank you for your letter and your explanation about the copyright on DOCTOR WHO monsters in the annual.

I noted that you you would be willing to consider original, unpublished Dr Who stories,so I have enclosed THE SEEDS OF DEATH and HOUSE THAT JACK BUILT.I hope you find them up to BBC standard,

yours sincerely,

Keith Miller

Keith Miller
(DWFC secretary)

Invoice
short story entitled
The House that Jack Built
for Dr Who Annual
3000 words @ £3 a 000 = £9-00
Job No 74/0456

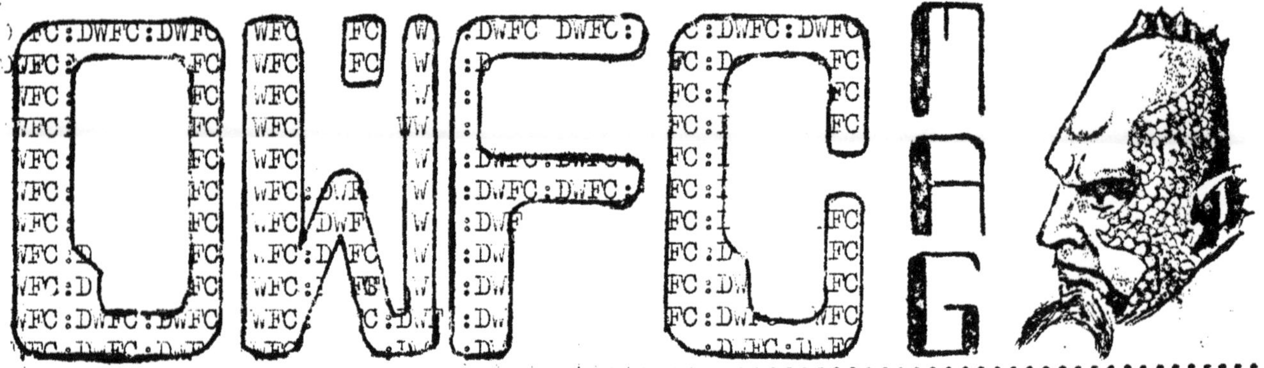

Number 15 April/May Edition Special Master Issue!!!!!

REVIEW:REVIEW:REVIEW:REVIEW:REVIEW:REVIEW:REVIEW

FRONTIER IN SPACE

by Malcolm Hulke

This adventure was a masterpeice of special effects and sets,but the story wasn't lively enough.I think the adult members of the audience would have enjoyed this one more than the youngsters. I still thought it was great,though.

Episode one was rather good and I liked the filmed excerpt on the screen when the Tardis was spinning through space.The speech made by the Draconian on the attacking ship bore a remarkable resemblance to that of the Daleks in INVASION EARTH 2150.I was rather surprised when the Doctor was shot.The ending was a bit unexpected,you might say.

Episode two started off with a huge chunk out of the ending of ep.one.Waste of time, I thought.The explanation about the six foot rabbit and purple horses was stupid.Should have been left out!Acting was good again in this episode,though there was a lot of walking back and forwards. The ending was pretty spectacular.

The Doctor certainly got about in this adventure,when in the third episode he was sentenced to the moon.It gave a good insight into what life might be like in the twenty second century.The sets gave the episode an extra sparkle.

The Master made a welcome return in episode four and I liked the remanicenses of the Doctor and Jo.And at last Jo realized she had been away from Earth for rather a long time.I liked the excerpt where the Doctor done the spacewalk.Very realistic.I also liked the part where the door was left open and the air was being sucked out.The spaceships looked good in the outer space film.Before I forget,I thought the makeup on the Draconians was splendidly done.Very realistic.

The forth episode was a little drawn out,but the acting of Jon Pertwee and Roger Delgado was superb.I liked the part when the Master tried to hypnotise Jo but failed.Then,the best of the six epsiodes was to come.

Episode six,the grand finale and truly a masterpeice.Again we saw the Doctor do a great spacewalk,although once,but only once, I saw the suspension wire glint in the lights.The adventure was proceeding at great pace when the battle betwe n the Earthmen and the Ogrons took place.I liked the look of that horrible squelchy thing on the hillside but it only had a small part.Pity. Then,da dan dan dan dan ta!The Daleks are back with us once mroe. And what Daleks!They are the originals from the first story and thank the Timelords they brought them back.Sheer perfection!

And the voices!Much better than the carrot grater they used in DAY OF THE DALEKS.The spell of the magic of the Daleks is being woven again,and I wonder just how long it will be before Britain is Dalek crazy once more.One thing is for sure.I think PLANET OF THE DALEKS is going to be fantastic.

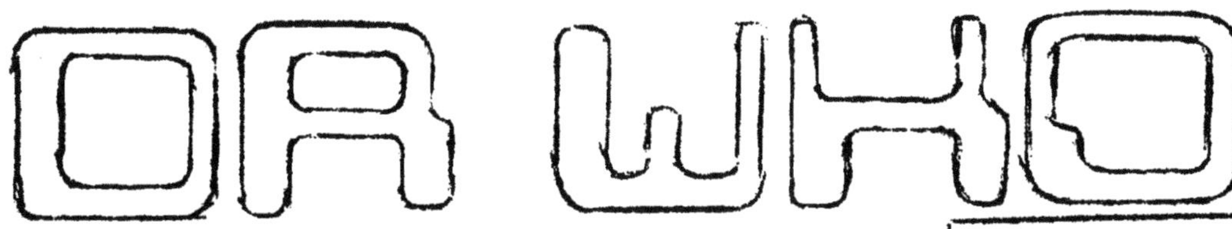

The D.W.F.C.,
c/o Keith Miller
109 Moredun Park Rd,
Edinburgh EH17 7HJ

Hi there,Timelord!,

Now that the mag's double the size,I've got lots more space to talk to you,so here's the first edition of DR WHO DATA which'll feature bit's n' peices of info which you might like to know.

I've just seen the first episode of PLANET OF THE DALEKS and I think it is fantastic!Seems as if my prediction on page one came true!

If there's any info you want printed in this column,drop me a line, will be only too pleased to help!

Actually,I was thinking of putting a comic strip in here somewhere,but decided against it.Do <u>you</u> want one here?

Now,During the summer hols,I'm going to try and get interviews with some of your favoutite DR WHO stars,and if I'm successful,I'll print the encounters here as special editions!

Now for news here,there and everywhere.

You may remember the scene in FRONTIER IN SPACE when the Doctor and Jo were being taken to their cells.Well,that big structure was in fact the South Bank of the Thames by the Festival Hall!

Christopher Storey of Carlisle wants to know if anyone is willing to sell him a copy of DR WHO'S SPACE ADVENTURE BOOK which was offered through Walls' Ice Cream products.If have one and are willing to sell it,send your book and price to me and I'll pass it on.

<u>FACT SHEET Number One</u>

<u>DOCTOR WHO AND HIS COMPANIONS</u>

This list displays the number of episodes the Doctors and companions occupied.

William Hartnell as Dr Who	131
Ian Chesterton	80
Barbara	80
Susan	50
Vicki	40
Steven	57
Dodo	21
Polly and Ben	40
Pat Troughton as Dr Who	116
Jamie	110
Victoria	40
Zoe	50
Liz Shaw	25
Jo Grant	63
Jon Pertwee as Dr Who	88

The last two figures were counted at the end of PLANET OF THE DALEKS

THE WINNER OF THE FIRST DWFC COMPETITION IS

<u>PHILIP ROBERTS</u>

Congratulations,Philip!You are now the proud owner of a super Jon Pertwee T-Shirt!Now,please send your size and I'll whip it off to you.

For all those who were stumped,the correct answers were

L-R

Dr Who-Patrick Troughton
Dr Tyler-Rex Robinson
The Brigadier-Nic Courtney
Dr Who-Jon Pertwee
Jo Grant-Katy Manning
Benton-John Levene
Mr Ollis-Laurie Webb

Remember-if anyone is is in Edinburgh during the summer hols and would like to pop up for a cuppa,don't be afraid to do so,but try and tell me way before hand,hear?

THIS IS THE YEAR OF THE DOCTOR!!

It is rumoured that Katy Manning might be leaving Dr Who,but it is only a rumour and there might be no basis to it.

Jon Pertwee had a special car made for him a few weeks ago.It was in the shape of a flying saucer and was built for a car show down in London.

Lots of people have been writing in asking what kind of surprises are in store for everyone at the end of the year.I don't want to tell you what they are,otherwise they won't <u>be</u> surprises,will they?

Over the years,there have been sketches on comedy progs and I thought you'd like to read some of them again.

MORCAMBE AND WISE:Relatives of a Mr MacDonald are gathered round the solicitors table listening to the reading of the will.The solicitor announces that he has left £50,000 to his neice.His woman and man servants are very annoyed and shout "What?After the way we looked after him?We served him loyaly for over th irty years?"

MORCAMBE:"Who's upset Dr Who and Batman?"

CHARLIE DRAKE AS DR WHO:"'Ello,my Daleks..."

Boom Boom

JON PERTWEE as

in

WHEN DALEKS RULED THE EARTH

Episode Three

featuring

THE DEATH OF THE DOCTOR!

The Doctor grabbed Jo by the arm.

"Run!"he yelled,dragging her out of the huge studio,into the corridors once more. Jo heard a bang behind her and glanced over shoulder to see that the Daleks were filing out of the hall after them at high speed.They stumbled into a lift and the Doctor stabbed at the door control.A Dalek hurtled forward as the doors slammed shut-the Dalek's sucker arm was trapped in the two doors.The Doctor pressed the Ground Floor button which activated the small room.The arm scrapped up to the roof;then with a loud grind, snapped from the alien and landed at Jo's feet.The doors glided open and all was quiet.

"It'll take them about another three minutes to get to the other lift.Come on..."said the Doctor,hurrying out into the huge hallway.He burst through the doors and into the silent streets of London.Jo began to cry.

"Oh,Doctor,I'm so afraid..."

"Never mind,my dear.I've defeated the Daleks in the past.I'll do so again."

They began to walk through the deserted metropolis.No sound was heard except two pairs of footsteps as they thumped out the last remaining spark of Londons heartbeat.

"What has happened,Doctor?Where is everyone?"

"I shudder to think,Jo,but to be frank, I think the Daleks have put into operation a world-wide extermination plan."

"Oh,no..."gasped the girl.

"Whatever's happened,we'll know for sure in here..."

The Doctor ushered Jo into a small building-the BBC Film Archives.They found themselves in a semi darkened room filled with seats.The Timelord told Jo to sit down as he picked up a reel of tape which was still spinning on the recorder.

"This must have been the last recording made before...it happened.Now,let's see what really happened..."

He fitted the tape in a playback machine and a large TV screen burst into life.The titles of the BBC NEWS faded as the newsreaders face appeared.

"The hi-jacking of the plane which disappeared about three hours ago is now over.UNIT,who are leading the investigation,said earlier today that the high ranking dilomats from all over the world have no recollection whatever as to what had happened.They were on their way to a Top Secret meeting on the new developments in the Human-Computer transference State..."

"So!"exclaimed the Doctor,"That is why the Daleks hi-jacked the plane.With the aid of this process,they could leave their machines for a short period and Robotise members from the World Government.That way,the Daleks had Robomen all over the world..."

"Doctor,look!"screamed Jo pointing to the screen.

A strange sound hummed through the speaker as the features of the man began to twist as if in terrible agony.He grabbed his throat as hair began to sprout from his face and hands.His forehead began to bulge forwards as his features took on the appearance of a Neanderthal man.His shape began to dwindle until he was a small animal struggling in a prison of the humans clothing.Then...there was nothing.The tape ran on,showing empty space.

"Doctor?"gasped Jo,"What on Earth happened to him?"

"I realize now how the Daleks finally exterminated the human race,Jo.They must have in their possesion a Time Controller -sort of a Kronos type machine-which can control mans time stream,sending him back into his past...so far back that he has faded into nothingness.The diplomats probably had some kind of miniture'pick-up' device planted on their Robodiscs so that the effect was world wide."

"Doctor..,that's horrible..."sobbed his young companion.

He put a cloaked arm around her shoulder. "Come on,Jo.We must strike a final blow in memory of the Earth and it's people.We must get back into the BBC and destroy that machine before it does any more harm.It could reverse all that's happened during it's existance... or it could destroy the very fabric of time forever!"

The Doctor and Jo watched the Dalek glide past the car park and into the huge circular building.They ran from

WHEN DALEKS RULED THE EARTH (continued)

shadow to shadow, stealthily hidding from any concealed eyes that may have been around. The duo pushed open the doors and entered. All was quiet as they padded along the corridors towards the main control area. They stepped into a lift and travelled upwards in silence. The doors glided open as a Dalek turned a corner and saw them.

"STOP! YOU CAN-NOT GET A-WAY!"

"Hurry, Doctor, close the doors!"

"What'd be the use?" asked the Doctor, wearily.

They stepped forward as the Dalek was joined by two more aliens. Their sucker arms jerked forward, pushing the duo down the corridor and into the studio they had fled from a few hours earlier. They stumbled in and took their place on a hexagonal platform, brightly lit in the centre of the hall. The Doctor hugged Jo close to him as the Black Dalek glided into the studio.

"The machine is over to our left..." whispered the Timelord, "I'll try and destroy it by smashing the neccessary components. Get ready..."

"SILENCE!" grated the Dalek leader, "YOU ARE THE DOC-TOR."

"Oh, don't let's go into all that again, yes, yes, Iam the Doctor."

He paused.

"So. You've won in the end, eh? The ultimate victory."

"YES. AND NOW WE HAVE YOU. YOU HAVE IN-TER-FERED IN OUR PLANS FOR TOO LONG."

"AND I'LL DO SO AGAIN!!" yelled the Doctor, grabbing the lens of one of the cameras standing trained on them and sending it spinning into the Black Dalek.

He lunged forward and sped across the hall towards the machine. Daleks crashed into the studio as Jo screamed "DOCTOR! LOOK OUT! BEHIND YOU!!"

The Doctor was about smash into the machine when a huge cloud of mist was fired at him from the guns of the aliens

The Doctors body turned negative as he let out a scream of pain, then collapsed onto the floor---lifeless. The Doctor had finally been destroyed by his most hated enemies whom he had been fighting for so long throughout the universe. And now he was gone. The Doctor was dead.

Jo was hysterical. She screamed at the Daleks, lurched forward and propelled a fully charged camera towards the line of murderous Daleks. Without thinking, they parted. The Black Dalek's dome spun round as it realized what the girl was doing. It grated out in it's mad alien monotone

"STOP THE GIRL! STOP THE MACHINE! IT IS HEADING FOR THE..."

The camera skidded on two wheels as it hurtled towards the Time Controller. The Daleks moved their clumsy machines forward but it was too late. The camera plunged into the intricate circuitry of the Time Controller.

She suddenly felt herself being thrown into the air and propelled faster and faster into space. Bars of light flashed, almost blinding her. Stars rushed by her as the hands of a clock began to retrace it's path.

Jo Grant stood outside the lab of the Doctor. She opened the doors of the lab with her elbow, due to the large wrapped parcel she held in both hands. She crept stealthilyup to the Doctor and shouted MERRY CHRISTMAS as the Doctors workpeice went flying over his head.

"What the devil...", he yelled as he spun round to see the box.

"From us to you,"

"Us?"

"Everyone at UNIT. Merry Chri..."

Jo looked round at the doors. She stared at them for a few seconds.

"What's wrong?" asked the Timelord.

"Nothing...it's just that I...I was expecting something to happen."

The Doctor put his hand on her shoulder.

"Merry Christmas, Jo."

THE END

Next month:-

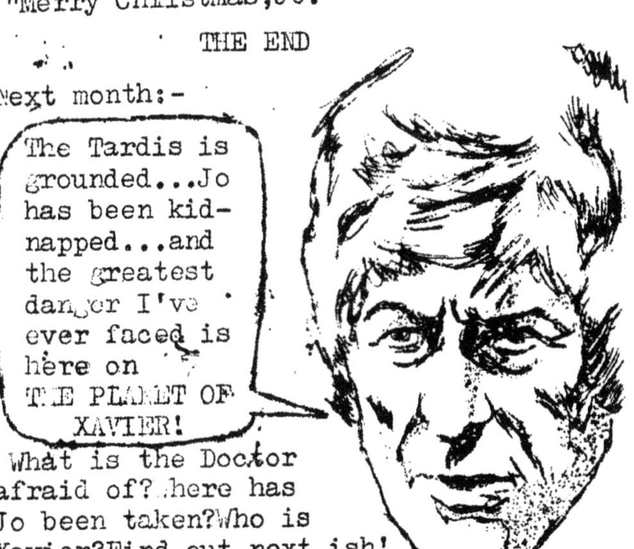

What is the Doctor afraid of? Where has Jo been taken? Who is Xavier? Find out next ish!

DR. WHO PEOPLE

Roger Delgado alias THE MASTER

Before deciding to do this dossier on Roger Delgado, I thought it would be a good idea if I wrote to him first,asking him personally what his likes and dislikes are.A few days later,I recieved a very courteous letter, but it also contained the sad news that the Master is not going to be with us for very much longer.But more of that later.

Roger Ceasar Marius Bernard de Delgado Torres Castillo Roberto -his full name- was born in London,within the sound of Bow Bells to be exact,making him a true Cockney,although his mother was French and his father Spanish!Before becoming an actor,Roger was a bank clark but turned to show biz in 1939.Since then,he has played numerous parts in films,TV programmes and in the theatre,usually as a villian because of his devilish looks.Then came Doctor Who where he couldn't be more evil,playing the part of personified badnnes!

The Master first appeared in TERROR OF THE AUTONS where we found out he was a Timelord from the same planet as the Doctor.He then created THE MIND OF EVIL after which he tried to help the Axons take over the Earth with the CLAWS OF AXOS. Then he tried to create havoc in a COLONY IN SPACE,where he failed and returned to Earth to summon THE DEAMONS.The Master next tried to coax the SEA DEVILS into war with the human race,but failing this,he summoned up Kronos,THE TIME MONSTER. He travelled to the future after that,trying,with the help of the Ogrons,to shatter the FRONTIER IN SPACE and cause a war between Earth and Draconia.

Roger Delgado is a much more peaceful man than the alien he plays on the telly. His favourite pastimes are reading Historical,autobiographical and science fiction novels!He loves his work,especially if it includes filming abroad,as he has recently done in THE ADVETURES OF DON QUIXOTE,where he worked with Rex Harrison and Frank Findlay.His likes and dislikes are simple.He likes good food and dislikes bad food!

As I said above,the Master will shortly be leaving us now.He'll be in one more story next year where at the end he'll either slip quietly away or go out in a blaze of glory!

During the filming of his latest adventure,Roger was taken seriously ill and had to have a major operation performed on his right kidney.He is getting better now after a holiday on Ibiza.

In his letter,Roger also enclosed a note for you.I leave the ending to him.

To the Doctor Who Fan Club-

I should like to say thank you for your staunch support these past few years.I hope you have enjoyed the shows as much as Jon and I enjoyed making them.Even though the Master may soon be no longer with you,he will be remembering with affection the time he spent chilling all your spines.

Sincerely,
ROGER DELGADO

NEW SERIES:NEW SERIES:NEW SERIES:NEW SER

How much do you know about Dr Who?Find out in this new series of questionnaires which'll feature questions about the Dr past and present.

DO YOU KNOW WHO?
Number 1

1)Who were the Doctors' first three companions? score 3

2)What is a 'Mechanoid'? score 1

3)Who are the actors that have played the Doctor? score 4

4)What was 'Liz 49'? score 1

5)Where did the scene below come from?

score 3

6)Who replaced Susan in the Tardis after she stayed behind in London,2064/score 1

7)Jon Pertwee has a radio show too.What is it called? score 1

8)The actor who played Steven Taylor now has another role in a famous TV prog.
a)Who is he?
b)What programme is it? score 2

9)What are the Primords? score 1

10)What was the name of the 'human zoo' in CARNIVAL OF MONSTERS? score 1

11)How many adventures have there been concerning the Daleks? score 2

12)What were the War Lords time and space machines called? score 2

13)Who shares the planet Skaro with the Daleks? score 1

14)What is Jo Grant's real name? score 1

15)In what year did Jon Pertwee become the Doctor?What adventure introduced him? score 3

16)What was the name of the gargoyle in THE DEAMONS? score 3

The answers to these questions will be printed next issue.

LAST WORD:LAST WORD:LAST WORD:LAST WORD

THIS IS THE YEAR OF THE DOCTOR

AND IT MARCHES ON WITH YET ANOTHER SUPER COMPETITION IN WHICH YOU CAN WIN AN EARTH SHATTERING TARDIS T-SHIRT!

All you have to do is match the following extracts to the correct adventures. Here we go!

EXTRACTS

1."WHO-EVER IS OPERA-TING THE TIME MA-CHINE IS AN ENE-MY OF THE DALEKS!ALL ENE-MIES OF THE DA-LEKS MUST BE EXTERMINATED! EXTERMINATE THEM!EXTERMINATE THEM!"

2."Well,the parties over now...you young men and I...must go back to our to our time zones..."

3."The tiger comes when he's around..." "Congratulations,Miss Grant!That was worthy of the late lamented Doctor himself!"

4."Jo...I'm liabel to sleep for rather a long time.If anything happens...anything at all,record it in the log..."

5."THE BOMB IS LOCKED ON COURSE.IT WILL DETONATE AT 30 RELS."

6."You say the cooks a Madrasy,Andrews? I find the Madrasies a bit idel,myself!"

ADVENTURES

A.The film:"DALEKS:INVASION EARTH-2150 AD"
B."THE TIME MONSTER"
C."THE THREE DOCTORS"
D."THE PLANET OF THE DALEKS"
E."CARNIVAL OF MONSTERS"
F."THE DAY OF THE DALEKS"

Write down the letter and number in which ever order you think is correct, write down your membership number,(Very important),then send it in to me at the club address at the top of DR WHO DATA. The winner will be picked on the 31st of May.

Now,after that rather difficult comp, let's see what little bit's of news have cropped up.

All those members who paid their years subscription and are thinking it should be running out soon,don't fret.The Beeb now pays for the mag!(Loud cheer for Auntie Beeb...)

Well,that's about it for the first bi-monthly issue.I'm dying to hear your reaction to it's new form,so write soon, hear?ONWARD TIMELORD.

KEITH

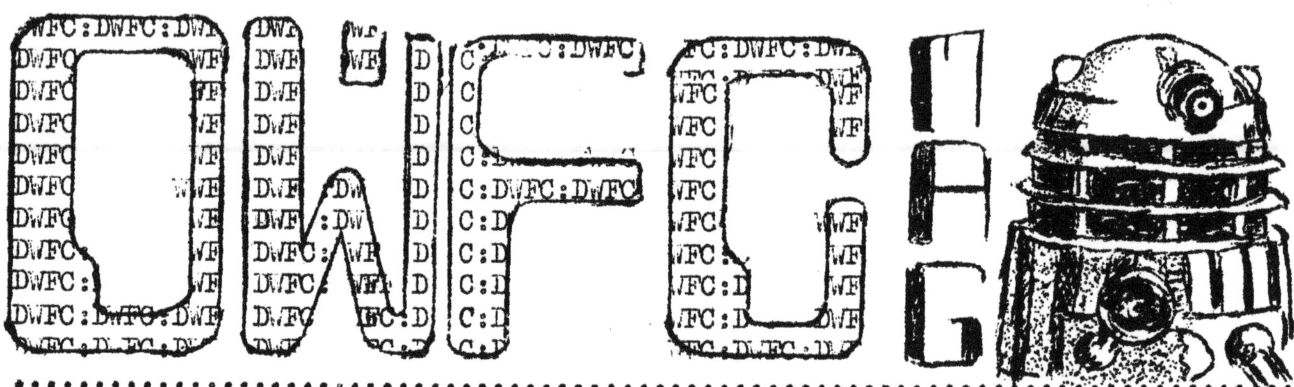

Number 16 June/July Edition D.W.F.C.

REVIEW:REVIEW:REVIEW:REVIEW:REVIEW:REVIEW:REVIEW:REVIEW:REVIEW:REVIEW:REVIEW:REVI

PLANET OF THE DALEKS

SHEEEEEESH! What an adventure! Truly a Dr Who Classic, the second to come out of the BBC studios this year, the other one being THE THREE DOCTORS, of course. In fact, I don't think I have anything bad to say about this masterpeice. Sheer perfection!

The sequence in the Tardis at the beginning was a good start, though I wish the Beeb would stick to one Tardis set, instead of adding and taking away whenever they feel like it, as in the "bed out of the wall" case.

I was thrilled when I heard that the Thals were coming back, and I hope the Doctor meets up with them again on Skaro some day. The tentacle extract was exciting.

Jon Pertwee's acting when he thought that Jo had been blown up was superb.

Then came the Dalek City. Mmm. Something missing there. It was a combination of two things; the sound that echoed through the corridors of the City on Skaro and the half circle doors were both missing. It would have created the original atmosphere if these two things had been included.

I thought the Doctors words of wisdom throughout the story were fantastic, first with his explanation that "Courage isn't a matter of not being frightened, you know. It's being afraid of what you have to do anyway."

I was indeed surprised when I saw the Dalek control room for the first time! About 12 Daleks crowded together! I thought only about 3 would be used.

Once again, the Doctor came up with the solution to all his problems. "Reverse the polarity." Off hand, I can remember him doing this in TERROR OF THE AUTONS, THE DEAMONS, THE SEA DEVILS and who knows how many more times!

The entrance gates to the Dalek City were super! Made up for the absence of the background noise.

The journey through the ice tunnels with the Thals was very good and while this was going on, the fight with the Dalek in the cell was heart-stopping stuff.

After escaping from their cell, the Doctor and Codal had that great adventure in the lift.

Later, when the Thals and the Doctor were trying to get to the refridgeration unit, the extermination of Marat was very unexpected. The sight of the millions of Daleks in the arsenal was breath-taking!

The ascent up the hot air shaft was cleverly done.

I enjoyed seeing the Daleks blow them-selves up when they

REVIEW:"PLANET OF THE DALEKS" (cont.)

tried to find the hidden explosives.

The breaking of the Doctors rope during the flight up the shaft was exciting with the Dalek coming up after him.I really enjoyed seeing the Dalek topple down the shaft when the rock hit him.

Terry Nation really brought back the human element into the story(and I think this has been carried on by Robert Sloman in THE GREEN DEATH) and this can be best illustrated by the Doctor and Jo reunion and it's aftermath.It seemed to be a flashback to the days of the Doctor Hartnell and Susan.

It was no surprise when Taron and Vaber started fighting,and later when Vaber was exterminated.

The skirmish with the Daleks at the ice pool **was again** perfect.

The death of Wester by the bacteria bomb was very sad,but his face when seen,looked remarkably like that of the monster that Omega sent to fight the Doctor in the 3 DOCTORS.

The landing of the Dalek spaceship was impressive,but what a suprise when the Supreme Dalek appeared!It looked like a variation on the film version and was very succesful too.When it was trundeling through the jungle,the music sounded remarkably like that in DR WHO AND THE DALEKS which I mentioned in Issue 8.

Now.The eruption of the Ice Volcano was spectacular!A fitting end to a great plot!All that molten ice pouring over the Daleks was great!

And so,the invasion stopped,the Thals returned to the Dalek spaceship and said their goodbyes to the Doctor and Jo. The Doctor's second talk was thought provoking.

"Be carefull how you tell this story, Taron.Don't glamourize it.Don't make war seem like an exciting and thrilling game."

I only wish more people could have heard it.

And so Jo turns down another offer of union,and the Thals make their way back. It was indeed a surprise to see the Daleks chasing the Doctor and Jo into the Tardis.

The final statement from the Dalek Supreme,or should I say the final threat, was spine chilling.

So with the Dalek adventure behind her, Jo hints that she is finally tired of life in the Tardis and wants to go back to Earth.Will she ever travel with the Doctor again?

DR.WHO PEOPLE

So far in this series,I have told you about the life and careers of the people who appear in front of the TV camera.

Now we go behind the scenes and look at the history of someone with which the programme couldn't do without.

BARRY LETTS - Producer

Barry Letts is the big man of the programme.He is the producer, which means he looks after everything that is connected with the programme. He even has to check that the DWFC is being run properly!

Barry first came into the world of Doctor Who during a Pat Troughton adventure called the ENEMY OF THE WORLD.He only directed this story,but he returned later to take up the position of new producer when Jon Pertwee took over the role of the Doc. So far,Barry has produced more stories than any other producer from the prog. Occasionally,he likes to direct as well as produce,as he did in TERROR OF THE AUTONS and CARNIVAL OF MONSTERS.

In the beginning,all ideas for stories come from the minds of Barry and Terry Dicks,the script-editor.Their ideas are then given to a professional writer and they transformed into the stories you see on the television.When it comes to the recording dates,Barry must be there to make sure everything is being run properly,and even when all the actors have gone,the producer still has lots of work/to do,making sure scenery is where it should be,arranging for costumes and special effects and so on.

Barry Letts career started as an actor, where he played parts in TV serials such as THE SILVER SWORD,THE THREE MUSKETEERS and in films like BOY,GIRL AND A BIKE and THE CRUEL SEA.

Then he thought he would like to write, and produced scripts for EMERGENCY WARD 10.Finally,he turned to directing THE NEWCOMERS and then DOCTOR WHO.

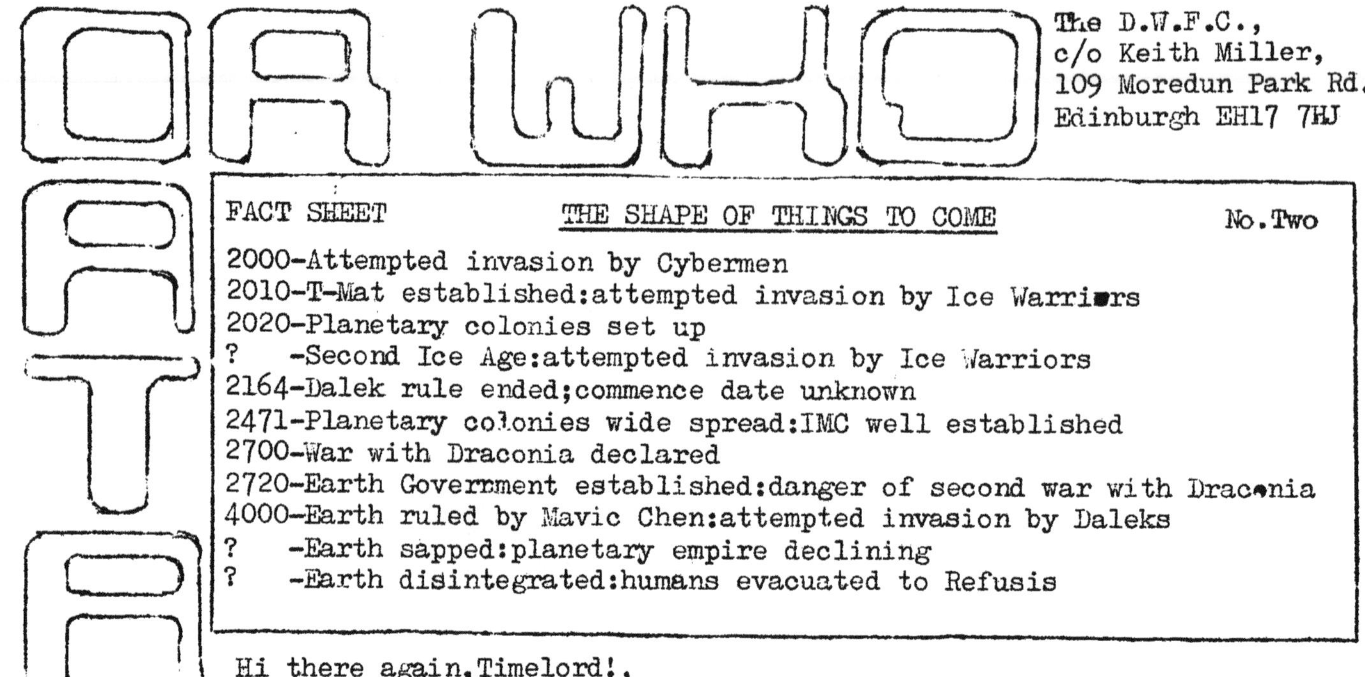

The D.W.F.C.,
c/o Keith Miller,
109 Moredun Park Rd.
Edinburgh EH17 7HJ

FACT SHEET — THE SHAPE OF THINGS TO COME — No.Two

2000-Attempted invasion by Cybermen
2010-T-Mat established:attempted invasion by Ice Warriors
2020-Planetary colonies set up
? -Second Ice Age:attempted invasion by Ice Warriors
2164-Dalek rule ended;commence date unknown
2471-Planetary colonies wide spread:IMC well established
2700-War with Draconia declared
2720-Earth Government established:danger of second war with Draconia
4000-Earth ruled by Mavic Chen:attempted invasion by Daleks
? -Earth sapped:planetary empire declining
? -Earth disintegrated:humans evacuated to Refusis

Hi there again,Timelord!,

Judging by your letters it seems you like the new style magazine.I'm glad about that,because it'll give me time to set up the goodies I have planned for later in the year.

Would you believe it?Two more Daleks have been stolen!These versions had the voice machine actually inside the shell,and this made the complete Dalek worth £500!

THREE SUPER NEW DR WHO BOOKS!Well,not exactly new - they are reprints of early Dr Who stories.The first one,DR WHO AND THE DALEKS is based on the original story by Terry Nation,and was turned into film form when seen last year on TV.

DR WHO AND THE ZARBI recreates the story of the Doctors struggle against the giant ants of Vortis and how he liberates the friendly Menoptera from their power.

DR WHO AND THE CRUSADERS is perhaps the least exciting of the three,but is still worth a read.

The cover illustrations are super and the drawings inside are good too,especially in THE DALEKS where the drawings are taken from photographs from the TV series. Each book costs 25p and are published by TARGET BOOKS.

And what about the DOCTOR WHO HOLIDAY SPECIAL then?Wasn't it super?All those great photos and articles.It made up for the rather disappointing annual this year. By the way,the DALEK DUAL story was a reprint from TV21,issues 11-17.

The Doctor Who Theme is now out on record again,and has the Tardis lift off sound half way through.Price 45p from most record shops.

Aren't there a lot of Dr Who products going around?Proof positive that THE YEAR OF THE DOCTOR MARCHES ON!

DOCTOR WHO COMPETITION NUMBER TWO has been won by IAN HUTCHINSON from Ryton-on-Tyne and BRYAN COOPER from Cheltenham.Well done!Your rings are on their way!

Derek Allen from Cheshunt wants to know if anyone is willing to seal any Dr Who Annuals or DWFC Magazines 1-4?If you have,write to me and I'll pass it on.

You may have noticed,in fact I'm sure you did,a rather ugly scrawl on this page last issue.I'm afraid that was due to the fact that I had printed info I shouldn't have.The day after I had finished scribbling it all out from every issue,I opened up my morning paper to see it covering half a page!I could have screamed!

The info is,and I'm sure you know by now,that Katy Manning is leaving Dr Who at the end of THE GREEN DEATH.(Sob!).She is getting married to Stewart Bevan who plays Clifford Jones in the current serial (lucky man).Katy made her debut in Dr Who three years ago when she ruined one of the Doctors experiments in TERROR OF THE AUTONS.Not a very good start,but the Doctor soon took her under his wing and there grew a fatherly love for her,perhaps for the first time since Susan left him to stay in London after the Dalek invasion.And now,as the Doctor sadly remarked, "the fledgling flies the coop".Sigh.A last farewell to Jo will be featured next issue when I review the final story of this season.

I think I've talked enough for now,so onward Timelord and remember

THIS IS THE YEAR OF THE DOCTOR!

FLASH:Have just heard that the two Daleks have been recovered!

How much do you know about Dr Who? Find out in this new series of questionaires!

DO YOU KNOW WHO?

Number Two

1)What is Bentons rank? score 1

2)Who composes the music for Dr Who? sr 2

3)What is the name given to the supreme leader of the Daleks? score 2

4)What is the name of the Dr's car/score1

5)Where did the scene below come from?/3

6)What is the Masters real name? score 1

7)What rock did the Doctor bring back from Meta-Benus 3? score 2

8)What part did Caroline John play in Doctor Who? score 1

9)Who were the Sensorites? score 2

10)In what adventure was a "simple peice of quartz" vital? score 2

11)Who was the Marshall? score 1

12)On what part of the body was the Auton daffodil programmed to cover? sr 2

13)The Axons brought a special substance to Earth

a)What was it called?

b)What were it's properties? score 4

14)In what adventure did the Guardian appear? score 2

15)What was Dr.Pat Troughtons last adventure called? score 2

16)How many adventures have there been concerning the Silurians? Name them. score 2

17)What was the name of Peladons High Priest? score 1

18)What adventure featured Gatwick Airport ? score 4

19)What was the name of Dr Hartnells last adventure? score 5

URGENT AND IMPORTANT: URGENT AND IMPORTANT

You will find in this issue six papers which will be used to send your next years supply of DWFC MAG. Please fill in your name and address on each one and send them back to me at the club address.

These will aid in the speedy delivery of the magazine, so please send them back as soon as you can or you may find your mag later than ever.

Thanks.

"DO YOU KNOW WHO?" ANSWER SHEET NUMBER 1.

1)Susan, Ian and Barbara
2)A Mechanoid is a small, hexagonal robot used by Earth to clear landing sites for landing of imigrants on Mechanus.
3)William Hartnell, Patrick Troughton, Jon Pertwee and Peter Cushing (1 mark each)
4)'Liz 49' was a spaceship in the adventure called THE SPACE PIRATES.
5)THE DEAMONS
6)Vicki
7)"The Navy Lark"
8)a)Peter Purves
b)"Blue Peter"
9)The Primords are transmutations of human body cells from slime beneath the Earths surface as featured in INFERNO.
10)The Scope
11)Eight(or 7 if you excluded PLANET)
12)Sidrats
13)Thals
14)Katy Manning
15)1970: SPEARHEAD FROM SPACE
16)Bok

Ratings:
20-30: You don't happen to be a relative of the Doctors by any chance?
10-20: Not bad! Try reading THE MAKING OF DR WHO...thirty times.
Under 10: Never mind. The Master only got -1...

---

20)Where did the scene below come from? score 3

JON PERTWEE as

in

"PLANET OF XAVIER"

The cosmic storm gained in strength as it spun through the universe like a giant animal searching for it's prey. A small but complicated spaceship suddenly appeared from the blackness of space and sped unknowingly towards the disaster area. The craft shook as it entered the outer reaches of the storm and was slowly dragged in towards the middle. The ship and chaos careered along the spaceways, until it plunged into one of the many black holes in space...into the world of anti-matter. The two energies met in a gigantic explosion which sprawled into the far reaches of the heavens, and then shrank back into a solid swirling mass. A new Genesis had occurred.

A light flashed, suspended in mid-air, until another form began to materialize below it. The shape of the Tardis slowly appeared.

One of the double doors slid open with a faint hum and two figures stepped from the darkness behind them. The two looked around them at the silent, barren world surrounding their time and space machine. A bright purple sky spread it's way above their heads, while on the horizon, volcanos smoked in little trails into the atmosphere.

The smaller figure of Jo Grant was the first to break the silence.

"I thought you said this was a blue planet?"

She waved a hand at the sky.

"Don't tell me you've missed again?"

"Missed?" shrilled the Doctor, "Certainly not!"

"Look, Doctor, why don't you just give up looking for Meta Benus..."

Suddenly, the ground at the duos feet began to tremble. The police box behind them rocked dangerously as the volcanos on the horizon burst into violent life and threw white, blinding light into the air.

The ground cracked under their feet as the Doctor jumped to one side.

"DOCTOR!" screamed Jo as she slipped on the crumbling ground around her.

The Time Lord shot an arm forwards and groped for her hand. Their fingers touched but the shaking increased. Jo's eyes were horrified.

"Doctor, I'm slipping...! Please, don't let gooooo...."

Their grasps released and Jo plumeted down into the abyss, her screams fusing with the dying sound of thunder.

"JO? JO, CAN YOU HEAR ME? JO?!"

The Doctors screams into the blackness were futile. Then, a voice boomed around in the air from some unknown source.

"The girl is safe, Doctor."

The Time Lord scrammbled to his feet and looked up into the purple sky.

"Who are you? Where are you?"

"I am Xavier," replied the voice.

An element of horror crept into the Doctors heart.

"Xavier?" he hissed in a horrofied whisper.

"I see you have heard of me."

Beads of sweat stood out on the Doctors forehead. He held a trembling hand in the air.

"Please...let my companion go. We shall leave immediately in my machine..."

"That is impossible," chanted the voice, coldly, "Your dematerialization circuit has been surrounded by a force field. You will never leave this planet!"

"But why? Why do you keep us here?"

There was a pause.

"You amuse me."

Silence.

"We have talked enough," continued the voice, "It is now you against me, Doctor."

"But you must know that it is nearly impossible for me to fight _you_!"

"Come, come, Doctor. It _is_ impossible. Let the game begin!"

A needle of lightning suddenly flashed across the sky as the volcanos resumed their belching of white light. The Doctor drew his cape over his eyes then bent down, picked up a stone and dropped it into the chasm. Moments passed that felt like years before the hollow echo of the falling stone reached the humanoids ears. He shook his head as he ran his fingers through his silver hair...then a thought struck him. Jo Grant had fell into the crack in the ground and yet it said that she was safe. Could this be some kind of conveyor down to the subteranian depths of the planet? He fumbled in his pocket for a moment then extracted his sonic screwdriver. He pressed a switch and the tip lit up with a glowing red light. He dropped it into the crack and watched it plunge into the chasm...then suddenly slow down as if travelling on a cushion of air down to the bottom. It was much shorter than he thought!

PLANET OF XAVIER (continued)

Swinging his legs over the edge of the abyss, the Doctor pushed himself off the edge and plunged into the darkness. Half way down, he estimated, he felt a force push from underneath to guide him slowly down to the bottom. He peered down at the tiny red light which grew bigger as he neared the end of his journey.

The Doctors feet glided to the crunchy soil at the base of the abyss and he bent down and picked up his screwdriver. Retaining his erect pose, he stared around him, his eyes quickly growing used to the darkness. Shining his illuminated screwdriver down at the ground, the Doctor could see drag marks leading into a cave mouth in the side of the crevice. Holding his only source of light well in front of him, the Time Lord stepped into the gloom and dank atmosphere of the tunnel.

As he progressed along the passage of rock, he could feel the ground begin to shake again. Rumbling began to echo through the chamber, and it seemed as if some maniacs laughter was mingled amonst the chaos. The Doctor felt something fall onto his head in a cloud. He looked up to see the roof of the cave crack and powder as the noise grew louder. Suddenly there was loud crash and the Doctor leapt into the darkness as the section of roof above him collapsed the ground. Rock and rubble crashed to the floor, and a few seconds later all was quiet.

The Doctor lay sprawled out on the floor, only a few yards from the rock fall. Looking up, he could see his screwdriver glow brightly a few yards ahead. He propped himself up on one elbow and said

"Round one to me..."

The silence was shattered by the voice of Xavier.

"Wrong, Doctor. Round one to me. You may have saved your self from an early death, but you now have no way of getting back to your spaceship."

"No way?" enquired the Time Lord.

"There is another," boomed the voice, "But you won't find it 'til you find the girl."

Silence drooped the cavern once more and the Doctor scrammbled to his feet, dusted himself down, then proceeded along the tunnel after collecting his torch.

After half an hour of walking, the Doctor heard what sounded like another rock fall up ahead. He turned a bend in the rock, and the sight that met his eyes took his breath away. He had stepped into a vast underground cavern which resounded to the sound of falling and boiling water, not rocks as the Doctor had first guessed. A lake of boiling water stretched out in front of him, and at the far end, a fall of water from some underground stream crashed to the lake in fury of foam and noise.

Then, the now familiar rumbling noise shook the ground below the Doctors feet and then a spectacular sight burst from the depths of the underground lake. A geyser shot from the middle of the lake to burst upwards and into a fracture in the roof of the cave. Erosion had made the crack smooth and round. As the spectacle had began, it stopped. Then, a new sound floated through the air. The Doctor looked around then listened.

"Doctor! Over here!"

The Doctor knew immediatley who it was.

"JO!"

He looked across the expanse of bubbling water and could see his companion wave at him from the other side. Now a new danger threatened. How was he going to reach her?

Looking down at the ground, the Doctor could see he was standing on a large, oval shaped rock which was a few feet away from the edge of the lake. Jumping down, he pressed his back against the edge of the rock and planted his feet against the wall of the cavern. Taking a deep breath, he pushed back at the object. It slid down the shore into the lake and stood quite steady amongst the bubbling waters. It began to drift away, but the Doctor managed to grab a thin but strong sliver of what looked like some kind of metal and leapt from the shore onto the raft. Plunging the metal into the lake, he began to paddle towards Jo at the other side. The heat from the lake make things even more difficult, but he reached the other side safely and beconed to Jo to jump on.

"But, Doctor," protested the girl, "I've timed the geyser. It'll be going up in a few minutes!"

"Exactly, that's just what I want! Now come on!"

Jo Grant jumped from the shore onto the rock and the Doctor made the raft float into the middle of the lake where the geyser had blown. Looking up, Jo could see a dot of purple sky in the black of the hole above.

"The geyser! It leads to the surface!"

The Doctor gave a faint smile as an answer when suddenly the water began to churn and bubble in white chaos.

"Hang on!" yelled the Doctor.

Suddenly, Jo saw the black hole fall down towards her as the raft was proppeled up towards the surface. The rock shook as they plummeted upwards. The G force pressed down on Jo's body and she could feel herself move towards the edge.

"Doctor!" she screamed, "I'M SLIPPING!"

Part Two Next Ish.

An End... and a Beginning

Wasn't that letter from Roger Delgado heart-breaking? His death was a great shock for everyone connected with the show, but especially for Jon. He and Roger really were great friends. I treasured his last hand-written note and filed it carefully away. Years after I shut the fan club down, I was introduced to a fan who asked if he could look through my collection of memorabilia. I said of course and left him to look through my collection. Some time later, I was looking for something else and came across the space where Roger's letter was filed. It wasn't there. He had taken it. This truly hurt. It was a final, hand-written note to me personally, and a fellow fan stole it. How can you be a fan of Doctor Who and behave in such a way? It's against its whole ethos.

It was at this time that Target Books - and a huge "wrong end of the stick" - was born. They had already reprinted the three old William Hartnell novels from the sixties and were about to embark on a series of novelisations. For the past few months, I had been beavering away, putting together a library of similar novellas, using the BBC synopses as a reference, and was about to announce the opening of the DWFC Lending Library. There was only one copy of each title, but members would be sent one title, read it, send it back and get another. Would Target be interested in these, perhaps to "fill in" between the titles they were going to publish. After all, they weren't going to publish *all* of Doctor Who history were they?

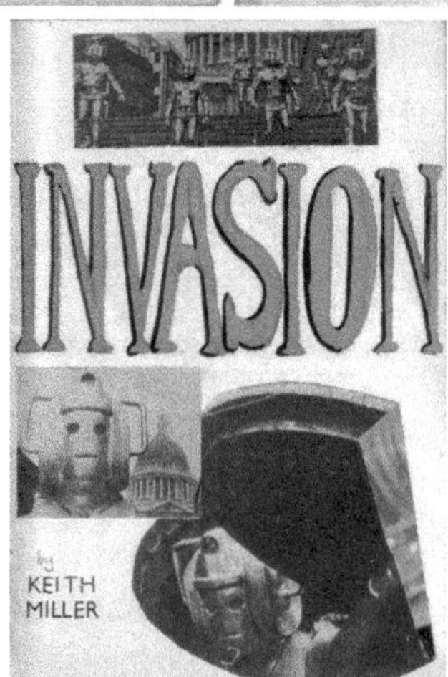

Tandem Books

UNIVERSAL-TANDEM PUBLISHING COMPANY LTD

14 Gloucester Road London SW7 4RD
Telephone 584 8766-7
584 6803-4

Reg. No. 898950 England Reg. Office: 99 Aldwych London WC2B 4JY
VAT Registration No. 238 4691 36

8th August 1973

Mr Keith Miller,
109 Moredun Park,
Edinburgh EH17 7HJ

Dear Mr Miller,

Thank you for your letter of July 30th.

We were very interested to hear of your DWFC editions of the Doctor Who scripts and wondered if it would be possible for us to see a sample copy, which would be returned to you.

Of the titles you mention, I would advise you that we have bought the paperback rights to 'Spearhead From Space', 'Colony In Space', 'Doctor Who And The Day Of The Daleks' and 'Doctor Who And The Daemons', which will be published along with two other titles in the same series next year.

Yours sincerely,

Eloise Logan.

Assistant to the
Children's Book Editor,
TARGET BOOKS.

Directors: Chairman Arnold E. Abramson (USA) Managing Director Ralph S. Stokes (UK) Robert J. Abramson (USA) Peter J. Abramson (USA) Edwin J. Harragan Snr (USA) L. George Coleman (UK) Brian A. Miles (UK)

Although every reasonable care is taken of material while in our possession we can accept no responsibility for any loss or damage thereto

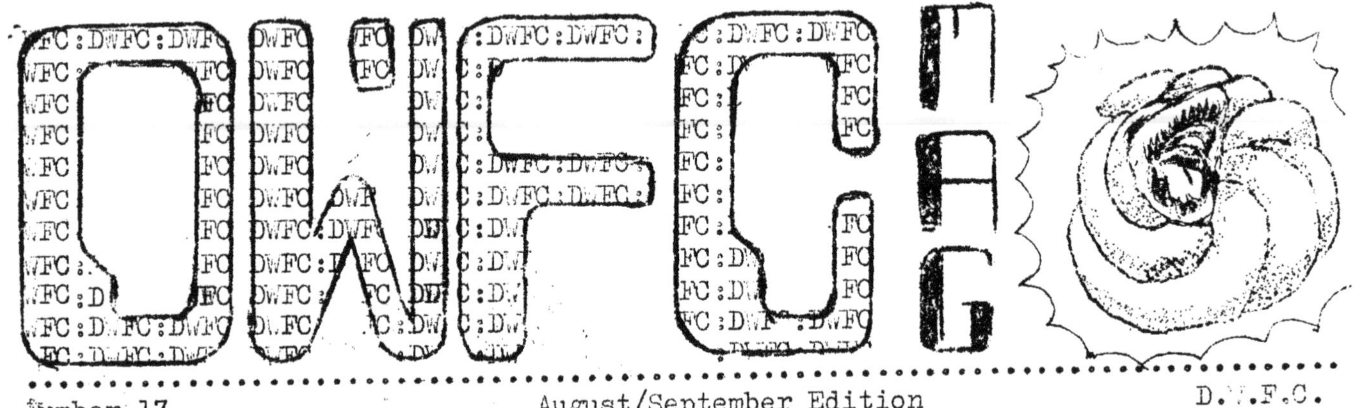

Number 17 August/September Edition D.W.F.C.

ROGER DELGADO

I'm sure you were all as deeply distressed as the BBC and I was at the death of Roger Delgado who played the Master for three years in the TV programme.Although he played a very evil character on the screen,off set,he was a very kind,well-mannered gentleman as Barry Letts and Jon Pertwee know,as they became great friends during his time as the Master.

It only remains for me to say that we shall miss you,Roger,but we'll never forget you.It is tragic irony,perhaps,that his last words to us were "Although the Master will soon no longer be with you,he will be remembering with affection the time he spent chilling your spines."

REVIEW REVIEW REVIEW REVIEW REVIEW REVIEW REVIEW REVIEW REVIEW REVIEW REVIEW

THE GREEN DEATH

Not a bad end to a brilliant series of adventures which I don't think will be equalled for a long time to come.

The first episode started rather sadly with the Doctor finding out for sure that Jo Grant has her own life to lead and wants to be independant.His comment 'So,the fledgling flies the coop',was a sad one as for three years he had been trying to turn her into a scientist.Then,at last the Doctor landed on Meta-Benus 3 and what a place!I thought it would a blue heaven but it seemed to be the exact opposite.It was quite terrifying to see that tentacle lash around the Doctors body and hear that unearthly scream pierce the silence.

When the Doctor at last reached Earth,Bessie made her return to transport the Doctor and company to the mine where those horrible,squelchy maggots were slithering to the surface.

When the Doctor and Jo had to 'paddle' through the sea of maggots in the mine, the effect was a bad one with the shimmery white outline blazing out like a halo. Only bad thing about it really.

At the end of episode three,it was sad the way Jo simply refused to take interest in the Doctors blue sapphire,after all the trouble he went to get it.The ending was good where the maggot slithered up behind Jo and prepared to attack.

Episode four saw the escape of the maggots from the mine which wasn't bad and the identity of the Boss was at last revealed as the giant computer intent on control of the world.The computer itself was great and I liked the huge disc where it's speech patterns jumped up and down in white lines.A good effect.

Episode five disclosed that the Boss,the computer,was linked to a human brain-Stevens.I don't think Jo could repair that radio transmitter,really.She just didn't seem capable to repair such an intricate peice of electronics with a nail file.The sight of Bessie trundelling through the maggots towards the cave where Jo and Clifford were trapped looked terribly false.The infection on Cliffords neck looked real and horrible.The glowing effect was brilliant!Then,when Mike was trying to kill the Doctor,the blue sapphire came in useful,which I might have known it would.Interesting to note that Mr James was played by Roy Skelton who provided the voices for the Daleks and Wester,both from PLANET OF THE DALEKS.

REVIEW: 'GREEN DEATH' (continued)

Then came the best episode of the whole adventure...episode six.

To begin with, the party at the Nuthutch find the solution to the maggot problem. The fungus! Next, we find the computer singing of all things, which I found rather amusing. When the Doctor and Benton started scattering the fungus over the maggots, the effect created was good, especially the close-ups of the mouths of the monster which was very realistic and a little horrific.

This is where the metamorphic fly came in which looked rather good on the hill-side and in mid-air. The crunch that it made when it hit the ground was a bit disgusting. Put me off my tea, but the over all sequence was very well done.

Now, the final confrontation with the Doctor and the Boss. The coaxing of Stevens by the Doctor to reject the Boss was a well acted out scene. Finally, when Stevens' hold is broken, his sacrafice for the destruction of the computer was rather sad, but perhaps a fitting end to both of them. Rather like Frankenstein and his monster.

With the terrific blowing up of Global Chemicals, we return to the Nuthutch where we find Cliffors fully recovered and the stage is set for the ending of the series. Jo discloses that she wants to go with Cliff to the upper reaches of the Amazon to search for this new fungus, and he reveals his intention to the Doctor to get married to Jo. And so the party gets under way, then we see the Doctor and Jo in a corner of the room saying their good-byes. Perhaps the most sentimental moments since Susan left the Doctor occured during this time. Then, Cliff tells the Doctor that he will look after her, and takes her to join the rest of the party, leaving the Doctor in the shadows. During the teast to the happy couple, Jo looks back to see the Doctor quietly slip away out into the cool, night air, leaving behind the sound of happiness...the sound that Jo had brought to him three years ago. Climbing aboard Bessie, the Doctor takes one last look back, alone with his thoughts of times gone by. Starting the engine, he slowly drives off into the distance, once more...alone.

And so the end of another companionship for the Doctor, and a very sad ending (which I liked) to a truly fantastic series. That final shot of the Doctor gave the feeling of lonelyness which the Doctor had experienced so many times be-fore. Now if you'll excuse me, I think I've got something in my eye...

EXTRA REVIEW EXTRA REVIEW EXTRA REVIEW EX

THE DAY OF THE DALEKS

Here we are with the final review of the series, but it will return when the new series of TV programmes begin in December.

Not a very good set of episodes, I thought to turn into a spectacular, but I was surprised how good it turned out to be. I enjoyed this cut down version much more than the first showing in four episodes.

Louis Marks is a writer I'd never heard of, and it seems he wasn't over-enthusia-stic in bringing out the evil of the Daleks.

Still, what was lost in the Daleks was made up for in the sets which were rather good and would have been better had the storyline been improved.

Here, it was plain to see that the BBC only had three Daleks and most of their time was spent in that tin can of a hide-out. Their voices were slow and you could almost tell what they were going to say before they said it. Not very impressive.

The introduction of the Ogrons was put to good use, by why oh why can't the writers have the Daleks doing the exter-minating instead of their pet apes.

If too many people are killed by the Daleks, then the BBC are swamped with letters saying that there is too much violence in the programme, but what about the age-old westerns you see on TV? In about the first ten minutes, you have a heap of dead bodies filling the screen from left to right, so why not buck your-selves up, BBC, and let's return to the ruthlessness that was shown in the earlier Dalek adventures.

I can't really say this was a good story, but I can't say it was bad. It was middle-of-the-road, which a Dalek script should <u>never</u> be, and considering it was the Daleks first appearance for five years, it was rather a flop. But all that was changed with PLANET OF THE DALEKS, and thank heavens for Terry Nation!

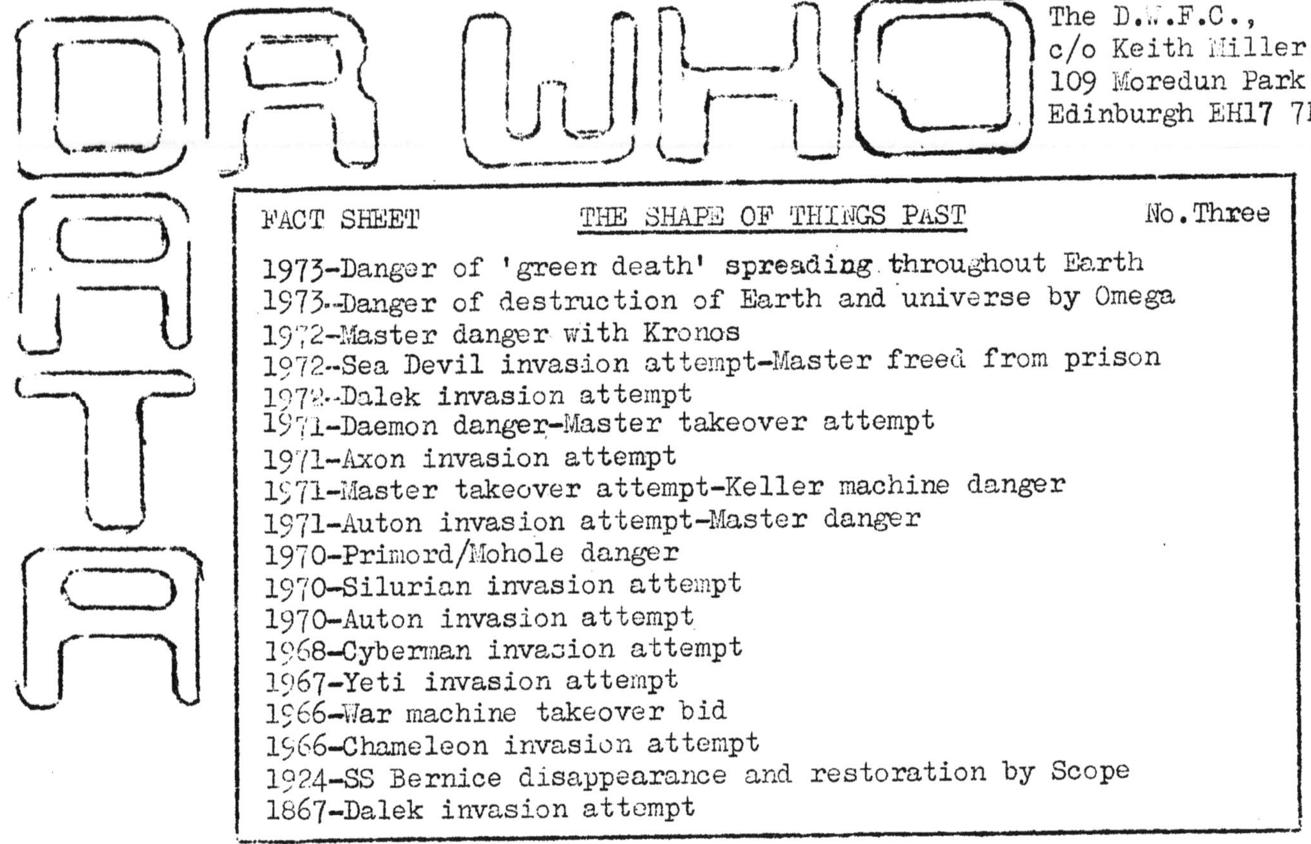

The D.W.F.C.,
c/o Keith Miller,
109 Moredun Park Rd.
Edinburgh EH17 7HJ

FACT SHEET — THE SHAPE OF THINGS PAST — No.Three

1973-Danger of 'green death' spreading throughout Earth
1973-Danger of destruction of Earth and universe by Omega
1972-Master danger with Kronos
1972-Sea Devil invasion attempt-Master freed from prison
1972-Dalek invasion attempt
1971-Daemon danger-Master takeover attempt
1971-Axon invasion attempt
1971-Master takeover attempt-Keller machine danger
1971-Auton invasion attempt-Master danger
1970-Primord/Mohole danger
1970-Silurian invasion attempt
1970-Auton invasion attempt
1968-Cyberman invasion attempt
1967-Yeti invasion attempt
1966-War machine takeover bid
1966-Chameleon invasion attempt
1924-SS Bernice disappearance and restoration by Scope
1867-Dalek invasion attempt

Hi There,again,Timelord!,

Well,now that the series is over,the magazine is the only link the Doctors fans have with him,and now that the day of the Doctor is looming up fast,next issue will be packed with exciting articles and things to do to celebrate the Doctors tenth birthday!I promise you an exciting time during November.

I've had news from Tandem Books that they intend to publish six more Dr Who paperbacks next year,including SPEARHEAD FROM SPACE,THE DAEMONS,COLONY IN SPACE, and DAY OF THE DALEKS.They will be published at two monthly intervals (to co-incide with the magazine) starting in January 1974.

Wasn't it a pity that TV Action had to disappear? The photographs from the programme were quite good,even if the comic strip wasn't too good,but which is continuing in TV Comic.

The DOCTOR WHO ANNUAL 1974 is now on sale.I hope it's better than last years. The cover is exciting,but you can't tell a book by it's cover.I've been told that this year there are two comic strips included.Price 70p from bookshops.

Sad news,I'm afraid,in that Barry Letts,producer and occasional director for the programme since 1970 is now leaving the Dr Who crew at the end of the year to deal with his successful brainchild MOONBASE 3,which is now being shown every Sunday night at 7·25 and the crew behind it is,in fact,the Dr Who boys.Well done on a super prog!

The first story of the new series later in the year will see the Doctor back in time,just to prove that the Tardis can still go back as well as forwards!

Recording has started now on the new series,so I hope a new series of REPORT will be starting soon.Now that Jo Grant has gone,she will be replaced by Sarah-Jane Smith played by Elizabeth Sladen,who hides aboard the Tardis hoping for an interview with the Doctor,but unknown to her,the controls have been set and the two are sent spinning back in time and into danger!

Over the years,the actors who have appeared in Dr Who usually go on to bigger and better things.Amongst the Doctors companions,William Russel (Ian Chesterton) was one of the board of directors for RADA for a few years,before venturing back into TV with "Harriets Back in Town".Peter Purves (Steven Taylor) has gone on to become one of BLUE PETERS' succesful presenters,while Michael Craze has played numerous parts in plays including Len Harvey in "Crossroads".His compaion,Polly, played by Anneke Wills,carried on her acting carreer as Evelyn in "Strange Report" More info about actors from the past series next issue!

Well,that's about all for now,so prepare to find out the identity of Xavier!

JON PERTWEE as

in

"PLANET OF XAVIER"

Part Two

Jo Grant slid perilously towards the edge of the rock as it plumetted upwards towards the surface.Her ringed fingers reached out for the Doctors' hand which fought against the G force that was keeping them apart.Just as the girls legs slipped out of sight over the edge,the Doctors fingers met hers.He heaved with every ounce of strength he could summon up and Jo hauled herself back onto the raft.

The hole of purple above them suddenly enveloped them.They had reached the surface.

"Jump!"shouted the Doctor as the duo leapt from the rock hurtling skywards to land in a heap on the ground.

Jo looked up at the gushing,white foam forcing it's way upwards towards the sky. Their craft of rock balanced on the top of the fountain for a few moments,then fell back into the crust as the geyser suddenly fell dead.

The Doctor helped Jo to her feet.

"Well done,Doctor.You are more amusing than I had even hoped,but don't worry. There are more 'games' on the way."

The voice of Xavier died away and the two stood in silence.Jo was the first to speak.

"What is that voice,Doctor?Who does it belong to?"

"It's a story that began many thousands of years ago,Jo.So long ago that this place is now only spoken off in legends. The voice belongs to Xavier,a highly intelligent creature who was drawn into a cosmic storm and then blown up in one of the black holes of anti matter."

"Blown up?"

"Well,not exactly.You see,Jo,Xaviers life force,the cosmic storm and the energy created by the explosion when matter and anti matter met,combined and solidified."

"Are you saying that Xavier is somewhere on this planet?"

The Doctor looked grim.

"Jo.Xavier is this planet!"

Jo Grant stood in stunned silence at the Doctors last remark.

"But...but you can't defeat an entire world..."she gasped at last.

"I do have an idea,Jo,but it means trying to get back to the Tardis.We seem to be a few miles away from her..."

The Doctor extracted his sonic screwdriver again and adjusted the control on the end.A low bleeping sound filled the air which grew in pitch as the Timelord revolved round on one heal.Suddenly, the bleeping smoothed out into a high, continuous tone.The Doctor pointed out into the distance.

"That's our direction,Jo.We had better get started.We may not have much time left."

The duo made their way across the plain towards a collection of green and purple pools,bubbling furiously and giving off an acrid smell.

The Doctor led the way along a small path which wound in and out of the pits of fluid.

Suddenly,a long,slimy tentacle splashed to the surface and wrapped itself around the Doctors legs,dragging him towards the bubbling froth.Jo screamed as the sound of Xaviers laughter echoed about her.The Doctor clawed at the purple soil to try and slow his journey towards certain death.

"Jo!Behind you...the metal rocks!"

She remembered at once how the Doctor had splintered one of them and used it as an oar to get across the boiling lake earlier.Jo Grant heaved at the shiny stones,lifted it high above her head and smashed it to the ground,sending splinters of metal shooting over the ground.Diving for the largest and sharpest sliver,she sprang over the ground towards the Doctor and sank the metal into the living slime around his legs.

The monster squealed,writhed,then quickly disappeared into the pool,leaving a stain of red to mingle with the green and purple.

The girl helped the Doctor to his feet.

"Thank..thank you,Jo.That could have been fatal.But come on.We still have a long way to go."

On the horizon,flashes of white light could be seen,and Jo knew that that was where the Tardis lay,and it seemed a million miles away.

Leaving the pools behind,they came to a bridge of rock over a vast crevice which plunged into darkness far below them.

"Doctor?How can this be here?Surely we would have seen it when we were below the surface?"

PLANET OF XAVIER (continued)

"This is Xavier,"the Doctor answered, "He can change the face of the planet whenever he likes."

The Doctor looked round and saw that the path veered off to their left into the distance until it came to the end of the crack in the earth then continued on it's way into the distance.

"To cross this bridge would mean certain trouble,but to follow the path would mean waste of time.What do we do,Jo?"

Before the girl could answer,a tremendous roar ripped through the atmosphere and they spun round to see a gigantic Pterodactyl swoop towards them,it's huge jaws wide,seeking blood and dripping saliva.

"I think the choice has been made for us!"yelled the Doctor,"Over the bridge fast!Don't stop for anything!"

The twosome ran as fast as they could onto the bridge as they felt the beating of leather wings above them.Two taloned claws ripped the cloak from the Doctors back,sending him flying towards the ground.Struggling to his feet,the Timelord felt the bridge quake as a new and more terrifying threat loomed up from the darkness below him.

A huge crab-like creature clamped a claw across the bridge as it discerned the two small figures desperately trying to get across to the other side.It's eyes moved on long,pink stalks and Jo again screamed at the horror of the monster.

Suddenly,another roar shattered the air and the Pterodactyl turned for another death swoop.The Crabs attention was wrenched from the two insignificant figures below it to the half monster, half bird flapping towards it.

The Doctor helped Jo to her feet and they scrammbled over to the other side into the thick,yellow bushes and safety.

Meanwhile,the Crab reached upwards and clamped a vice-like claw around the neck of the flying terror and dragged it down into the crack in the earth.A scream echoed around the walls for a few moments,then silence drooped as the crack slowly closed.

The Doctor and Jo were still running when the noise of the battle faded behind them.Jo Grant slumped to the ground in exhaustion as the Doctor pressed his back against a wall of rock and tried to regain his breath.

"But why?"asked Jo,"Why did those two creepys kill one another?"

"Xavier may control many things here, Miss Grant,but he can't control the life forms which inhabit it,thank goodness.We wouldn't be here otherwise."

"DOCTOR!"

The Timelord opened his eyes to see the girl stare behind him.He turned and looked round the large rock he was resting on to see

"The Tardis!"

The duo raced over to the blue box and pushed open the doors.Hurrying into the control room,Jo Grant dusted the purple powder from her black mini-skirt while the Doctor closed the doors.The brightness of the control room hurt Jo's eyes at first as they had become accustomed the dark,purple light of Xavier.She stood at the opposite control panel from the Doctor.

"Can we get out of here?"

The Doctor looked up for a brief moment

"No.It's true what Xavier said.There's a force field around the dematerialization circuit."

"What a pity,Doctor,"boomed the voice of Xavier,"After all your trouble and delightful little tricks,you get a prize that's useless.But I am in a generous mood,Doctor.I will let you stay on my planet for the rest of your lives.You can keep me company."

"Hah!"exclaimed the Timelord,"You haven't beaten me yet!"

"Excellent!"answered the voice,joyfully "I *am* glad you landed here,Doctor."

The voice fell silent as the Doctor switched on the scanner.The horizon of volcanoes filled the screen with their belching of white light.

"What are you going to do,Doctor?"

"I can't tell you,Jo.He may be listening."

The Doctor then disappeared into one of the many store rooms in the Tardis and emerged with a long,needle like machine with a cable which he fitted into a socket in the control console.Opening the doors,he plunged the machine into the soil and raced back inside.

"I do not like the look of this,Doctor I wish to know what you are doing."

The Doctor ignored the voice.

"Hold on tight Jo."

The girl grasped the end of the table as outside,the volcanoes burst once more into life.

At the same time,the Doctor threw a switch on the control console as a scream of pain shrieked through the air.The Tardis shook eretically as the Doctor disconnected the lead and threw it out onto the planet,closing the doors on a world breaking up outside

How much do you know about Dr Who? Find out in this series of questionaires!

DO YOU KNOW WHO?

Number 3

1) Who sang "WHO IS DOCTOR WHO?" score 1

2) What is the Time Rotor? score 2

3) Has Peter Barkworth ever appeared in Dr Who as a Monk? score 2

4) Who was Marat? score 1

5) Has Dr Who ever met a) Dracula
b) Frankenstien
c) The Mummy
d) The Werewolf
score 4

6) Where did the scene below come from?

score 3

7) The Keys of Marinus weren't keys at all. What were they? score 2

8) How many Dr Who complete story specials have there been on TV ? score 1

9) Can a Dalek survive underwater? s.1.

10) Who played the Celestial Toymaker? s.3

11) When was the IMC creating trouble for the Doctor and what do the letters stand for? score 4

12) Name at least three stories concerning the Cybermen. score 3

13) What part did Verity Lambert play in the first episodes of Dr Who? score 2

14) When did the Doctor and Jo meet a hemaphrodite exopod? score 1

15) Has Dr Who ever met the Emperor Dalek score 1

16) Were the Doctor and Susan telepathic? score 1

17) What is the name given to a Daleks human slave? score 2

18) Who was Mavic Chen? score 1

"DO YOU KNOW WHO?" ANSWER SHEET NUMBER 2.

1) Sergeant
2) Dudley Simpson
3) Emperor
4) Bessie
5) "DALEK INVASION EARTH; 2150 AD."
6) Roger Delgado
7) Blue sapphire
8) Liz Shaw
9) Telepaths from another world who were saved from a deadly disease by the Doctor.
10) "THE TIME MONSTER."
11) Leader of a team of Mutant exterminators from Skybase in orbit about Solos.
12) Mouth and nose.
13) a) Axonite
b) To duplicate any substance perfectly.
14) "COLONY IN SPACE."
15) "THE WAR GAMES."
16) Two: "THE SILURIANS" and "THE SEA DEVILS"
17) Hepesh
18) "THE FACELESS ONES"
19) "TENTH PLANET"
20) "THE CLAWS OF AXOS"

Ratings:
20-30: Very good
10-20: Not bad
Under 10: Oh...

PLANET OF XAVIER (continued)

The Tardis suddenly lurched as the planet began to disintegrate and the weak voice of Xavier drifted into the control room. The shaking eased off, then all was still.

"So...it has happened at last...You were the only one, Doctor...the only one to realize that the white light was cosmic energy which came from the very heart of the planet I once was...and so using your machine...you turned that energy against me...but I thought I had at last found company for the future..."

"I...I'm sorry," whispered the Doctor.

"No, no...do not be sorry, Doctor. Though I dared only hope for company...you have brought me something far better...something I dared not even hope for..peace."

The voice began to fade.

"...thank you, Doctor...and goodb..."

Silence again reigned in the control room as the Time Rotor began to rise and fall. The Doctor propped himself up against the control console as Jo moved to comfort him. His head hung low as he thought of the saddness in the heart of Xavier that must have existed for centuries. But now he was free... and at peace. The tiny box whirled through space and time barriers, leaving behind the dust of Xavier and heading towards the planet of Earth.

THE END

Tandem Books

UNIVERSAL-TANDEM PUBLISHING COMPANY LTD

14 Gloucester Road London SW7 4RD

Telephone 584 8766-7
584 6803-4

Reg. No. 898950 England Reg. Office: 99 Aldwych London WC2B 4JY
VAT Registration No. 238 4691 36

September 25th 1973

Mr Keith Miller,
109 Moredun Park Road,
Edinburgh EH17 7HJ

Dear Keith,

Thank you for your letter addressed to Miss Logan. I do want to show your excellent paperbacks to the people involved with the Doctor Who programme and I shall be seeing them early next week. I shall post the books back to you as soon after that as possible.

For the time being,

Yours sincerely,

Richard Henwood

Children's Book Editor,
TARGET BOOKS.

BBC tv

BRITISH BROADCASTING CORPORATION
TELEVISION CENTRE WOOD LANE LONDON W12 7RJ
TELEPHONE 01-743 8000 CABLES: TELECASTS LONDONPS4
TELEGRAMS: TELECASTS LONDON TELEX TELEX: 22182

Dear Keith, Sorry but I can do nothing more as regard to sending more of this. When a stencil is duplicated twice it can't be used again because of splitting. So I'm afraid we'll just have to forget it. Sorry. 'Day of the Daleks' - 3rd Sept.

Dr Who map - November. Write to Peter Cushing via Thames T.V. He's recently done a series there. Sorry about maps, but the 'little darlings' will have to miss this one.

SARAH

P.S. Frankly I've always run off 350. I didn't realise you need 450 now.

I was a HUGE Peter Cushing fan. Not only had he played the Doctor on the big screen, but I thought his portrayal of Professor Van Helsing in the Dracula movies was terrific. So towards the end of 1973 I started to try and pin him down for an interview, which was like trying to pin down fog...

But I got postcard after postcard from Joy Broughton, Peter's secretary for 35 years. And delightfully camp things they were too, with "Peter Cushing" embossed in bright red (natch!) at the top, but even better was the "joined-up-handwriting" font of her type-writer! These were the days when Courier reigned supreme, so to see this product from someones typewriter was a thing of wonder and delight.

And I never did get to meet the great man.

PETER CUSHING

October, 1973.

Dear Mr. Miller,

Mr. Cushing is away filming in the Far East, and I am dealing with his mail during his absence.

He is heavily committed for some considerable time, but if you care to write again in the New Year, he may be able to arrange the interview you request.

With all good wishes.

Yours sincerely,

J.M. Butler

Secretary to Mr. Peter Cushing.

PETER CUSHING

January, 1974.

Dear Mr. Miller,

Mr. Cushing is now away filming in France, and will be back March/April, when he is to make a picture for Tyburn Film Productions Ltd., Pinewood Studios, Iver Heath, Buckinghamshire (Slough 33441).

If you care to get in touch with the Publicity Department there sometime in early April, they may be able to arrange an interview with Mr. Cushing.

With all good wishes.

Yours sincerely,

J.M. Butler

Secretary.

I was getting bored waiting to hear from Target Books, I thought I'd ask Sarah if she had heard anything. And I tried to blag free phone calls (for interviews) and see if the BBC would pay for my jaunts down south. She was having none of it...

BRITISH BROADCASTING CORPORATION
TELEVISION CENTRE WOOD LANE LONDON W12 7RJ
TELEPHONE 01-743 8000 CABLES: TELECASTS LONDONPS4
TELEGRAMS: TELECASTS LONDON TELEX TELEX: 22182

4th October 1973

Dear Keith,

No we haven't seen Mr. Henwood this week. I'm afraid you must have got the wrong end of the stick as regard phoning outside the BBC and us paying for it. Never! Travel warrants,you must be joking. Sorry. PROPS - another no. We keep them here for emergencies as you will understand I'm sure. I'm afraid this letter 'aint much good so I apologise again. But travel warrants are only granted if someone is being paid by the BBC on commission.

...and I must've gone off on a massive strop and sent her a letter saying I was feeling I was putting all this effort in for nothing (It was not to be the only time that happened!). A reply was quick to appear...

BRITISH BROADCASTING CORPORATION
TELEVISION CENTRE WOOD LANE LONDON W12 7RJ
TELEPHONE 01-743 8000 CABLES: TELECASTS LONDONPS4
TELEGRAMS: TELECASTS LONDON TELEX TELEX: 22182

1st November 1973

Dear Keith,

I was sorry to receive your letter. I realise that you must have felt 'ignored' on several occasions but for a letter to arrive like that on our desks ....well, what is the world coming too! Anyway, let's try and make up our differences and try and settle down again. As regard envelopes it has been impossible to send them to you as we have a strike at the BBC stationery offices. However, I will try and get some through . I'll go up to th Braodcasting House place and see if they can spare some. You see we can only use them at the moment for our quota in the offices, and to send you a whack, I felt offices here came first. I expect you'll agree. The other thing is, I know it's a cliche but we have been busy. Doing two programmes is no holiday.

Anyway, if you feel you have put up with a lot these last two years why on earth didn't you give it all up? The last guy doing it did he found he didn't have time with exams and all that so why didn't you say something or at least cut down the newsletters.

I send you little picutres of Lis. These are all we have and they are bad pictures anyway so we are having some more taken. Next season starts, 15th December, first one is about the Middle Ages, the next is about Dynosaurs in London present day, the following is returning to Peladon and the one before the last is Daleks and the last about giant spiders. Be grateful if you keep these to yourself. Send yo back the right picture I hope of the Fan Club. Yes, we proof read your story for Mr. Henwood. I think everything is going through isn't it. Not sure because he doesn't consult us much .

Yours, (formal now I see!)

Sarah

I read and re-read the last bit with barely controlled hysteria. "Yes, we proof read your story for Mr Henwood. I think everything is going through, isn't it?" I had told Sarah how I hoped he would use my stories to "fill in" the major stories. And the BBC had approved my writing. I was about to become one of the first Target authors!

On target with Gordon

I was well excited and had to tell someone. My mum was always totally underwhelmed by anything I did, so I decided to tell Gogs, or Gordon McClean Stewart. I had managed to bag a best pal somewhere along the way, when he pushed me down a flight of steps at school. I landed in a heap at the bottom and he found this absolutely hilarious and decided I was best pal material. He likes the odd and eccentric does Gordon, and I was both. We share the same sense of humour and can reduce each other to desk-slapping hysterics. Even though he is an ardent fan of New Who, back then he looked upon it as one of my eccentric idiocyncracies.

I ran to his house (a prefabricated bungalow built in 1948 to ease the pressure of deman for housing after the war) and breathlessly told him the news.

"They're publishing my books! Target! Publishing!"
"How much are they paying you?" Gogs asked.
I was momentarily perplexed. It didn't occur to me they would actually be paying me.
"Don't know, "I replied eventually, "We haven't got that far yet. But it's "definately going through" " I said, as if reading it from the letter back in the house, "The BBC have proof read them and everything. Probably get about £2k."

Don't ask me where that figure came from, Well, that was it. Why wait for the cheque when you can spend the money in your head right now? Using £2,000 as our budget, we planned and listed all the things we would get when the dosh arrived. And as a thankyou to Gogs for being my BF, I told him I would buy him the electric guitar he'd always wanted. He was well chuffed.

Days went past and the list grew ever longer. We converted the spare room in my house into a den where all the loot would be stashed and we awaited the letter from Target Books, telling us what was to happen next.

TEN YEARS OLD!
Number 18
October/NOVEMBER Edition
DWFC
DWFC
SPECIAL EDITION

On Saturday 23rd,1963,as the clock neared quarter past five,a programme called "Juke Box Jury" finished and the announcer broadcast that in half an hours time, there would be another "Dixon of Dock Green" adventure,but first,he continued,a new science fiction serial was about to start with the peculiar name of "Doctor Who".

Then,for the first time,the public of Great Britain heard the weird,haunting music and saw the hypnotic,swirling patterns which marked the beginning of what was to be the most popular programme on TV for children,then for adults,and was soon heralded as a cult by young and old alike.

The first story told of Barbara and Ian who,suspicious of Susan Foremans actions follow her to and break into the police-box time and space machine,Tardis.They are then transported through time to the stone age,beginning their first adventure with the mysterious owner of the Tardis - the Doctor.

The programme recieved instant recogintion,but the boost to audience figures really came when the Tardis took them out of the Stone Age and threw them into the far reaches of the Galaxy to a planet called Skaro where machine-like creatures known as Daleks tried to destroy the Doctor and his compaions.Although they lost their battle against the crew of the Tardis,they won their way into the imaginations of millions of viewers who wrote and demanded their return.

And return they did,time and time again,trying to take over the world by mass-extermination of everyone in London,then setting out to take over the universe by using the ultimate weapon - the Time Controller.In the end,the Doctor destroyed their home planet and,their Emperor,but not before they had developed time and space machines which meant that the Doctor could come up against them wherever and whenever he went.

But in between his fights with the Daleks,the Doctor ventured back in time to Marco Polo's time,to the French Revolution and many other centuries where he helped but didn't disturb the balance of time.

Originally,the Doctor was an old man,and after his first skirmish with inhuman creatures called Cybermen,he changed his form,rejuvinated himself into a younger, though slightly more eccentric being,It was in this form that he met many more alien life forms,including the Yeti and the troublesome Ice Warriors,until he was recaptured by his own people,the Time Lords,where we found out that he had stolen the Tardis becuase he was sick of simply observing the evil in the universe. He wanted to go out and fight it with a sword of truth,the sword he has had by his side all the time we have known him.But the Time Lords were still displeased and sent the Doctor to Earth in exile,where he once again changed his form,and lost the secret of the Tardis.

During the last couple of years,the Doctor has found the secret of the Tardis once more,and can roam freely through time and space,taking us with him to new and wonderous lands,where the unbelievable becomes believable and the unexpected, expected.

We have travelled with the Doctor to the far-flung reaches of space and through eons of time for ten years.It was originally scheduled to run for less than half a year,and when William Hartnell,the original Doctor,suggested that the programme might run for five years,he was laughed at.Ten years have passed since the first episode when,through the gateway of your TV screens,we first stepped into the wonderous world of Doctor Who,and who knows how many more times we shall travel to other worlds with him?Here's to the next ten years.

On the other side of the universe, a sun rapidly grew in brightness, throwing out huge tongues of brilliant white flames to clash with the inky blackness of space. Suddenly, a micro-speck appeared at it's heart as it exploded into pure energy, turning the sun into a super-nova. The tiny box was forced through space at such a speed that it broke all known barriers, sending the police box into an unknown dimension at an incalculable point in time.

The Doctor shakily reached out for the control console and pulled himself up from the floor, his forehead bleeding from the injoury he sustained as he was thrown against the corner of the control table. Wiping the smear of blood with the back of his hand, the Doctor flipped the switch which operated the scanner. A room appeared, completely devoid of furniture with walls of pure white that shimmered with brilliant light.

Pinching his lower lip, the Doctor depressed the door control and stepped outside onto the white floor.

"Welcome, Doctor." said a voice, as the Doctor spun round, his black cloak spreading out like a pair of ravens wings behind him.

A small, thin man stood in the centre of the room, dressed all in black except for a large medallion which hung around his neck.

"You! I thought I had seen the last of you the last time I was here!"

"Ah!" he shrieked bursting into a smile, "I see you remember!"

"I could hardly forget the Mindmaster after you nearly turned Zoe and Jamie into two of your imagination creatures. But we destroyed your world..."

"You did, Doctor. Although you won the battle, destroying my world and all of my creations...I calculated that one day you would return to what once my own personal dimension, and although I would be no more, I couldn't bear the thought of you winning without the reassurance that one day I would have my revenge. That is why I built this android with my own brain patterns. This room is all that is left of my world, but through it, I will destroy your mind. Goodbye, Doctor."

The figure faded into nothingness like an image upon a screen, and almost instantly, the Tardis disappeared and the walls fell away to reveal a huge web-covered corridor the Doctor had seen once before.

"It can't be!" gasped the Doctor.

"Doctor, help!" someone screamed... a voice he recognised.

He sped along the corridor until he came to a large arch in the corridor and burst through into a vast control room where a teenage girl struggled to free herself from the grip of four giant ants.

"Susan!" yelled the Doctor in amazement.

"Doctor, help me!" she screamed, tears streaming down her cheeks.

The Doctor fumbled below his cloak and extracted from his pocket his sonic screwdriver. He turned the end and a piercing note sang through the air. The Zarbi ants ripped their claws from the girl and scurried out of the room

PAPERBACK LIBRARY

Announcing the official opening of the DWFC Library with 12 exciting adventures which have taken place over the ten years "Dr Who" has been on television! Each book has the full story plus additional information in the introduction. Now, each book has approximately 45 pages, so it won't take you very long to read through them. Three days per book is aloted, but you can send them beforehand if you wish. The quicker you return it, the quicker your next choice will arrive!

If you wish to join the library, simply send me a letter with each of the titles in the order in which you want to read them. Send for all twelve if you like, but please remember that they will be delivered one at a time and there may be a lapse of time between each one.

There is no charge for this service, but would you please enclose a 3½p stamp every time you return a book for your next order. This includes your first book.

DWFC 1: "THE DALEK INVASION OF EARTH"
This story is the original version upon which the film was based. Ian, Barbara and Susan find themselves fighting the Daleks again with the Doctor played by William Hartnell. (C)

DWFC 2: "THE CHASE"
The Doctor and his three companions are chased through time and space by the Daleks until it seems there is no way of escape!

DWFC 3: "THE DALEK MASTER PLAN"
A bigger story than the others, this paperback follows the Doctors battle against the Daleks as they attempt to control the universe with their deadly Time Destructor!

DWFC 4: "THE TENTH PLANET"
William Hartnell plays the Doctor for the last time in this story where the deadly Cybermen make their first attempt at trying to take over the Earth by using the base at the South Pole.

DWFC 5: "THE POWER OF THE DALEKS"
Pat Troughton makes his first appearance as the new Doctor to fight the Daleks on Vulcan. (C)

DWFC 6: "DR WHO AND THE MOONBASE"
The Doctor, Jamie, Ben and Polly meet up with the Cybermen again, this time on the surface of the moon where they have captured a weather controlling computer and threaten to cause havoc on the Earth if their plans are opposed!

DWFC 7: "THE FACELESS ONES"
This adventure is a personal favourite of mine, where aliens who can take the form of human beings, the Chameleons, plan to take over the entire population of Earth! The whole adventure takes place against the background of Gatwick Airport.

DWFC 8: "THE EVIL OF THE DALEKS"
The Doctor is forced to plant the human factor in three Daleks and finally returns to Skaro where he battles with the gigantic Emperor Dalek!

DWFC 9: "TOMB OF THE CYBERMEN"
The Doctor, Jamie and Victoria land on the planet Telos where the tomb of the Cybermen is being uncovered, but all is safe until something stirs in the honeycomb of tombs... (C)

DWFC 10: "WHEEL IN SPACE"
The Cybermen return again, this time to take over a space station with the aid of the terrifying Cybermats!

DWFC 12: "THE WAR GAMES"
This is the last of Pat Troughtons series in which he gets involved with the War Lord, intent on building a huge army composed of soldiers from different wars. The ending is an acurate account of the Doctors trial by the Time Lords.
(Notes: DWFC 11 will announced next issue as it's late in it's preparation. Those marked with a (C) are Dr Who Fan Club Classics)

Please send your lists to: Dr Who Library, c/o K. Miller, 109 Moredun Pk. Rd, Edinburgh

as the girl hurried over to the Doctor and threw her arms around him.

"Oh,Grandfather,I thought I had lost you..." she sobbed.

"But,Susan,what are doing here?Has the Mindmaster got anything to do with this?"

"Doctor,quickly,the Zarbi have got Ian and Barbara in another section of the Web."

"Susan,will you please tell me what is going on here?"asked the Doctor sternly.

"Please,Grandfather,don't ask questions,there is little time left...LOOK!

Susan pointed towards the entrance where the frightening form of a Mire beast slithered into the room,it's six tentacles reaching out for the Time Lord while it studied him with two blood red eyes.

"It can't be possible..."gasped the Doctor,"There weren't any Mire Beasts on Vortis..."

A tentacle suddenly shot out and wrapped itself around one of the Doctors legs,pulling him to the floor with a loud thud.He cried for help from his female relation,but when he stared about him,she had gone...disappeared like a ghost.

Confusion and terror mingled in the Doctors mind as the slobbering mouth of the Beast drew nearer.By this time, five of the living tentacles had wrapped themsleves around the Doctors body,the final limb wrapping itself around the throat of the humanoid.It's grip grew tighter until suddenly it gave off a gurgled yelp and the limbs fell limply to the floor.The Doctor recovered his senses and saw a man and a woman standing above the monster,the former with a Zarbi weapon smoking in his hand.

"Ian!Barbara!But..but I don't understand...first Susan...and now you.."

Ian Chesterton gave the Doctor a hand up.

"There's no time for explanations now, Doctor,the Zarbi are right on our heels. There's a transporter at the end of the main Web corridor.We must reach it before The Web Centre is alerted."

They made their way down the corridor and the Doctor was about to ask Barbara a question when she jerked a finger to her lips and hissed the Time Lord to be quiet.

Towards the end of the corridor,the trio pressed themselves up against the wall of the corridor as Ian gave a quick glance round into the Web Centre.

"Look..."he whispered,"That disc on the far wall..that's the transportation unit.Our best bet would be to make a dive for it.If all three of us go together,we stand a good chance of getting away from here..."

The Doctor had grown tired of his fruitless questioning and nodded.

"Ready Barbara...Doctor?Right,NOW!" he yelled as the trio shot from the darkness and sped across the Centre, attracting the attention of the hoards of Zarbi ants skuttling to and fro, but before the creatures could do a thing,the party leapt at the shimmering white disc upon the wall and disappeared simultaneously from view.

The Doctor out on the other side alone.He rolled for a few moments,then once he had stopped,he dusted himself down and looked around.

He was in a jungle he vaguely recognised from some past adventure.Too puzzled to think of the disappearance of his two companions,the Doctor was suddenly startled by two figures crashing their way through the jungle. They stumbled to a halt and gasped

"Come on,Doctor,they're right behind us..."

"Steven?Vicki?I think I must be going mad..!"

"RUN!"screamed Vicki as she saw the dumpy shape of a robot menace from the Doctors past burst through the trees and speed towards them.

"Mechanoids!"breathed the Doctor, but was grabbed by the arms by Steven and Vicki and forced to run into the jungle.

The hexagonal robot drew nearer,it's gun firing deadly radiation beams at the party as they sped towards some unknown destination.

Suddenly,Vicki stumbled and with a squeal,she fell to the ground,tripping the Doctor up who fell on top of Steven, dragging him down with him.

"DOCTOR!"screamed Vicki as the Mechanoid blazed it's gun at them and the Doctor felt a horrible burning sensation flood through his body and cloak his mind with darkness.

The Doctor lay alone in a corner of the white room.The Mindmaster bent down on one knee and feltthe Doctors pulse beating in his neck.

"Still alive are you,Doctor?Is your mind still intact?Let me warn you then, if somehow you can hear me,the game has just begun...and this time Doctor,the outcome will be different!"

CHAPTER TWO

The Doctor awoke to find a hand dabbing a white moist cloth over his forehead.He struggled to focus upon the figure above him.

"Dodo...not you too..."mumbled the Doctor,heaving himself up onto one elbow,"What on Earth is going on here? Wait a minute...oh,no...not again."

He looked around and saw that he was in a room suspended high above London in the gigantic building called the Post Office Tower.

"I must have time to think...what am doing here? How did I get here? What happened to the Mindma..."

Dodo suddenly became agitated and said to the Doctor

"We must get out of here,Doctor..."

"Not until I can figure out what's going on..."

"But Wotan's War Machines are on their way up here!"she sobbed.

"Wotan?But...but I destroyed that war-mad computer years ago."

"Please,Doctor,you can think later. The lift is almost here!"

The Time Lord leapt to his feet and studied the guage on the wall.

"It's passing the 33rd floor.We have about half a minute before they reach this level.Help me over with this computer bank,Dodo..."

The Doctor and Dodo crossed over to a large machine situated to the left of the doors.He planted his back on the adjacent wall and forced the heavy machine forwards with his feet.Dodo helped by pulling but the Doctor felt she was giving no ease to the strain. Reluctantly,the box slid grittly forwards until it was directly in front of the double doors of the lift.

Kneeling down on his haunches,the Time Lord removed a metal plate from the wall and reached in,pulling two red and black wires sharply from their terminals.There was a small implosion and Dodo gave a tiny squeal.

"It's alright,Dodo,"reassured the Doctor,"I've just fused the doors."

"But the Machines will just burn through them..."

"My dear girl,I want them open,not shut."

He pressed his fingers in the small crack between the doors and forced them apart.They slid open easily and the Doctor stared down the shaft to see the lift only five floors below them.

"Quickly,Dodo,we don't have much time.Get in front of the machine and push..!"

"Doctor,I don't think I can..."

"Do as I say,girl!"

Dodo disappeared round the back of the box and the Doctor gave her the order to push while he prepared to manouever it into the shaft.It was now only threefloors below and rising.

"Dodo!Push!"urged the Doctor but no force was applied.

He rushed round from his post to see the girl was gone.Growing frantic,the Doctor pushed against the machine and it slowly inched it's way forward.

Suddenly,it tilted then toppled over into the shaft,smashing itself onto the roof of the conveyor,sending it smashing to the basement far below.

Mopping his brow,the Doctor felt a hand clamp onto his shoulder.He spun round.

"Ben!Polly!"he exclaimed.

"Follow us,Doc,"said the sailor,"We know the way out of here."

The duo led the Time Lord out of a door onto a flight of steps that led down,down,down until it emerged onto the deserted streets of London.

"It's odd,"remarked the Doctor,"I never noticed a door when Dodo was up there..."

Ben and Polly walked on as if they hadn't heard the Doctors question.He grabbed Polly by the arm and spun her around.

"Listen,Polly,what's going on here? You can't have recognised me as I was in my other form when you left me!"

Suddenly,a red beam of light of such high intensity that it hurt the Time Lord's eyes shot between them.He glanced round to see five seven foot aliens stride towards them.Their skins gleamed with a metallic glint,their features were no more than holes cut in a metal facemask,their hands had ten,pointed silver fingers,and a box of flashing circuitry throbbed upon their chests.

"Cybermen!"breathed the Doctor.

"Make for the Underground,Doctor!Run!" shouted Ben as they dispersed into different directions.

The Doctor decided to take the young mans advice as another beam zoomed past his head.He sped around a corner and suddenly skidded to a halt.Another three Cybermen were lunging towards him.

"Doctor...over here!"shouted a Scots voice.

The Doctors brain had hardly taken in the identity of the owner of the voice when he was speeding along another London street towards an Underground Station.

"Down here.Victoria's waiting down there.She may need help..."

"What about the Cybermen,Jamie?"

"I'll deal with them...now hurry!"

The Doctor sped down the stairs,his black cloak flowing out behind him.

CHAPTER THREE

The Doctor emerged onto the platform of Piccadilly Station and looked about him. All seemed quiet until a scream pierced the silence and three figures emerged from the darkness.Two Yeti were dragging a girl he recognised as Victoria along the tunnel.She screamed again and the Doctor leapt down onto the lines and sped down the tunnel towards the attackers.The sound of his footsteps alerted the aliens attentions and they turned,emitting a fiercsome roar which echoed down the dark passageway.

The Doctor gave the first monster a sharp Venusian karate chop on it's chest which fused it's control box,making it slump to the ground lifeless.

The remaining Yeti clamped two three-fingered hands onto the Doctors shoulders and began to crush them when the Doctor wrenched himself free by quickly deflecting the arms with his own limbs and delivering the deadly karate blow which cuased the explosion on contact.

"Victoria?"wheezed the Doctor after he had recovered from the battle.

He peered into the darkness but could see nothing.Suddenly,another scream filled the air.

"Oh,no,"groaned the Doctor,"not again..."

He limped along the tunnel towards the entrance and emerged to find Zoe with an Ice Warrior towering high above her with a deadly stranglehold about her neck.

The Time Lord seemed to regain his energy and scrammbled up the side of the line onto the platform.The Ice Warrior looked slowly round,it's reptilian skin glinting olive green in the artificial light and its huge triangular eyes,glazed and menacing,gazed down at the humanoid desperately trying to break it's hold by hammering down on it's arms.Zoe choked and the Doctor sobbed with hopelessness as the Warrior increased the pressure.

Suddenly,a beam of white light whizzed past his head and struck the monster in the chest.It hissed in pain and collapsed to the ground,releasing it's death grip upon the small female.The Doctor helped her onto her feet and looked behind him to see

"Liz!Thank heavens you are here..."

Liz Shaw looked at the Doctor strangley.. and then vanished before his very eyes.

"LIZ!"yelled the Doctor.

He returned his gaze to Zoe and saw her too disappear,as if she was never there. The Doctor broke out in a nervous sweat and ruffled his silver hair with his hand.

Then,out of the corner of his eye,the Doctor saw a bright spot appear in the wall of the station which grew in size and brightness until it was a few inches higher than the Time Lord himself.He stood motionless,waiting anxiously to see what was to happen next.At first he thought it was trick of his eye...but then he saw it again.Something was moving behind the light!The figure of a human appeared in silouette then stepped through the veil onto the platform.

"Jo..."the Doctor gasped.

"This way,Doctor,"she said in monotone.

Her eyes seemed to look right through him as she turned to re-enter the light-doorway.

"Jo,wait!"

She hesitated and turned,her eyes fixed on an invisible spot in front of her.

"Just follow me,Doctor."

With that,she disappeared into the light,closely followed by the Doctor.

When he emerged at the other side,he found himself back in the room of the Mindmaster when all his friends had assembled in a line on the one side.In the centre of the room,the Mindmaster turned and grinned an evil smile at the Doctor.

"So you didn't just disappear after all?" commented the Doctor in a matter-of-fact way.

The Mindmaster lost his smile as the Doctor wiped the sweat from his brow with a large red hankerchief and returned the grin.

"I thought you would give up this stupid game once you saw I was "cracking up"."

The Mindmaster scowled.

"I haven't finished yet,Doctor."

Saying this,he pointed a finger towards the wall to the Doctors right where a portal appeared and three more aliens glided into the room,their metallic armour glinting in the white light as their domes swivelled to and fro as the Doctor had seen them do so many times before.An element of fear crept into the Doctors heart.

"Hah!"exclaimed the Mindmaster,as if he could sense the Doctors fear."I see you aren't very pleased at the appearance of my little slaves."

"The Daleks are slaves to no-one!"urged the Time Lord.

"In my world,Doctor,everyone is my slave!"

"Everyone except me,"triumphed the Doctor.

"Exactly.That is why I am delivering this ultimatum to you.Surrender your mind willingly to me...or I will order the Daleks to exterminate your friends!"

The Doctor pinched his lower lip.

"Hurry up,Doctor.I want your answer now!"

PLEASE REMEMBER AND SEND YOUR LABELS TO ME AS SOON AS YOU CAN,BECAUSE ALL THOSE MEMBERS WHO FAIL TO RETURN THEM BY THE TIME ISSUE 19 IS READY FOR SENDING WILL BE CLASSED AS THOSE WHO DO NOT WISH THE MAGAZINE TO BE CONTINUED TO BE SENT TO THEM.IF YOU DIDN'T GET LABELS,PLEASE TELL ME.THANKS.

SUPER NEW MAGAZINE
THE DIMENSIONS OF DOCTOR WHO

PHOTOGRAPHS • ARTICLES • MONSTER PAGES • COMIC STRIPS • COLOUR ART

All these things are in the new DWFC Publication "THE DIMENSIONS OF DR WHO", a new magazine which will be brought out at irregular intervals during the coming eons of time!This magazine is part of the great,new DWFC Lending Library and the same rules apply,but please send a 5p stamp for this super colour magazine.

FIRST ISSUE CONTAINS:Full colour cover,comic strip version of UNEARTHLY CHILD, the first Doctor Who adventure,colour Monster Page of the Autons,Visiorecord of "THE THREE DOCTORS" and an article on the club itself!

NEXT EDITION OUT SOON!

"DOCTOR WHO MUST BE DESTROYED!"(continued)

The Doctor gave another knowing smile.

"Thank you,my dear chap."

"Thank you?For what?"

"Giving me time to think."

At that remark the Mindmaster suddenly became agitated.

"Ah,I see I've hit a weak spot.All this the Doctor said,waving a hand about in the air,"is,as you said yourself,all you have left.Therefore,how is possible you can send me to different planets and times,mm?"

"I AM ALL-POWERFUL!"screamed the alien.

"Youre nothing but a fake!"retorted the Doctor,"I don't suppose I've even left this room?All these people from my past I keep seeing...they were nothing but instruments to try and keep me confused while my past enemies were there to terrify me into maddness...and that is where you made your mistake!"

"EXTERMINATE THEM!"yelled the Mindmaster.

The Daleks swivelled round and pointed their guns.

"NO!"yelled the Doctor,screwing up his eyes in concentration as the Daleks guns fired.

Nothing happened.When the Doctor reopened his eyes,he found the Daleks and his companions gone.The Mindmaster stared about him franticly.

"How apt!I've defeated you with the thing you were trying to gain...my mind. All I needed to do was admit to myself the they weren't really there...and what do you know...they weren't!"

"No...no,I can still defeat you!"hissed the Mindmaster.

"But that can't be,can it?How can a figment of someones imagination destroy a living being...becuase that is all that you are...you were created in the Mindmasters brain,therefore you are nothing but a product of imagination.You don't even exist!"yelled the Doctor in triumph.

"NO!NO!"screamed the alien.

"YOU DON'T EVEN EXIST!"

"NOOOOOOoooooooooooo......"

The Mindmaster faded before the Doctors eyes like a ghost...like the figment from some tormented brain,which he,of course,was.

EPILOGUE

The Tardis materialized in UNIT H.Q. and the Doctors lab.The Time Lord opened the doors to find the Brigadier waiting for him.

"Bean anywhere exciting,Doctor?"

"Just visiting olf friends,Brigadier", the Doctor replied,"...visiting old friends"

THE END.

AND NOW, TO CONTINUE THE ACTION, THIS IS WHERE YOU TAKE OVER AND FIND OUT ...

DO YOU KNOW WHO?

SPECIAL

The last and greatest edition of the present series.

1)Where did the scene opposite come from? score 2

2)In which adventure did the Master make his first appearance? score 1

3)What is the science of the Cybermen called? score 1

4)What was leader of the Yeti called? score 2

5)What was the name of the Queen in THE TIME MONSTER score 2

6)Pat Troughton played another part in a Doctor Who adventure besides the Doctor. Who was it he was portraying? score 3

They're like goldfish in a bowl, aren't they? Going round and round forever...

7)What famous comedy stars played
a)Tom Campbell in DALEKS INVASION 2150
b)An Ice Warrior in SEEDS OF DEATH
score 4

8)What connection was there between Victria Waterfield and Professor Traverse of the Yeti adventures? score 4

STOP EVERYTHING! SUPER NEW RECORD OUT CALLED "THE WORLD OF DR WHO"! IT'S THE 'B' SIDE OF "THE MOONBASE 3 THEME" on the BBC Record Label! GET NOW, TIMELORDS!

9)The War Lord had some connection with Dr Who. What was it? score 2

10)What connection is there between todays Dr Who and Jean Marsh, a former companion from THE DALEK MASTERPLAN? score 2

11)Who, what or where was Wotan? score 3

12)Terry Nation wrote the TV script for "DR WHO and the DALEKS". Who wrote:
a)the film script?
b)the book? score 4

13)Who designed the Trojan Horse? score 4

Answers next issue.

"DO YOU KNOW WHO?" ANSWER SHEET NUMBER 3

1)Frazer Hines alias Jamie
2)The clear column of glass in the centre of the Tardis console.
3)No, Peter Butterworth played the Monk
4)One of the Thals in "PLANET OF THE DALEKS"
5)a/Yes, b/Yes, c/No, d/No
6)"PLANET OF THE DALEKS"
7)Small wrist time and space machines
8)Three
9)Yes
10)Michael Gough
11)In "COLONY IN SPACE, the Interstellar Mining Corporation
12)TENTH PLANET, THE MOONBASE, TOMB OF THE CYBERMEN, WHEEL IN SPACE, INVASION
13)Producer
14)In "CURSE OF PELADON"
15)Yes, in "EVIL OF THE DALEKS"
16)Yes
17)Roboman
18)Ruler of the ninth Galaxy who tried to trick the Daleks into working for him to try and take over the universe.

Ratings:
25-35: Very good, 15-25: Not bad, Under 15: Better luck with the one opposite!

COMING SOON! ·NEW·

DR. WHO INFOSHEETS

Illustrated dossiers on the actors and the characters they portray!

BACK ISSUES!

The following numbers are available to any member who wants them:-
6(1st 2 pages), 7(last 2 pages), 8, 9, 10, 11, 12, 13, 14 and 15

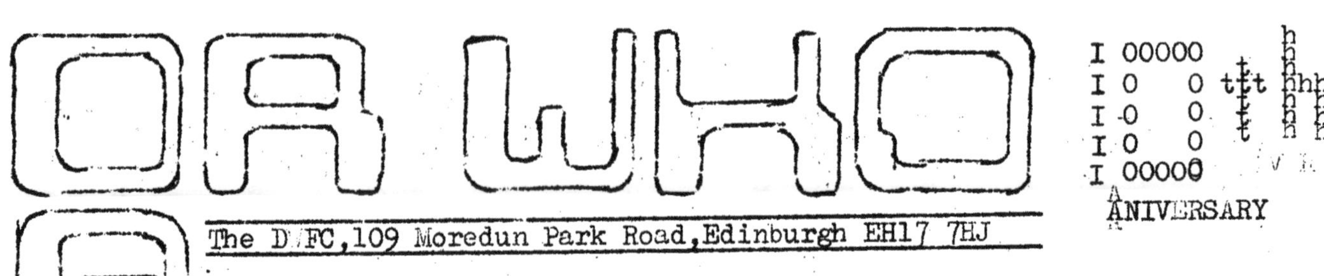

DATA

The DWFC,109 Moredun Park Road,Edinburgh EH17 7HJ

Hi,Timelord,

And first let me say how great it is to be presenting this special issue of DWFC MAG on Doctor Who's tenth birthday.I hope you are enjoying the extravaganza,and next issue will be something rather special too,as it will be celebrating Christmas,the second birthday of the Fan Club,and the return of the prog to our Tv screens! And if that isn't worth celebrating,I don't know what is!

Now,may I apologise for the extreme delay of issue 17.There was a strike at the BBC stationery offices,so we couldn't get the envelopes in which to send your hallowed magazine.

I hope you ALL saw that fantastic edition of BLUE PETER on the 5th of November where Jon Pertwee drove in his super new cosmic car.As Peter Purves said,the new car will be featured early in January in the new series.Then,surprise,surprise!A great run-down on the history of Dr Who with excerpts from the very first Dr Who adventure,which I thought had been lost forever!It showed the final moments when the Doctor,Ian,Susan and Barbara were escaping from a band of howling savages from the stone-age.Further excerpts included THE DALEK MASTERPLAN,THE TENTH PLANET,FURY FROM THE DEEP,THE THREE DOCTORS and the great ending to the WAR GAMES when Pat Troughton played the Doctor when he was on trial by the Time Lords and the "shopping list" of monsters appeared on the screen behind him.May I give my thanks to BLUE PETER for giving half their programme to Dr Who as a birthday present.

Last issue,I started a list of names who were once companions of the Doctor but who have now left to go onto other things.Continuing the list,you may remember Maureen O'Brien as Vicki,the girl who took Susans' part when she left.Well she has gone over to Canada,where she has recently been portraying Alayne in the series THE WHITEOAKS OF JALNA which is currently being seen in many regions in this country.Doctor Who Mark 2 alias Pat Troughton has been appearing in Family at War, The Goodies,Colditz,films such as THE SCARS OF DRACULA and FRANKENSTEIN AND THE MONSTER FROM HELL and other parts in films and TV plays,too numerous to mention. Frazer Hines who played Pat's companion,Jamie,now stars in Emerdale Farm,while his other companion,Victoria alias Deborah Watling,starred recently in DOCTOR IN CHARGE.Victorias replacement,Zoe,played by Wendy Padbury,is now starring in FREEWHEELERS,and last but not least is the Doctors latest loss,Jo Grant who was played by Katy Manning,who now has turned presenter of a Sunday prog named after the theme of THE GREEN DEATH -"Serendipity".That about completes the list,but if I find out more,I won't hesitate to tell you!

The Doctor Who Annual is now out on sale,let's hope that 1974 is better than the '73 edition.Although I've tried in vain to get a copy in the bookshops,I have heard that there are two comic strips in it this year,which might make it a little better.I'll have to see it first to say if there is to be a REVIEW on it or not.

Also out on sale now is the DOCTOR WHO SPECIAL printed by Radio Times.As the annual,I haven't seen it yet,but what I've heard about it,I think it's going to be really something.I think I can really guarentee a review.

Starting next issue is a brand-new series called DR.WHO DICTIONARY where all major events,monsters,machines and people will be listed with an easy-to-look-up format,with everything from Auton to Zarbi.

Over the past two years there have been a number of series in the magazine, including Dr.Who-In the Beginning,Tardis Talkbox,Dalek Data,The Dr's Drawing Board, Dalek Dominators,DWFC Crossword,Dr Who People,Report,and Do You Know Who?.I was wondering if there was any of the old series' you would like back,or if there was something you would like to see,but isn't yet in the magazine.After all,the fan club is for your pleasure,and so I would like the magazine to be composed of things you would like to read.Send me a letter or a po stcard and I would be very grateful.

Well,that's it over.Rather sad really,it's like the feeling you get when Xams has gone,but I hope you've enjoyed this as much as I have,and I'll see you next issue, or before if you send me a letter.Here's to the next ten years,Doc!

KEITH

BRITISH BROADCASTING CORPORATION
TELEVISION CENTRE WOOD LANE LONDON W12 7RJ
TELEPHONE 01-743 8000 CABLES: TELECASTS LONDONPS4
TELEGRAMS: TELECASTS LONDON TELEX TELEX: 22182

19th Nov.

Dear Keith,

No new pictures of Jon yet. They should be coming through sometime next month. Next season will start with a four part 'The Time Warrior' then a six part 'Invasion of the Dinosaurs' then a four part 'Return to Peladon' then a six part 'Planet of the Spdiers'. Barry will be directing the lastone. The new producer will be joining September next year. I'll be leaving in May I expect. By the way I'm getting married on 4th May! As regard Richard Henwood, he's a doozy old devil. If I were you Iwould get in touch wi~~t~~th him yourself. We had the birthday party early on this year. In June actually. We had the old regular actors and previous writers and staff. It wasn't very exciting.

Love,

SARAH

Awww,cheers. They had a 10th birthday party and I wasn't invited. Perhaps Sarah didn't enjoy it, but can you imagine what it would've been like for me to mix with previous writers and staff?!

And then, three weeks after Sarah told me the deal was "going through", the letter arrived from Richard Henwood at Target Books...

Tandem Books

UNIVERSAL-TANDEM PUBLISHING COMPANY LTD

14 Gloucester Road London SW7 4RD

Telephone 584 8766-7
584 6803-4

Reg. No. 898950 England Reg. Office: 99 Aldwych London WC2B 4JY
VAT Registration No. 238 4691 36

21st November 1973

Mr Keith Miller,
109 Moredun Park Road,
Edinburgh EH17 7HJ

Dear Keith,

Many apologies for being so late in returning the enclosed books. I have, as you know, been showing them to various of the BBC people involved with the programme, who applaud your interest and initiative very much.

However the Script Editor of the series did ask me to warn you gently of the rules regarding the sale and distribution of this sort of material, which presumably comes from taped recordings. It is, as you know, copyright material, and therefore illegal to reproduce it in any form, certainly for sale.

Anyway we all admire your enthusiasm very much, and I thought you might be interested to see a list of Doctor Who publications, published, and in the pipeline. This is a confidential document, the contents of which should not be disclosed outside of your club.

One final note : I am hoping that we will have Jon Pertwee on the Edinburgh/Glasgow Children's Book Train next October (for the Children's Book Show in Glasgow), and that we can all meet up then.

Please continue to keep me in touch with your activities.

Yours sincerely,

Richard Henwood

Children's Book Editor,
TARGET BOOKS.

Well, I was gutted. Rather than being one of Target's pioneer authors, I was being told off by Terrance Dicks, who obviously didn't want me muscling in on his cash cow!! I was royally pissed off. Later, I would have a laugh with Terrance about it on the set of *Planet of the Spiders*, but there was only one thing on my mind now. How on earth am I going to tell Gogs his dream of a guitar has just gone up in smoke?

DWFC MAG

Number 19 SPECIAL REVIEW EDITION D.W.F.C.

Hi, there once more, Timelord!,

This is just an in-between edition of the mag to prove to you that we haven't forgot you or anything like that, and it gives me a good oppertunity to have a run-down on the adventures we have seen. I'll be back to talk to you later, but meanwhile let's starts by Reviewing:

INVASION OF THE DINOSAURS
by Malcolm Hulke

As always, let's take it episode by episode.

First episode opened with the Tardis returning from the middle ages where the Doctor had been battling Linx.

The deserted London Streets created a brilliant atmosphere, and set the scene for what I thought was going to be the Malcolm Hulke version of "Dalek Invasion of Earth"but with Dinosaurs.

The scenes that followed were very good, what with the public telephone being out of order and the streets being devoid of any bus service.

The looter in the jewellery shop was brought to a quick and mysterious end when his car crashed some distance down the road. Very good, I thought. The mystery deepens.

Then came the pterodactyl which was quite well done, but it's wings didn't flap enough.

The Doctor and Sarah being arrested was a novel twist, and the photography scene brought back some of the Pat Troughton humour.

After escaping, they came up against their first Dinosaur and oh dear, shades of Basil Brush! A glove puppet nervously sking about London streets didn't exactly fill me with fright.

Second episode ebgan rather well with peasant from some time in the past trying to force the Doctor and Sarah (whom I think is getting better by the episode) to return him to his own time. The ray effect of the time ripple was great, when the monsters appeared and disappeared.

The other monsters weren't so bad, the Brontosaurus being the best I think. It's interesting to note that the baddie Grover (the MP) is in fact Noel Johnson, known to everyone during the war years as Dick Barton-Special Agent of BBC Radio. Then came the moment when it is revealed that Captain Yates is the double agent which was rather a pity as I don't think he really would do such a thing after he had been with the Doctor for so long and should have known better. The ending comes when the Doctors gun refuses to fire and lo and behold, it's Basil again.

After Yates had a change of heart and rescued the Doctor, episode three opened with the Dinosaur being shot down. The part I really enjoyed of this episode was when Basil broke look from his chains, bumped his head against the roof of the hanger, smashed his tail through a window and knocked Sarah unconsious. After she had recovered, Grover is shown as being one of the those pioneering the Golden Age. The idea of the filing room lift was good. Then after a pause, the ending comes as the revelation that she is on board a ship which left Earth three months beforehand.

Episode Four introduced the Doctors new car which was brilliant but wasn't seen for long enough I don't think. Then came the return of the pterodactyl which was only a shadow on the wall this time. After a lot of theexplanation as what is going on, the story ends with the Doctor being accused of conjuring up the monsters.

Episode Five began with a long, drawn out run-about as the Doctor escapes from UNIT. This part seemed to take up half the episode. And how did it end? You guessed it. The re-return of Basil!

After the battle of the bendy toys with Basil and Bronty, the Doctor guides UNIT down to the Underground station where he combines forces with the elders and brings about the ironic ending of all the baddies being tranpsorted back to the time they wanted to bring forwards.

The story, on the whole, was well written, but the effects let it down badly, I'm sorry to say.

The DEATH TO DALEKS

On the morning of the day this story was to start, I picked up a copy of the 'Sun' newspaper to read a disturbing report by Chris Kenworthy about the past Dalek stories.This one proved him wrong anyway.

The opening shot of the arrow was quite well done and we got our first glimpse of the marvellous sets and locations that were to be seen throughout the adventure.

I thought the 'death' of the Tardis was very well done,with all sounds being stopped and echoes brought in,but once again,they've brought in more cupboards which will have miraculously diappeared by the next time we see the control room.

The scenery where the Tardis landed with the huge rocks and swirling mists gave it a very mysterious and creepy atmosphere. The position of the Tardis made it look like the old,darker police box they used to use.

The oil lamp the Doctor brought out added to the whole segment,creating a very good beginning.As Sarah paniced to open the Tardis door,I thought it was great the way the Exxillon hand grabbed her ankle and she tried to fight it off.

Afterwards,when I saw the light and heard the organ music,I thought Sarah was seeing something holy,and I asn't far wrong.What a superb sight! The Citadel was a magnificent masterpeice of alien architecture. Really terrific.After Sarah had been captured,the Exxillon singing was great and frightening.

The ending of the Dalek spaceship(which didn't look too real then)landed and they trundelled out,firing their guns was predictable.

This provided the opening for episode 2, but what an odd sound the Dalek guns made. Sort of a slurping sound.The idea was good though.

This time,the Dalek spaceship really looked huge.When they developed their new guns and glided out of the ship,the murder of the Exxillons on the ridge was very well done.The guns sounded quite good too.

Luckily,the Doctor managed to save Sarah from sacrafice,and when they were trying to escape through the tunnels,the following of Bellal,then unknown to us,was creepy.I had my doubts when the Doctor left Sarah to be attacked by the Root,as it looked rather like a Hoover tube!

The tube looked rather better in the third episode where I enjoyed seeing the Dalek being blown to bits.The actual idea of the "Root" was a good one.I liked Sarahs' repulsion at Bellal (soon to be repeated with Alpha Centauri).It was a very 'human' touch to the story.

The Root was to appear again at the mine workings,and this time it looked better than ever as it rose from the lake,destroying another Dalek before it itself was destroyed.The effect of the Exxillon on fire must have been dangerous to do.

When we returned to the Doctor,we found him trying to get into the citadel,and I liked the idea of different puzzles to graduate into it.Rather like "The Celestial Toymaker" when William Hartnell was the Doctor.After they had escaped the Daleks outside,the first room looked a bit forboding with two skeletons lying there.The test of the maze was well thought out.The ending of the Doctor shouting "Stop,don't move" was a bit puzzeling as I had no idea why they should want to stop,but all was revealed in part four.

Venus must rate pretty highly in the Doc's book,what with Venusian measurements, karate,lullubies and now hopskotch!The lightning bolts as the Dalek skimmed over the floor were well done,as was the floor repairing itself.

The Daleks seemed prettystupid at this stage when they simply glided over the hopskotch without a second glance.

Then came the first sighting of the alien in front of the giant viewscreen,which looked great.The ultimate test was the best with the city attacking their minds, Then came the appearnce of the door to the brain centre where that alient slipped down into dust which was very good indeed.

The anti-bodies,described in Radio Times as zombies,was a noveland quite searey twist,especially when the Daleks couldn't shoot them down.I liked the ascent of the citadel from the outside by the Earthmen and suicide of the Dalek when he found his prisoners had escaped.The breakdown of the citadel was very well handled with the eratic doors etc.When the Doctor got back to the others,the explosion of the Dalek spaceship looked a little false,but the death of the citadel made up for it with it's agonising screams of pain echoed around them. In general,I thinkeveryoone should get top marks on a first class story. Hooray for Terry Nation!

The MONSTER OF PELADON

by Brian Hayles

When I first saw the workers of the familiar planet of Peladon,I thought they might have some relation to the Menoptera of Vortis,with their furry, multi-coloured heads.This was how the first episode of this adventure began, and right from the start I had doubts.

The Tardis materialized again slightly off-target,as Sarah said "In another gloomy ol' tunnel!"

The Doctor and Sarah-Jane are then captured and taken to the Queen.Here was a good touch,with Thalira having the slight lisp that her father (David Troughton) had.

Then came the re-introduction of the story of "CURSE OF PELADON".Ortron has taken the place of Hepesh,the ruler has changed sex,but the story was almost the same,with Ortron trying to show the Queen how wrong she is,trying to get rid of the Doctor and anyone else who dared to defy his ways. Then Grun,the kings champion was reincarnated as the kings champion again.It seemed as if it was just going to be CURSE drawn out into six episodes.How disappointing!

To end episode one,the spirit of Aggedor pops up and zaps Preba,the k.c.

Second episode threw some hope onto the story,with the refinery door posing some trouble for Sarah with the machine that attacked her mind. Rather reminicent of the last story DEATH TO THE DALEKS with the Exxilloin citadel.

The story plodded wearily on until once more Ortron strated up again,then ended epside two by throwing both the Doctor and Sarah-Jane into the pit where an old enemy awaited...old Aggy himself.

After a roar and a claw,the Doctor managed to subdue him with his eyeglass cum key-ring.

I did like the part where Sarah gives the Queen a little tutorial on Womens Lib.

Apart from this episode Three seemed to be rather uneventful,apart from the end where the Doctor opens the door of the refinery to find an Ice Warrior staring him in the face.

This is where we find out that the Ice Warrior cheif,Azaxyr,has given the excuse that they are police from the Federation.The Ice Warriors then turned out to be the enemies again,with Azaxyr threatning to kill a Peladoian every day the strike is on,and if that didn't work, he'd blow up the whole planet!

So,the menace of the Ice Warriors unite the Peladonians against them,apart from Ettis who eventually goes mad in the cave with the sonic lance which was pointed a pretty picture of the citadel which wasn't really very convincing.

Then came a very realistic part...the sword-fighting sequence.

In all of the Dr.Who's,even those which were set in the past with swashbucklers etc.,I've never seen a really convinging sword fight.But this one was excellent, except for rather a bad shot of Terry Walsh at one point when a fall was neeessary.Then,the sonic lance blew up, obviously killing Ettis,and for all we know,the Doctor!

Episode Five strated by giving us the welcome news that the Doctor hadn't been killed in the explosion.I think I had better comment now that I think the Ice Warriors get-up or costumes were not too good,with their nobbly heads bobbing about like those dogs in the back of car windows.I think they must have been taken from different series in the past, as on example had the small head and large body while another was the opposite.

I did like Azaxyrs' costume with that large bulbous helmet,but I think the hands or claws or whatever they were spoiled him.

It was a pity Ortron had to be zapped, as he seemed to be proving himself better than his predecessor by saving the Queen.

The noise at the end of this episode was deafning,my whole TV set was shaking, but it added to the good effect of the door melting.

The Ice Warriors were,of coarse,dealt with in the next episode,as I suspected, by the spirit of Aggedor The mind attack on the Doctor was quite well handled and the aftermath of his 'death' was excellently acted out by Liz in her role as Sarah.

Then came the climax of the deaths of Azaxyr and his fellow Martians and the chase between the Doctor and the miners and Eckersley with the Queen.This section was very well acted out,but I don't know what's happened to Aggy.He seemed terribly tatty and false,but it was a rather ignoble way to die,being zapped at the back of the head by the ray gun.

Still,I did like the ending with the goodbyes and the Doctor and Sarah at the Tardis,and the stage is now set for the Review and Report next issue of THE PLANET OF THE SPIDERS!

BOOK REVIEW:BOOK REVIEW:BOOK REVIEW:BOOK REVIEW:BOOK REVIEW:BOOK REVIEW:BOOK REVI

'DOCTOR WHO AND THE AUTON INVASION' by Terrance Dicks.

The first thing that struck me was the change of cover artist.Jon Pertwees' face seems to topple over to one side,but apart from that,it was fine.At least for the cover illustration.The black and white drawings inside were badly done,I'm afraid to say.But to get onto the book and it's story,I liked the Prologue where the Doctor in his guise as Pat Troughton,is banished to Earth.I think this interpretation of the TV series "Spearhead From Space" was very good indeed.Liz Shaws' stubborness at first to join UNIT was well brought out.The Doctors reunion with a puzzled Brigadier was very good.The highlight of the book,I think,was near the ending and it's climax where the Autons smashed through the shop windows to occupy London.The invasion itself was taken into more detail in the book,with details of how even the Government reacted.This is one advantage the book has over the TV series.

'DOCTOR WHO AND THE CAVE MONSTERS'by Malcolm Hulke.

As before,the cover illustration was quite good,but the other drawings inside weren't too hot,but I think they were better than those mentioned above. I did like,though,the map of the research centre complex.The Prologue was well done, setting the scene for an average story.In my opinion,Chapter 8 "Into An Alien World",was the best,with it being written from Morka's point of view.As I said, the story itself was average,which was hardly surprising as the TV series was run-of-the-mill too,but the ending was good with the Doctor's dissapproval of the caves being blown up.One last word for these two introduction books,why did Tandem bother to change the titles?"Spearhead from Space" and "The Silurians" seems okay to me!

DR. WHO & THE DOOMSDAY WEAPON
THE DAY OF THE DALEKS

OUT NOW! TWO NEW TITLES FROM TANDEM! REVIEWED NEXT ISSUE! 25p per COPY! OUT NOW!

THE MAG RETURNS SOON

YES,IT's TRUE,TIMELORDS!,

DWFC MAG will be back at the end of May/the beginning of June,better than ever with new features and old favourites! The first issue will mark the beginning of the Colden Age of Doctor Who with an article called "GENESIS" heralding the return of one of the best loved series the Mag has seen! I'll keep you in suspense as to what it is. New series' include "TALKABOUT",with interviews with the Doctor himself,and his companion,Sarah-Jane Smith alais Liz Sladen. "THE COMING OF THE REVELASIANS" will continue,after which "WAR AGAINST THE PLANET SKARO" will see the Doctor and Sarah-Jane,traversing the Universe to find the planet of the Daleks,meeting old enemies on the way! Then,news about TOM BAKER, the NEW Doctor Who! "REPORT" returns with more news about coming series and the making of new Dr Who series,going into more depth than ever before!

Now that that exciting peice of news is over,another bulletin to interest all members of the DWFC Library! New envelopes have arrived and the Library is back in full swing! No need to send envelopes now.

A piece of sad news,I'm afraid THE DIMENSIONS OF DR WHO,has had to be cancelled. All stamps will be returned with the first issue of the NEW DWFC MAG!

Now,an appeal to all those of you who have any questions,any questions at all which you are not sure about,concerning the Daleks,Cybermen,Ice Warriors or any of the other monsters which have intrigued or frightened you out of your wits!Send them to me,I'll print the answers in another new series starting soon.The first subject:THE DALEKS. If you have any queries on the Dalek City,Emperor,how they move,talk,reproduce,kill,anything,then send your letters to me: "THINGCHECK",DWFC, c/o Keith Miller,109 Moredun Park Road,Edinburgh EH17 7HJ.

Well,Timelord,I guess that's about it for now.When I see you again,it'll be in the new format.Keep your letters coming,especially those for Thingcheck.Okay?

Seeyasoon,

KEITH.

031- 225 - 2433

BRITISH BROADCASTING CORPORATION
TELEVISION CENTRE WOOD LANE LONDON W12 7RJ
TELEPHONE 01-743 8000 CABLES: TELECASTS LONDONPS4
TELEGRAMS: TELECASTS LONDON TELEX TELEX: 22182

5th January 1974

Dear Keith,

No recordings on these dates I'm afraid. Am going away on holiday so short letter as I want to get things done.

Love

Sarah

DWFC

NUMBER 19 JANUARY 1974 D.W.F.C.

INTO OUR THIRD YEAR!

And so as we say hello to 1974,let's take a look back at the past year and see what the Year of the Doctor brought us.

The beginning of '73 saw the return of all three doctors in the spectacular adventure of the same name.Many of you, I know,herald this as being the best story for quite some time.The magazine, then "DWFC Monthly",celebrated the story by printing a special issue detailing the Making of the Three Doctors.

At the same time in London,the BBC TV Special Effects Exhibition brought onto view many of the monsters and sets from the programme including the Daleks,Ogrons Sea Devils,Axons and their spaceship Axos with Skybase,the Tardis and Liz 49.

The most unusual thing to happen,perhaps was the theft of the Daleks from the diffrent department stores around London.

Next came the story "When Daleks Ruled the Earth" which many members said was the best story the DWFC have yet printed.

Then came the big move for the DWFC when it went bi-monthly.This gave a wider scope to the events that the magazine could cover and gave space for special features like "Dr Who Data" and "Dr Who People".

Then during the Summer Holidays came the "Dr Who Holiday Special",the giant spectacular "Day of the Daleks" on TV, the publication of the three Dr Who books the publication of the Radio Times "Dr Who Special" and then the other TV giant "The Green Death".

All in all,it has been a very,very exciting year to celebrate the Doctors' birthday,and let's hope 1974 is a repeat performance!

NEW SERIES REVIEW

THE TIME WARRIOR
by Robert Holmes

Oh,dear,not a very good series to start off the new Tv series or this third series of Review.

Taking the story episode by episode, the first installment started off badly with the terrible effect of the space-ship falling to Earth as seen from Irongrons castle.However,when Irongrons' small party of men found the ship in the forest,it did look impressive.

Meanwhile,I found Sarah-Jane Smith very promising as the Doctors new assistant.Her acting was very good,showing she has a mind of her own,unlike Jo who tended to just follow the Doctor.I was rather disappointed with the names of the scientists in the Research Centre, including Matthew Dinkle and what sounded to me like a joke from Morcambe and Wise, Rubeish.I did like the proton particle detector and at last,they've brought back the key to the Tardis.Adds a touch of safety to the Ship.At the end of episode one when Linx removed his helmet, I thought the make-up looked terrible, but once I could see him better in part two,it did look rather good.

Sarahs' reluctance to admit she had been transported back in time was well handled.It seems TV Actions statement that the Doctor came from a planet called Gallifrey was true after all.

Episode three wasn't too bad and I liked the effect of the lightning bolts when the Doctor tried to break away from the control panel at which Linx had imprisoned him.

Undoubtedly,the last episode was the best one of all,mainly because it was the end,I think,but the last fifteen minutes were great,where Linx was shot at the back of his neck,the Doctor and Sarah escaping by that fantastic swing from the balcony to the door,and lastly the explosion of Irongrons castle.

Overall,I thought it was an average adventure,but let's hope things pick up before next issue when I review INVASION OF THE DINOSAURS.

NEW SERIES:NEW SERIES:NEW SERIES:NEW SER

BOOK REVIEW

This year is going to be one when there will many Dr Who Publications out on the bookstalls, therefore a new series starts this month and will continue through the year, looking at new books and magazines! This month: THE RADIO TIMES DR WHO SPECIAL

Overall, this publication was a great tribute to the Doctor on his tenth birthday, with it's fine layout and colour photography.

The cover photograph was very good, but didn't seem to balance itself out, somehow, perhaps because of the blue triangle at the right hand side.

The contents pages gave a sneak preview of the new titles and what a work of art they are (see REVIEW). It's good to have a photographic record of them.

The interviews with the three Doctors was fascinating, giving their views of the programme as it grew up. The one thing that surprised most of you, by your letters is that Jon Pertwee loathes the Daleks. A very surprising comment.

Then came the records of the History of Dr Who from the beginning, with the super photographs from past adventures. There were, however, quite a few mistakes with the titles, and I'll attempt to correct them now. The very first adventure had no title at all, and so it had to have a name so the editors called it "UNEARTHLY CHILD" This was the first episodes name. Next, "THE DEAD PLANET" was originally called "THE MUTANTS" and the two episodes afterwards had no names collectively, and so they were called "THE EDGE OF DESTRUCTION and "THE BRINK OF DISASTER". "THE ROOF OF THE WORLD" was, again, the first episode, but the adventure itself was called "DR WHO AND MARCO POLO". "THE SEA OF DEATH" was the first episode of "THE KEYS OF MARINUS" and "TEMPLE OF EVIL" the first episode of "DR WHO AND THE AZTECS", with "STRANGERS IN SPACE" originally titled "DR WHO AND THE SENSORITES". "A LAND OF FEAR" was "REIGN OF TERROR" and at last they got one right with "PLANET OF THE GIANTS". But back the first episodes with "WORLDS END" which was originally "THE DALEK INVASION OF EARTH". "THE POWERFULL ENEMY" was "DR WHO AND THE RESCUE" with "THE SLAVE TRADERS" ebing called "DR WHO AND THE ROMANS". "THE WEB PLANET" was correctly titled, but "THE LION" was called "DR WHO AND THE CRUSADES" "THE SPACE MUSEUM" was fine, but the "EXECUTIONERS" was called "THE CHASE". "THE WATCHER" was "THE TIME MEDDLER" and "400 DAWNS" was "GALAXY 4". "MISSION TO THE UNKNOWN WAS correct, but "TEMPLE OF SECRETS" was once "THE MYTH MAKERS". Next came "THE DALEK MASTERPLAN", the original name for "THE NIGHTMARE BEGINS", with "WAR OF GOD" originally being called "THE MASSACRE OF BARTHOLOMEW." "THE STEEL SKY" was DR WHO AND THE ARK", but they got the next one right, "THE CELESTIAL TOYMAKER". Returning to the mistakes, "A HOLIDAY FOR THE DR" was originally televised as "DR WHO AND THE GUNFIGHTERS" which, I'm glad to say, is the final mistake. All the others were corredt. Besides these, it was a very good summary of the the Doctors adventures, and the photographs made it even more interesting.

In between these "revision" pages were the articles about the Doctors companions which was amusing, sad and nostalgic and made excellent reading.

The interview with Terry Nation was something I had hoped for for ages. It was great to see what he had to say about his own creations and the programme.

Then came his story "WE ARE THE DALEKS" which was well written, but I think the Radio Times printers must have thought we are all short sighted or something due to the size of the printing, but nevertheless, a very good story, even although I had guessed the ending at about the second last page. The illustrations I didn't like at first, and now I'm crazy about them. It seems they grow on you.

"HOW TO BUILD A DALEK" was a good blueprint as to how to contruct one of your favourite monsters, but the price would be too much for anyone to attempt individuallym I think. Still, if anyone has a school working on one, I would like to hear from them if possible.

Finally, we come to the dossiers on the "Behind-the-scenes" people, which took up where "Dr Who People" left off but I would have liked to see a brief interview with Barry Letts and Terrance Dicks, instead of that minute paragraph at the beginning on the contents page.

And so, the great event is over. The Dr is ten and I'm glad I've got this souvenir to remind me that 1973 was indeed THE YEAR OF THE DOCTOR.

OUT NOW

"DR WHO AND THE AUTON INVASION"

TWO SUPER NEW TITLES to start off a terrific NEW series of Dr Who Paperbacks. In your bookshops now! Published by Tandem Books.

"DR WHO AND THE CAVE MONSTER"

25p each

These two books will be the subjects for next months BOOK REVIEW!

BEGINS THIS MONTH!FIRST LETTER IN A SUPER NEW SERIES!

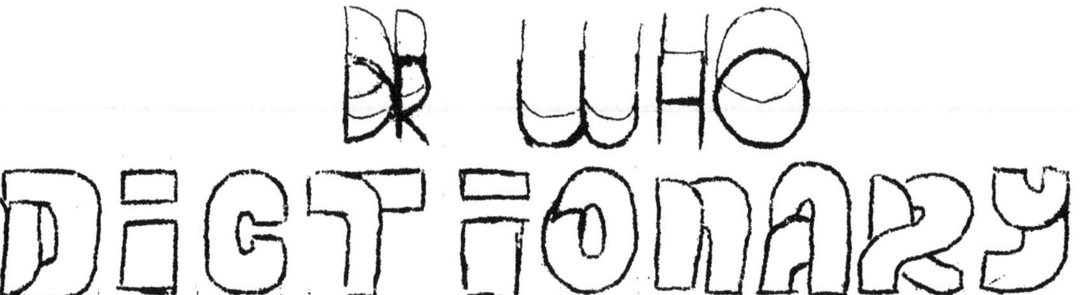

ADJUDICATOR-A Judge of the future who deals with inter-planetary troubles.

AGGEDOR - Large ape-like monster originating from the planet Peladon where it is the royal creature.

ALPHA CENTAURI - Planet which is one quarter of the Galactic Federation and name given to their delegate.

ALYDON - Leading Thal in the Dalek war on Skaro .

ANIMUS - Name given to an alien intelligence that controlled the ant-like Zarbi on their planet of Vortis.

ANTI-MATTER - A black hole in space where everything has a double but is reversed in it's structure. An object from either world cannot come into contact with it's counterpart,becuase if they do,it would result in a tremendous explosion.

ARCTURUS - Another delegate of the Galactic Federation.Small,rectangular robot which transports a tiny being which is no bigger than a clenched fist.

ARIDIANS - Tall,bronzed people of the planet Aridius who wear the skins of the Mire Beast which scourges their nation.

ARIDIUS - The planet,as it's name implies is one vast desert,caused when the worlds double suns moved closer to its surface and evaporated the seas.The inhabitants moved underground and sledom venture into the daylight.

ARK - Huge spaceship used for transporting humans to Refusis when the Earth finally disintegrated.

ATLANTIS - City beneath the sea where a mad Professor tried to drain away the worlds sea.

ATLANTIS - Classical city and home of the crystal of Kronos.

AUTON - Android form of an alien,disembodied intelligence which work to the orders of the Nestenes.

AXONITE - Material of living tissue which has the ability to duplicate any object or material fed into it.

AXONS - People or creatures of Axos who can take on any form to hide their own hideous features.

AXOS - Spaceship made up from the living material Axonite which provides power for the Chameleon-like powers of it's people.

AZAL - The fallen angel and last of the inhabitants of Daemos,capable of great power but they can use it unwisely.

BATTLE CRUISER-Spaceship used during and after the Draconian war.

BEN-Companion of the Doctor,sailor and adventurer with a short temper and a strong mind.

BENTON - Sergeant of UNIT whom the Doctor first met in a skirmish with the Yeti, then again with the Cybermen and has become one of the Doctors helpers.

BESSIE - Yellow T-Ford which the Doctor chose as his means of transport when he was exiled to Earth.

BLACK DALEK - Second in command of an invasion fleet,it is an all black Dalek shell or a blue shell with black dome.

BLACK HOLE - Area of anti-matter where nothing is meant to exist except a point of singularity.Also a power source for the Time Lords planet Gallifrey.

BOK- Servant of Azal and the Master,it is a small,evil featured gargoyle which can summon up enough energy to destroy and defend itself,but it relies upon it's frightful appearance as a defence.

BOSS - Biologic Organic Systems Supervisor.A huge computer which linked itself to a human brain,Stevens,and planned to take over the world for it's own sake and for the sake of "production" despite the terrific pollution it was causing with the Green Death.

Part Two of this new series,next month

JON PERTWEE as

in

"THE COMING OF THE REVELASIANS"

Chapter 1

The streets of London were quiet and dimly lit as somewhere,a clock chimed out midnight.Paula Martin shivered as the cold night air swept over her and her companion.Richard Warrington placed a comforting arm about her shoulders as she looked up into the night sky.A tiny streak of light scratched a white line across the blue ceiling of night and Paula whispered

"Look...a shooting star.Make a wish."

Rick Warrington closed his eyes and smiled when suddenly,a tremendous crash shook the very ground they stood upon.It echoed about them for a few moments then died into the night.

"What...what was that?"stuttered the girl.

"I don't know...it seemed to come from the next opening.You wait here and I'll run on ahead..."

"I want to come with you."

"Stay here!"ordered Rick as he sped up the street and skidded to a halt at the corner.

There,he saw a taxi,halfhidden in one of the big stores windows,while sprawled across the road was a jack-knifed lorry, it's wheels spinning furiously as it lay on it's side,pumping petrol out of it's gashed tank which oozed out over the road and down into the sewers.The driver of the lorry opened his door upwards and managed to climb out with the aid of the taxi driver who seemed to have a cut on his forehead.

Rick shook himself and darted back to Paula who waited anxiously to hear the news.

"Well?"

"A pile up in the middle of the road..." panted the man,"...drivers seem to be okay...don't think they had anybody with them.We'd better get to a phone quick. There's petrol all over the place and it could go up at any moment..."

"Where's the nearest telephone box around here?"

"Don't know...we'd better just scout around."

The duo walked along the pavement again, past the accident where a few people had gathered.Rick tapped one on the shoulder.

"'Scuse me,but do you know where the nearest telephone box is?"

The little man swung round and pointed further up the street.

"Sure,mate.Saw one of 'em old police boxes up the road there...don't know if it'll be workin' though..."

"Can but try.Thanks.Come on Paula."

Rick and the girl set off up the road, the cold wind blowing Paulas' blonde hair across her face.

"Look,there it is..."said Rick,pointing to a blue box positioned in the recess of the wall of a bank.

Taking Ricks arm,the two hurried over to the police box and pushed open the doors.A blinding light hurt their eyes at first,but then it died down to the light of a sunny day,and revealing a huge control room,the walls pitted with huge circles in a regular pattern,broken by a wall of three foot squares and a TV scanner.In the centre of the room a six sided control panel with a cylinder of glass in the middle which housed delecate components,glowed with a bluish tinge.A figure could be behind the control panel,looking down and adjusting some of the instruments.

"Sarah,I thought were never going to get he..."

The Doctor looked up and stopped in mid-sentence.

"Oh,no..."he gasped.

The Time Lord pressed the control stud for the door mechanism and they hummed to a close.

"What on earth are you doing here?"he asked.

Paula smiled a nervous grin.

"Sorry,we thought it was a real police box...not an entrance to your..eh..house!"

The Doctor decided to go along with her explanation and added:

"That's all right,my dear.Perfectly natural,I assure you..."

Just then,the doors hummed open again and Sarah-Jane Smith rushed in.

"Doctor,there's been an accident...oh, hello.Sorry.Didn't know you had company."

Sarah gave the Doctor a questioning

glance.

"Could we use your telephone,please.As your friend said,there's been an accident and there's danger of fire..."

The Doctor returned to the control console and drew up the microphone to his lips.

"UNIT H.Q...UNIT H.Q...This is the Doctor here."

A voice crackled over some unseen loudspeaker.

"Go ahead,Doctor."

"There's been an accident near co-ordinate 320 590.Please notify the police and the necessary authorities."

"Will do."

There was a click then all was silent. Suddenly a piercing note cut the air and the Doctor dashed round to another panel.

"The Time Warp circuits!"he yelped stabbing at the door control.

They swung to a close and Sarah moved round to the Doctor.

"What are they doing here,Doctor.I thought you didn't like too many people knowing about this Tardis of yours."she whispered.

"Oh,don't bother me just now...if the temperature doesn't rise soon,then the safety self-operating soldering operation of the circuits won't function and blow the lot!"

"Oh..."

"So be a good girl and explain to them will you?"

"Fetch,doggy."mumbled Sarah.

She crossed over to find Paula looking at her rather nervously in Ricks arms.

"Well,now that the police are informed I think we'll be on our way.Do you think you could ask your friend to open the doors?"asked Rick.

"Well,it's a bit difficult at the moment.You see,he's conducting some kind of experiment at the moment,and if he opens the doors,it'll ruin it completely."

"Oh..."squealed Paula,looking a little frightened.

Sarah gave her a reassuring smile then disappeared into the clothing section of the Tardis to change.

"I wish we could be rid of this place." said Paula,"There's something not quite right about it.Is there way out of here?"

"Let's talk to this Doctor chap."

Rick left Paula and joined the Doctor who was observing the experiment through a raised section of the control panel.

"Doctor..."

"Mmm?"

The Time Lord didn't look up.

"Doctor,we can't stay any longer.Thanks for everything,but could you open the doors now?"

The Doctor straightened up.

"My dear chap,I thought that Sarah explained everything to you.The soldering has begun and I can't open the doors until it has finished as the reduction in temperature will ruin the lot of it. I'll open the doors in about an hours time..."

"An hour!"exclaimed Rick looking alarmingly at Paula.

"Yes,an hour!"retorted the Doctor,"now you really must excuse me."

Saying this,the Doctor returned to his work.Rick returned to Paula and said

"I'm not sticking around here for an hour.Don't worry.I think I can remember the door switch..."

Rick returned to the control panel, which was hidden from the view of the Doctor.He could remember it was a black control,but there black buttons and levers dotted over the entire panel.

"The others are probably only light switches or channel selectors..."Rick thought to himself.

He stabbed at three of the black buttons and pulled down on a set of levers.The Time Rotor suddenly burst into life, rising and falling as the Doctor suddenly jerked his back straight,glaring at the intruder upon his work.

Outside,the light on top of the box flashed with regular pulses until the box and light faded into nothing...or rather into somewhere else.

"You young fool!"shouted the Doctor as the sound of dematerialisation died away.

He pushed Rick out of the way and began resetting the controls,but they jerked to a halt.

"Blast!Solder has melted into the dematerialization circuits.Why couldn't you leave things alone?!"

Sarah-Jane appeared at the door of the annexe section of the Ship.

"Doctor?Where are we going?Why have we taken off?"she asked.

"I..I was only trying to get out..." stuttered Rick.

"What's happening?"screamed Paula,"What do you mean we've taken off?"

"You'll soon see,my dear.We're landing now...but I've no idea where."

The Tardis reformed itself...in the recess in the wall of a bank.The doors cricked open,and the foursome stepped out into strong mid-day sunlight.

"This can't be...it's past midnight!"

Paula screamed and her outburst echoed down the deserted streets.Her companions turned and saw a fleet of five saucer-like machines glide towards them,suspended four feet in the air,transporting a large metal dome,devoid of features,apart from a thin slit in the metal,through which alien and hostile eyes studied them intently!

DATA

D.W.F.C.,
c/o Keith Miller,
109 Moredun Pk Rd.,
Edinburgh
EH17 7HJ

FACT SHEET — **DALEK TIME-SCALE** — No.Four

1867-P.T.-Daleks attracted to Earth to find the Dalek Factor
1967-P.T.-Daleks capture Dr Who's Tardis
1972-J.P.-Daleks try to steady the course of time
2020-P.T.-Daleks attempt to wipe out Earth colony on Vulcan
2164-W.H.-Daleks rule Earth but are destroyed
2300-J.P.-Daleks rule but are stopped by change of events
3000-W.H.-Daleks pursue Tardis in newly built time machines
4000-W.H.-Daleks attempt conquest of universe with Time Destructor
11964-W.H.-Dr Who destroys Daleks on Skaro
12164-J.P.-Daleks prepare invasion force on Spiridon but are stopped
Date unknown-P.T.-Daleks try to implant human factor:Skaro destroyed

Happy New Year,Timelord!,

Before I go any further,may I say a big thankyou to everyone who sent me Christmas cards ,including Barry Davies,Brian Smith,Geoffrey Dunn,David Brown,Richard Lane,David Sandford,Paul Bennet,Donald gottke,John Bradley,John Connors,Stephen,Susan Prakash,Philip,Beverley Manton,Jean Pilbeam,Andrew Veasey and a big thankyou to Tracey for the super Christmas decor!

Now,last issue there was a reminder to all members about the six labels that were to be returned.If you didn't get the labels,not to worry.The magazine will still be delivered.

Speaking about last issue,some of you might not have recieved the Special Edition. If you didn't,then send a sae to me at the address above and I'll get it to you as quick as you can say Linx!

Another reminder about the two super new paperbacks now on sale from Tandem Books at 25p each.First in this new series is "DR WHO AND THE AUTON INVASION" telling the story of the Doctors first few days of exile on Earth,when strange alien life forces arrive on Earth and build ultra-modern,plastic bodies for themselves.Can the Doctor stop them in time?

Second in this pair is "DR WHO AND THE CAVE MONSTERS".The story of the Silurians who emerge from caves in Derbyshire and are determined to take back the planet that the apes who grew into humans have taken from them.Can anyone prevent them?

DO YOU KNOW WHO? Answer Sheet No.4:1)CARNIVAL OF MONSTERS 2)TERROR OF THE AUTONS 3)Cybernetics 4)The Intelligence 5)Galea 6)Salamander 7)a/Bernard Cribbins b/Bernard Bresslaw 8)They are,in fact,father and daughter,Jack and Deborah Watling 9)They were both Time Lords 10)They were once married 11)Wotan was a power mad computer that built War Machines and tried to take over London.12)a/Milton Subotsky b/David Whitaker 13)The Doctor when he was played by William Hartnell.

DR WHO FAN CLUB PAPERBACK LIBRARY:Please,please,please remember to enclose another 3½p stamp for your next book.when returning one which you have read,otherwise your order will have to be cancelled for the remaining titles.I know it's a bit drastic, but it's been a bigger success than I thought it would have been and so all the books are very much in demand.

I hope you all saw "BILLY SMARTS CHILDRENS CIRCUS" on Sunday the sixth of this month with Jon Pertwee starring as Dr Who in the super new Whomobile as it's now called.And talking about starring parts,did you know that Jon starred in the rock opera "TOMMY" a few weeks back?Just another example of his many talents,but of course he would feel at home because the part he played was called "The Doctor".

I've had a few letters from Peter Capaldi in Glasgow saying that members didn't get any chance at all to entre into the club,that is why I am you now,who's stories would you rather read.My own or other members? I'll collect letters together if you would be so kind as to write to me and if the interest is there,then all you budding writers will have your chance.But be warned."The Dr's Drawing Board" had to close down because of lack of interest.

Well,that's it again for another two months.I'm sure the Revelasians will make a big impact on you,so please write and tell me what you've thought of the mag,and anything you care to write to me about,I'll be glad to know.Bye for now! KEITH

Every so often, people would complain that the fanzine was late (which it nearly always was) and Sarah would defend me to the hilt, saying exams come first etc., but a particularly narked parent took me to task in a letter to the BBC, resulting in:

BRITISH BROADCASTING CORPORATION

TELEVISION CENTRE WOOD LANE LONDON W12

TELEPHONE 01-743 8000 TELEGRAMS BROADCASTS LONDON TELEX

CABLES BROADCASTS LONDON-W1 TELEX 22182

16th Jan.

Dear Keith,

Am very sorry but due to the enclosed I'm afraid we are going to have to stop the newsletters for the time being.

Awful blow to you I'm afraid but I think it has to be so

A birthday present from my new best friend! Katy who...?

From one Aquarian to another! Elisabeth Sladen

Your Lucky Stars
by John Naylor

Aquarius
(January 20 to February 18)

Day-by-Day forecast
March 21-September 22
1974

Tandem Books

UNIVERSAL-TANDEM PUBLISHING COMPANY LTD

14 Gloucester Road London SW7 4RD
Telephone 584 8766-7
584 6803-4

Reg. No. 898950 England Reg. Office: 99 Aldwych London WC2B 4JY
VAT Registration No. 238 4691 36

1st February, 1974

Keith Miller, Esq.,
109 Moredun Park Road,
Edinburgh EH17 7HJ

Dear Keith,

Thank you for your recent letter and accompanying newsletter, and before I say anything more, do please ensure that we are on your monthly list for it as from now.

The publication of DOCTOR WHO AND THE AUTON INVASION and DOCTOR WHO AND THE CAVE-MONSTERS has suffered a little delay due to the newsprint shortage, but finished copies are now available and are due for distribution through February. Meanwhile, I have pleasure in enclosing two review copies, and look forward to hear of your reaction to our first originals. I believe that I have previously advised you on forthcoming titles which you will find appended to this letter.

As things stand at the moment, we are likely to have Dr. Who present at the Glasgow Children's Book Show. It has not yet been decided whether or not he will appear on the Book Train from Edinburgh.

By the way, I have put you on the Standing Order list for our DOCTOR WHO books as they are published.

Yours sincerely,

Richard Henwood

Children's Book Editor
TARGET BOOKS

ENC.

Woah! A directive from the big man himself to come down and see him one last time.

Jon Pertwee

4th February, 1974.

Dear Keith,

I am sorry it has taken me so long to reply, but I have been up to my eyes in work recording and rehearsing the new series, making personal appearances, and doing cabaret work, etc.

Enclosed is a photocopy of a press release issued by John Stanley. He, however, is no longer representing me, so please do not write to him in the future on anything that concerns me.

Would you please write to Sarah Newman at Barry Letts office asking her for recording dates, and to arrange a suitable day for you to come along to the studios. Tell her I have asked you to do this. Let me know when you are coming along, so that I may be expecting you.

Thank you so much for the magazine, which I foubd mos t interesting.

Yours sincerely,

115 CASTELNAU LONDON S.W.13

World Distributors *Publishers*

Head Office: P.O. Box 111, 12 Lever Street, Manchester M60 1TS
Telephone: 061-228 3841 *Telex:* 66 8609 *Cables:* Sydpem, Manchester
London Office: 36 Great Russell Street, WC1B 3PP. *Telephone:* 01-636 5544/9476

18th February 1974

Keith Miller Esq
109 Moredun Park Road
Edinburgh
EH17 7HJ

Dear Mr Miller

Thank you for your letter, received today. No decision has yet been reached as to whether we shall be publishing another edition of the Dr Who Annual. If we need any material I will contact you again.

Yours sincerely

M Broadley

Mae Broadley BA (Mrs)
Editor

WORLD DISTRIBUTORS (Manchester) LTD. A member of the Marshall, Morgan & Scott Group
Registered in England No. 468030. Registered Office: 12 Lever Street, Manchester M60 1TS.

BRITISH BROADCASTING CORPORATION

TELEVISION CENTRE WOOD LANE LONDON W12 7RJ

TELEPHONE 01-743 8000 CABLES: TELECASTS LONDONPS4

TELEGRAMS: TELECASTS LONDON TELEX TELEX: 22182

20th Feb.1974

Dear Keith,

Could you come up on 17th April to Tel. Centre at about 1245 hours and write and tell Jon so that he can meet you there. There will be several other people there too.

all love

Sarah

BRITISH BROADCASTING CORPORATION

TELEVISION CENTRE WOOD LANE LONDON W12 7RJ

TELEPHONE 01-743 8000 CABLES: TELECASTS LONDONPS4

TELEGRAMS: TELECASTS LONDON TELEX TELEX: 22182

28th March 1974

Dear Keith,

Thank you for your letter. Tom Baker is very busy at the moment. I'expect you will hear something soon. Send you more envelopes. I'll meet you in Reception at 1215 if that's okay, at Television centre on the 17th. I've got to organise a monster being transported earlier so won't be able to make it earlier. I think Stewart Money already knows you are coming!

Goodbye, Jon Pertwee...
Planet of the Spiders Set Report

I braved the coach journey to Victoria and arrived in London on the morning of Wednesday April 17, but thankfully it was breaking into Spring, so my time-wasting spent in Kensington Gardens was lovely, and not sub-zero like my last visit.

I got my taxi at mid-day to the TV Centre, and was surprised when the taxi slowed down at the security gate and the security man looked at me and then just waved me through. None of the usual "having to prove I was me"! I wondered who he thought I was... I remembered to tip the taxi driver this time, so I escaped unscathed and with Mum still married to my Dad, and Sarah was waiting for me in Reception. She was chatting to Richard Franklin who played Mike Yates. There was a rushed introduction, but Richard was still filming and hurried away.

"Recording has started early on this one, Keith, so I'll have to leave you here for a while," said Sarah, "But I'll tell Jon you're here..."

So I sat in the Reception foyer and watched as the world filed past, including chat-show host Michael Parkinson, journalist and "Film Night" presenter Philip Jenkinson, and of course the ubiquitous Ronnie Barker - did the man live in this building?! This was the third time!

Jon made a very theatrical entrance into the foyer and warmly shook my hand. He was in full Doctor gear and cut a fair dash. "We're all recording just now, Keith. Are you hungry? Why don't you get something to eat in the Restaurant. Do you know the way?" I replied that I did, but I got lost and ended up having to ask the way. It wasn't the first, nor the last time I did that. A circular building is very confusing.

In the Restaurant, I found my fellow Who fans were already there and eating, Stu Money and John Hudson looked sheepishly at me. I said hello to Brian Smith who supplied the telesnaps for me to copy in the club magazine. Brian had visited me at home in Edinburgh as he didn't stay too far away from me in Fife, so I chatted to him for a while. There was another fan I hadn't met before, a ginger-haired girl called Alexandra. She was some kind of student, doing a theatrical subject at college. Nice girl, very excited to be there.

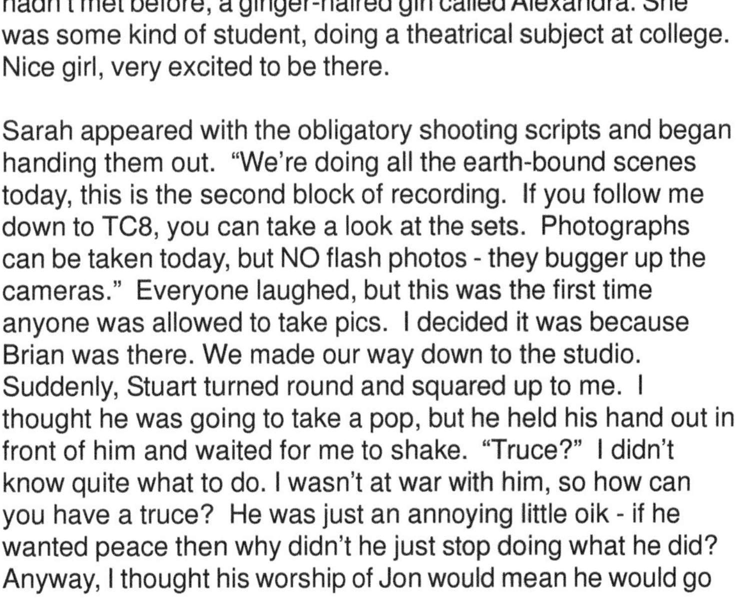

Sarah appeared with the obligatory shooting scripts and began handing them out. "We're doing all the earth-bound scenes today, this is the second block of recording. If you follow me down to TC8, you can take a look at the sets. Photographs can be taken today, but NO flash photos - they bugger up the cameras." Everyone laughed, but this was the first time anyone was allowed to take pics. I decided it was because Brian was there. We made our way down to the studio. Suddenly, Stuart turned round and squared up to me. I thought he was going to take a pop, but he held his hand out in front of him and waited for me to shake. "Truce?" I didn't know quite what to do. I wasn't at war with him, so how can you have a truce? He was just an annoying little oik - if he wanted peace then why didn't he just stop doing what he did? Anyway, I thought his worship of Jon would mean he would go with him.... But in the meantime, I decided there was nothing to lose so I shook his hand. Stu smiled, but behind his back, John Hudson looked at me with barely concealed distaste, but to be fair, I think that's just how his face fell naturally. Poor soul. When we entered the studio, the air was filled with men chanting, "om mani padme hum" very loudly, whilst in the corner of the studio, a large yellow-screen area had been set up, with men on step-ladders manipulating giant spiders, hanging from control bars on thin lengths of wire. Jon appeared and greeted us with a stage whisper. "We'll get together in my dressing room in about an hours time, but in the meantime, if you could stay behind the cameras and not take any photographs when the cameras are turning. If you have to have a conversation, make it quiet. I'll see you soon." And with that he disappeared back on set.

I spotted something familiar and looked about for Brian. I whispered for him to follow me round the back of some flats (scenery), where the Tardis police box stood. It wasn't until 2010 that I was reading DWM - an article about the Tardis police box prop - that I found out that this was the original box. The one that took Ian and Barbara out among the stars. If I knew that then, I probably would've cried. We waited for a break in filming, then Brian took a shot of me stepping out of the box, then I took the camera and took one of Brian. This was access all areas indeed - I was so used to being cooped up in that little box upstairs. I watched as filming progressed, then spotted Lis Sladen standing on her own to one side. I went over and introduced myself. "Jon said you were coming," said Lis, "Very nice to meet you." I'll be honest and tell you I wasn't a Sarah Jane Smith fan up to that point. My heart still lay with Jo Grant and time hadn't healed the wound of her going, but by the time the day was out, Lis Sladen had totally turned that opinion around. Very easy to talk to, Lis and I chatted about the show, theatre, film, lighting techniques, coach trips and cooking. I had found talking to show biz folks a bit hard work, but here was a woman I could chat to quite normally, and from that moment on, Lis Sladen was to become my rock, a shoulder to cry on as stress began to mount, especially when the Doctor Who family broke up and Philip Hinchcliffe took the reigns. But I'm getting ahead of myself.

I was having such a nice time with Lis, I was quite peeved when Brian came up and said, "Jon's ready for us now. He's taking us down to his dressing room." Lis picked up I was a little annoyed and hugged my arm. "I'll see you later. We'll have a coffee."

We crowded into Jon's dressing room with much shuffling about as stools were ferried in for us to sit down.

Between scenes, there were occasional tea-breaks that everyone takes advantage of and heads out the studio where the Mrs Mop tea ladies were. However, I took this opportunity to get a closer look at the Mummerset monestary set. I had managed to get myself a steady girlfriend by this time - Wendy - who was a practising Buddhist (but not a Who fan). However, she was well impressed when I told her how accurate and detailed the set was, with its mandalas, cotton scarves and so on. She was particularly impressed when I told her I spun a drum-like affair with ribbons tied to it. This was a prayer wheel apparently, each ribbon holding a prayer or loving thought which was spread each time the drum was spun.

Anyway, I then saw Kan Po, actor George McCormack, sitting in a high backed chair, watching me. He smiled. "Did I hear a Scottish accent earlier, young man?" he quietly asked. "Aye, ye did that," I replied. "Are you not having tea?" He shook his head. I sat down on the floor beside his chair. I noticed he had make-up on to make him seem even older than he already was.

"Where are you from?" he asked. "Edinburgh", I replied. "Really?" he said, obviously delighted, "I was brought up in Edinburgh. I was born in Stonehaven - in 1907, a long time ago - but brought up in Edinburgh. Do you know Infirmary Street?" "Know it, I work there!" I replied. I had a job in a bookseller. "You work in James Thin?! I used to be in there every weekend with my pocket money!"

We spent a delightful break as he regaled me with stories of old Edinburgh, and as he went on, I suddenly realized I was sitting at the feet of the Doctor's mentor, "the old man who lived half way up a mountainside." Twas a very nice feeling indeed, and he was a very sweet, erudite old chap.

JP: Got the latest batch of photographs, Brian. Well done, you've really got that down to a fine art now, haven't you? Whose got a match, anybody?"

I had taken up the dreaded weed and was cock-a-hoop I had one up on Money and Hudson!

KM: Yes, I've got one.

JP: Have you? Oh, well done. (sparks up). If we've got any chatting to do on tape recorders or what have you, let's do that now, eh? Let's get all the mics up and going at the same time. Is everyone okay for sound?

SM: When do you open in your new play, and what's it about?

JP: The new play that I'm doing is a play under Ray Cooney's management. Ray Cooney's the actor and playwright - he used to write a lot of plays with John Chapman. He did *Not Now Darling, Move Over Mrs Markham* and those sorts of plays, so they were very successful comedies, and it was a play that originally went out on the road once before under the very different title of *That Was No Lady, That Was My Husband*, so it has been around some of your areas before, with Francis Matthews playing the lead, but its now been rejigged and rewritten and is now called The Breadwinner, and I start my tour at the end of July. I start rehearsing the 8th of July. I think we open in Norwich, we go to Leeds, Liverpool, Preston, Brighton, Richmond, Bournemouth - I think it may have been up in Edinburgh once before, so we might miss you, Keith. So I don't know if we're going to Scotland with it.

I tried to look as disappointed as I could.

SM: When do you finish here with Doctor Who?

JP: My last two recordings I finish on May 3rd, though I have already filmed the change-over between Tom Baker and I - we did that previously to help Tom out.

KM: How are you going to change over? Is it going to be the same as the previous one?

JP: No, not really. I go to face my fear. Remember I gave Katy, Jo Grant, the crystal from Metebelis 3? Well she sends it back to me, it had been causing her lots of problems up the Amazon on her expedition. She sends it back to me, it's then nicked from me and we find out it is desired by the Great One, the queen of the Spiders, and I have to return it to Metebelis 3 and in doing so, I lose my present life. I die, but I go on forever being a Time Lord and I'm taken over by Tom.

SM: How does the change-over occur - the actual effect?

JP: Well, its done by laying Tom down alongside of me, in exactly the same position. They take a picture of me, then they overlap his camera and they say "Move up a bit - more sideways a bit" until we're absolutely overlapping, then they just fade from My camera to the other camera.

SM: That was the same as William Hartnell's...

JP: Was it? I can't remember that far back...

SM: Is it in the Tardis, this change-over?

JP: No, I fall out of the Tardis. The Brigadier and Lis think I've gone and will never came back, but the Brig says "Don't be so stupid, he's likely to come back at any moment and when he does he'll probably look like somebody completely different. I've seen it happen before!" (Laughs) And she says "Well, that's no consolation, he's the one I was fond of..." and he says "you mustn't worry too much", then bang, the Tardis appears, and I fall out of the Tardis, and then have a little dying speech and I'm off!

SM: You said you had a lot of chase sequences in this one...

JP: Yes, there's a really magnificent chase sequence with Barry giving me my head once again with my love of gadgetry. We had a speedboat chase, where I chase a high powered speedboat, which I was so impressed with I have now bought. A lovely 16ft powerboat that does 40mph, which I being rebuilt and taken out to Ibiza. I chase it in a hovercraft, then we have the Whomobile in it, my new space car, that's in the chase too, and Bessie and all sorts of things.

KM: So you're not going to peter out then - you're going in a blaze of glory!

JP: A blaze of glory, yes! We've also got gyrocopters - when we were making the picture, the gyrocopter crashed!

KM: With you in it?

JP: No, without me in it, thankfully. The pilot was flying it and he started the prop up - the pusher prop - as it's a gyrocopter as opposed to a helicopter, and it took off with him sitting on the end and he managed to throw himself clear and the thing went charging along on its own and tipped up and wrote it off. So one of our shots looks very peculiar with a bent rotor-arm.

SM: Have you got any favourite Doctor Who stories over the past five years?

JP: Yes, undoubtedly the one we did at Marlborough, *The Daemons.* The other one was the one with the Drashigs, where we were in the ship going round and round, *The Carnival of Monsters,* which I liked very much indeed. *The Green Death* I liked although it was a sad one to do.

SM: How much say do you actually have in the script? If there were lines that you don't like, have you the right...

JP: Oh, absolutely. They never make me say things I adamantly wont say. It depends on the writers. Certain writers... The writer of this one, *Planet of the Spiders*, I like very much the way he writes. Barry has a lot to do with this one - he's directing as well - and I just went straight through and didn't alter a line. Others I alter a great deal. I don't like a lot of scientific jargon, I never have done. 'Cause if I don't know what I'm talking about I'm sure the viewers won't either.

JH: Have you any films in mind for when you finish?

JP: I haven't got time, unfortunately, John. Because my commitment... it is John, isn't it?

JH: Yes.

JP: Sorry but you gave me a dirty look!

Even JP has noticed! Poor soul.

JP: Soon as I've finished this I'm off to Ibiza for six weeks for a rest and see if I can get my back straightened out a bit. I have a man out there who hopes to perform some miracles on it. Then I come back and do a series for Thames Television called Whodunnit?, which is a bit of an unfortunate title. (Laughs) I'm certain the press are going to take that to task pretty quickly. I'm doing that for six weeks, overlapping my three week rehearsal period. With maybe some more later in the year, and then I go out in the play, so I won't have any time for films at all.

JH: You were in a horror film a few years ago...

JP: Yes, *The House That Dripped Blood*, because it happened to fit in just right, but these rarely fit in their shooting schedules. They usually overlap. I was doing Doctor Who at the same time.

SM: We've read a lot of contradictory reports about how you got the part of the Doctor, we would like to know how it actually happened.

JP: It actually happened when Tenniel Evans, who plays Taffy Goldstein in *The Navy Lark* with me said "Why don't you put yourself up for Doctor Who?" and I said "Why, what's wrong with Patrick Troughton?" and he said "He's leaving I hear". So I rang my agent and said "I've got a silly thing to suggest - I can't think why they'd want an eccentric comic to play Doctor Who, but they might do", and he thought it was as silly an idea as I thought it was. "But I'll do it if you like" and so he rang up and spoke to the then producers, Peter Sherwin and Derrick Briant, and said "I've got a suggestion for Doctor Who". They said "Who's that?" and he said "Jon Pertwee." And there was sort of a pause at the other end and he said "Okay forget it..." "No, no" they said, "There's something rather interesting here, do you mind if I read you my short-list?" He said the first name on the list was Fred Flange or somebody and the second name was Jon Pertwee. They had thought of me to play Doctor Who some four years previously. Which I never knew at all. It was a complete accident.

Once I got the part I said, "How do you want me to play it?" And they said "As Jon Pertwee." But I said "Who's Jon Pertwee?" I had never played myself in anything - I've always hidden under a green umbrella. And even in plays like *There's A Girl In My Soup* I wore glasses...

KM: If they ever have story called The Four Doctors, would you return?

JP: We got away with The Three Doctors but I don't think we'd get away with it again. Poor old Bill is not well enough to do it any more. We had to shoot him on film on the last one and put it through the monitors. I suppose it's possible. But because I'm leaving now doesn't necessarily mean I'm leaving forever. The great joy of Doctor Who of course is you can always come back. That is, if they want me. And that is if I want to do it. At the moment, I feel I want to go away and do new things and tread new ground, but I don't know how I'm going to feel in two or three years time. In two or three years time, maybe nothing else has come up on television, none of the plans I've got - I have some very interesting plans for things I want to do in the future - if they don't happen, I may come back and do another series of Doctor Who and play

it like that with Tom and see if he wants to play it like that..."

There was the sound of collective jaws hitting off the floor...

SM: IN *TV Life*, you said your wife has just had a book published...

JP: Yes, she's here today actually - she's in the Beeb being interviewed on a new afternoon programme. It's a book called *Together.* A novel - her first novel. And she's had a tremendous amount of publicity, you may have seen in the papers. And she was down at HTV in Wales talking about it. She's on air at half past two today, then tomorrow we do *Pebble Mill at One* in Birmingham. We'll talk about it there. It's being published by Hamish Hamilton, one of the best publishers in the country, and she has a cookery book coming out in September as well, which she wrote as an exercise when we were in America when I was doing *A Girl In My Soup* there.

SM: Do you know what's going to happen to Doctor Who next year?

JP: No idea at all - I don't want to know either. I might upset myself. I don't really want to think about that.

SM: But is Lis staying on?

JP: Yes, of course Lis is still in it. And the Brig. And John Levene.

SM: Do you have any favourite locations that you've worked on?

JP: Yes, I think one of my most favourites is the location we did in the last story *Death To The Daleks.* It was a marvellous location which you may have seen. It was a sandpit in Dorset near Lulworth Cove, and it was down about seventy feet from ground levels and it was like the Grand Canyon down there. You remember all those high shots through pinnacles that looked like rock? That was in fact sand - if you leant against it it would fall over - and the rain runs down and makes crags and cracks and rivulets down the sides and looked absolutely marvellous.

JH: Is there anything in particular you liked about *Doctor Who*, anything you enjoyed?

JP: I always enjoyed locations, when they're not too cold. Usually, we're out on location in winter, up to our crotches in mud, which can be a bit irritating. When we were down doing *Colony in Space*, we were in the china clay pits down in Cornwall and that went all over the inside of my car. I didn't realise - I washed the outside but not the inside and when I got back to London, I found the heat off my car had baked all the china clay all over the chassis of the engine block and it cost me £100 to get it all chipped off with hammers and chisels. Tremendous amount of harm. No, I like location work as this is where I get free reign to race motorcycles about and do all my speedboat chasing and things like that. I have this lovely stunt double, Terry Walsh, who's here, you'll be able to speak to him today, he's a very interesting bloke. He and I have got a great working arrangement. He always says to me before I do a stunt that he's meant to do but I won't let him because I want to do it myself, he says, "Alright, governor, but make it look difficult."

It was at this point I noticed Stu and John joined in at the end of Jon's stories, they had obviously heard them numerous times before...

JP: And we've used it as a catch-phrase which caught on as, unlike most stuntmen, he never ever shows his face. You can take a fall that Terry will do - I can't fall because of my back - I'll do everything else, I'll ride the motorbikes, I'll ride the speedboats, I'll do all those things, but I won't actually be thrown, because you can't... you don't know how you're going to land. He can take it, he wears pads, you know - shoulder pads, elbow pads and everything. In fact if you saw Saturday's, I did all my own sword-fighting but when it came to all the bits where he goes over *bang* on the floor, that's Terry.

JH: There was a bit of a bad shot where you could

see it was him.

JP: But only you would notice that. My own family didn't notice it. You mean when I stand like this and he passes in front of camera full face? We could not work it out camera-wise any other way. He kept his head down but you could still see it was him, but only you would notice that. Did you notice anything, Alexandra?

A: Yes.

JP: You did. Well not many people do. My own kids didn't, cause they said "Cor, papa was that you? Taking all these whacks?" and I said "Aw, that's because your papa's brave!" and my wife Ingeborg said " You're very stupid doing that" and we often kid her along, and sometimes she gets frightfully cross with me and I have to bring Terry along to prove it, and say him, "Go on, tell her it wasn't me."

One marvellous one - the one with the daffodil men *Terror of the Autons* - that was one of my favourites, again one of Barry's. I had to jump off a bus when its moving and do a tremendous roll-over fall and nobody could tell that was Terry at all, then I did the last part of the roll on the cut in, and my wife was absolutely convinced it was me and said, "Well no wonder you've got a bad back, you bring it all on yourself!" I had to get Terry along to promise faithfully it was him and not me.

SM: Which story were you doing when you were chosen for *This Is Your Life*?

JP: It was *Colony in Space*. I remember Barry saying, "We've got to do this shot and its very important" - this was a little trailer they were going to show - and there were heaps of things that told me it wasn't true. First of all, they were shooting with OB cameras, which you don't shoot film on. Secondly, BBC had been taped out on the side of the cameras, so I should've realized that had Thames written underneath. Thirdly, Barry was directing instead of the director Mike Briant.

There was a knock on the door and a shy little man with glasses popped his head round the door. It was Jon's dresser with his velvet jacket.

JP: "Come in, Charles. And Barry was directing it like Cecil B DeMille, and I thought "He's overacting a bit" and I never twigged it at all. And he said "Keep looking to the left and when you hear the car draw up, don't turn round. Then Jo says, "What's that over there, Doctor?" and I keep looking, then I heard "Brrrrrmmmm!" and if you watched it you see the eyes slowly going round and I was nearly the first person on air to say a four-letter word. There was Eamonn sitting there like a perishing pixie in

that duffle coat with a hood on - and he's a bit of a goon sometimes, Eamonn - and he's just as likely to come roaring into someone elses shot, "Hello there! How are you?!", and I was just about to say "Eff off!" and then I saw that damn red book in his hand. It was great fun, I enjoyed it tremendously.

I decided to Join Jon in a ciggy and was casually lighting up when I became aware of an ominous silence.

JP: Keith, anything you want to say?

I was taken totally off the hop and just about swallowed my ciggy. I was quite happy to leave the interviewing to Stuart. I desperately wracked my brains and then hit upon:

KM The Whomobile!

I think I shouted that a little too loud, but nevertheless I went on:

KM: Done by two guys from Norwich, was it...?

JP: The Whomobile is my own property - doesn't belong to the BBC at all, its my own property and its designed by me and a chap called Pete Farris and he comes from Nottingham. Its my own car, I go where I want in it and the BBC ask when they want to use it. It won't be in any more Doctor Who's unless I want to lend it to them. And that depends if that's going to help me any by getting it more shown - if I think it will help the situation along, I will loan it to them to get it more coverage on the air. Then it'll probably put the value of the car up. You see it quite a lot in this series.

KM: Were you pleased with the end result? Was it just as you wanted?

JP: Oh, yes. It's magnificent. It handles beautifully - goes at 100mph -sticks to the ground like a limpet. Doesn't shift at all. We had teething trouble with the hatch cover that lifts up - that whole top has been redesigned now, but it's got everything in it. Twin track stereo, television set, telephone,

everything. And it's very comfortable to drive too.

I was on a roll now!

KM: Do you find it draws a lot of attention?

JP: Too much, yes. Cars crash into each other! I don't crash, although the first time I took it out, I ran straight into a motor cyclist who stropped dead in front of me when he saw it. Then a German Volkswagon bus, full of students, pulled up dead and a great big Evening Standard delivery truck ran straight up the arse of it (laughs). This happens all the time, unfortunately, where people leave their cars to have a look then someone shunts them up the back. People say, "I didn't know hovercraft were allowed on the road." because it looks like a hovercraft.

SM: Looking at the clothes there, did you choose your own style?

JP: Yes, I did. It was all done by accident. They asked me what would I like to wear for Doctor Who and I had all sorts of ideas which nobody seemed to be very definite about and then I had an early photocall and they said, "Put something on." I found my grandfather's old Inverness cape, which is a sort of half-cape, and an old smoking jacket I had, and a frilly shirt from Mr Fish, and a few other bits and pieces and I put this on and I appeared in this and they said, "That's marvellous!" and I said "How the hell can we explain it away? Why am I dressed like that?" That was why, when we did the first one, *Spearhead From Space*, when I was in the hospital trying to escape, I went into the doctors dressing room and nicked all the different bits of clothing - I had a coat from there, and something from there, and that old banger car that I had to give back and I said, "I'll only stay on if you promise to get me another car..." and that is how Bessie came in.

KM: You've had a number of costumes, is there any special one you liked?

JP: I had eight or nine changes in all. A lot of them got worn out. A lot of them have disappeared. To strange places. Like my home (laughs). My present dress designer who designs all my costumes, I said to him, "I desperately need a black one...." and he said, "I think we'll have a black one this season!" (laughs)

A: Who are the designers for the show we're seeing today?

JP: Set designer or costume designer?

A: Well, both!

JP: I'll introduce you to them. What's her name, Charles?

C: Rochelle. Rochelle Hudson.

JP: Rochelle Hudson, she's the set designer...

A: Had quite a nice lot of women recently!

JP: Yes we have! And Roland Warne is the costume designer, who is a super guy, a lovely man.

JH: He did the masks for the Exxilons.

JP: Yes, he did. Very good weren't they? Marvellous. They were always popping out and Charles and I were rushing around tucking those Exxilon masks in...

C: Beautiful costumes, though.

JP: Marvellous costumes. They looked good no matter how skew-wiff they were, as long as the camera didn't stick on them for too long. That's why Mike is so good, he keeps moving the camera all the time and not hold on anything too long. Like the Ice Warriors, which I think are awful costumes. If you hold on them, you can see all the flaws on them. You need to be quick, to give an impression. Like on the dinosaur one, which was very good - if it was to be criticised it was they held too long on the models. We hadn't the time to animate. Normally you have a bendy toy and you animate there, and you photograph them there, and you do it together on film. That's how animation is basically done. We didn't. We had to actually move them with wire as they were being filmed. It was alright with the big dino when he turned his head round - that was fine - or when we had that one that came up through the building going "Raaaargh!" - it should've been cut immediately so everything is subliminal. That's much more effective to me and they just held onto them much too long. But their argument was "Well, they cost us so much money to make these models, you know, it seems so silly to throw it all away." Well, my argument is you're not throwing it all away, you're getting a marvellous effect. Hang onto it too long, like Aggedor. You can't hang onto that face of Aggedor, you see old Nick Hobbs peering through the gullet to see where he is (laughs). You can see his eyes shining in the back of his throat. He could only see by opening the mouth.

SM: You've never had a Cybermen story.

JP: No, I've never had one. I think they're doing one next season. I heard that they are. Now, you really must excuse me, I've got to get changed, I'm recording in half an hour. I'll see you on the floor.

Stools were put away and we were herded out of the dressing room and back into the studio. I had a brief conversation with stuntman Terry Walsh, who explained the next big stunt recording was in a couple of weeks time with the Metebelis stuff. Barry Letts and Terrance Dicks stopped by to say hello, then Lis whisked me off for the promised cup of coffee. My new best friend. "You know what I would like is a note of the address of the fan club, so I can pass it on when I reply to fan mail and I can tell them all about you, Stuart." Through clenched teeth I growled, "He's Stuart Money..." pointing to the oik across the way, "...I'm Keith Miller!" "Oops, sorry," guffawed Lis, "How could I get that wrong? My husband is Brian Miller. We Millers must stick together," To quickly change the subject I told Lis how I had ideas for releasing more merchandise through the club magazine, and one thing I wanted to do were small sculptured busts of prominent cast members, would she like to be the first? "What do I have to do?" I explained all I needed were some reference photos which could be taken there and then. Lis said okay and the photos were taken, but the sculptures proved too difficult for me and was quickly forgotten.

Another idea I had was to offer copies of the Tardis key. I explained this to Jon and he replied, "Okay, but I want 50% of the profits." I'm not entirely sure he was joking. He scooped the key out of his waistcoat pocket and I produced a shoe-polish tin full of clay. I pressed the key into the clay, getting a successful impression. This was to be used as a mould. This was another failed enterprise that would never see the light of day.

Jon then introduced to me to his wife, Ingeborg, a very glamourous lady and exactly what you would expect Jon Pertwee's wife to be like. She introduced me as "the man who sent you the T-shirts" to daughter Dariel and ten year old son, Sean. I had screen printed two T-shirts for the kids some time earlier and Jon was very impressed with them.

"We're just going for something to eat, would you care to join us?" she asked. I replied I had better make a move as I didn't want to miss the bus back to Edinburgh. "I'll say goodbye then," said Jon reaching out and shaking me warmly by the hand, "Very nice to have seen you." I suddenly realised this was the last time we'd see each other and I wanted to thank him for being such a fine Doctor, even if he had occasionally been a thorn in my side. "Thanks for everything." he said, but I couldn't find the words to say and simply replied, "Yes." It was so sad, and with a wave of his hand, Jon and his family left. They passed Barry and Terrance. They were all going. Sarah too. Nothing was ever going to be the same again. With heavy heart, I returned to Edinburgh.

BRITISH BROADCASTING CORPORATION
BROADCASTING HOUSE LONDON W1A 1AA
TELEPHONE 01-580 4468 TELEX: 22182
TELEGRAMS AND CABLES: BROADCASTS LONDON TELEX

Ext; 2535/5331

13th May, 1974

Dear Mr. Miller,

Thank you for your letter pointing out to us that Eric Winstone did not write the Dr. Who theme. We realised that in the studio very shortly after Steve Race had finished his piece and by that time there really wasn't very much we could do about it.

You will have to admit Steve Race doesn't really make many slip-ups like that and we promise Ron Grainer won't get mis-represented again.

All good wishes.

Yours sincerely,

Christopher Serle

(Christopher Serle)
Producer
Light Entertainment, Radio

CBPS

Keith Miller Esq.,
Dr. Who Fan Club,
109 Moredun Park Road,
Edinburgh,
EH17 7HJ

In May of 1974, I had a brain wave. A weekly magazine devoted entirley to Doctor Who. Not unlike the club magazine. I decided to tout this to the current holder of the comic book license for the show, Dennis Hooper. Mr Hooper was already renowned as being a cantankerous old git, but I didn't know this, and was quite taken aback at the curt reply...

Polystyle publications limited

Publishers of TV COMIC, PIPPIN, PLAYLAND and I-SPY
Polly Perkins House,
Paddington Green,
382-386, Edgware Road,
London, W2 1EP

Telephone 01-723 3022

May 29, 1974

Mr. K. Miller
109, Moredun Park Road,
Edinburgh.
EH17 7HJ

Dear Keith,

Thanks for your observations, but I'm afraid I can't altogether agree. To be blunt, I have the experience to prove it. You as the secretary of Dr Who Fan Club are obviously too close up to your favourite programme. When one has been in popular commercial publishing for as long as I have, one learns to be more objective. It is all very well to question the age groups of TV Comic against the BBC programme, but only one point is relevant. Eleven-year -olds buy comics, teenagers do not. I will also contest the validity of your statement as to whether more older children do watch the programme than their younger brothers and sisters. My own family is considerably younger and are avid fans, together with many of their similar aged friends.

As to your suggestion of a weekly based entirely on the subject, the answer has to be a negative. Taking none of the programme's excellence away, one is compelled to point out its age and lack of novelty. I use the latter word to describe the necessary freshness required to persuade a publisher to invest many thousands of pounds that would be needed to launch it.

I hope you take my straight speaking in the manner it is intended. I have no wish to offend yourself or the programme, but one has to keep things in perspective.

Yours sincerely,

Dennis Hooper

Dennis Hooper

Editor

And five years later, Marvel bought the license off Mr Hooper, and *Doctor Who Weekly* was born, which would eventually regenerate into *Doctor Who Magazine*, still on the go today. Unlike Polystyle Publications. LOL.

BRITISH BROADCASTING CORPORATION
TELEVISION CENTRE WOOD LANE LONDON W12 7RJ
TELEPHONE 01-743 8000 CABLES: TELECASTS LONDONPS4
TELEGRAMS: TELECASTS LONDON TELEX TELEX: 22182

10th June 1974

Dear Keith,

I'm afraid I'm not even allowed a quater of 2400 labels! You must be joking. Stationery here is not open ended for my use! Sorry. I wish it was. I suggest you write to the Marx people yourself and them if you get those toy things free since you started the correspondence! Yes we have recorded one story already. We don't start again till November now. They have all gone on hols.

Yours sincerely,
(Sorry forget who I was writing too!)

Love,

I still felt awful I hadn't thanked Jon for being a terrific Doctor on the *Planet of the Spiders* set, so I sent him a letter. Jon's ego was annoying, certainly (There was a song around at the time by Carly Simon, I think it was, which had the line "You're so vain, I bet you think this song is about you...." which I used to hum every time he annoyed me), but he was a great bloke nonetheless and his Third Doctor personae has a special place in my heart. He would insist on smoking all my fags though.

Jon Pertwee

18th June, 1974.

Dear Keith,

Thank you so much for your very nice letter which I have just received on return from holiday. I agree with you THE PLANET OF THE SPIDERS was probably the best I have ever done.

You kind remarks and best wishes are much appreciated, and I would also like to thank you for your continued interest while I was playing the part of the Doctor.

All good wishes,

Yours sincerely,

Have you noticed Peter Capaldi has disappeared? I thought that with Jon going, Stuart Money would disappear too. But no. Sigh.

BRITISH BROADCASTING CORPORATION

TELEVISION CENTRE WOOD LANE LONDON W12 7RJ

TELEPHONE 01-743 8000 CABLES: TELECASTS LONDONPS4

TELEGRAMS: TELECASTS LONDON TELEX TELEX: 22182

20th June 1974

Dear Keith,

At this moment in time my sympathies are with you as regard S.Money. It has come to my knowledge that the beast is trying very hard indeed to oust you out of your job as Fan C. Sec. However, I have written him an abosulte stinker telling him that you are the Official F.Sec and that until <u>you</u> decide to give up your responsibilities there is no other official fan club. And only when you decide to give up your duties that we will appoint another fan club sec. Okay. Now I would be grateful if you would control your anger and not write to him at all until I get a reply from my very 'to the point and angry' letter to see his reaction. So please bear with me and don't get involved. This is strictly between you and me and a rather underhand, childish little boy. I will certainly let you know the outcome as soon as he replies. If he dares. But don't worry. You are the one and only official FCS. Okay? Give us a ring if you are feeling insecure!

[signature]

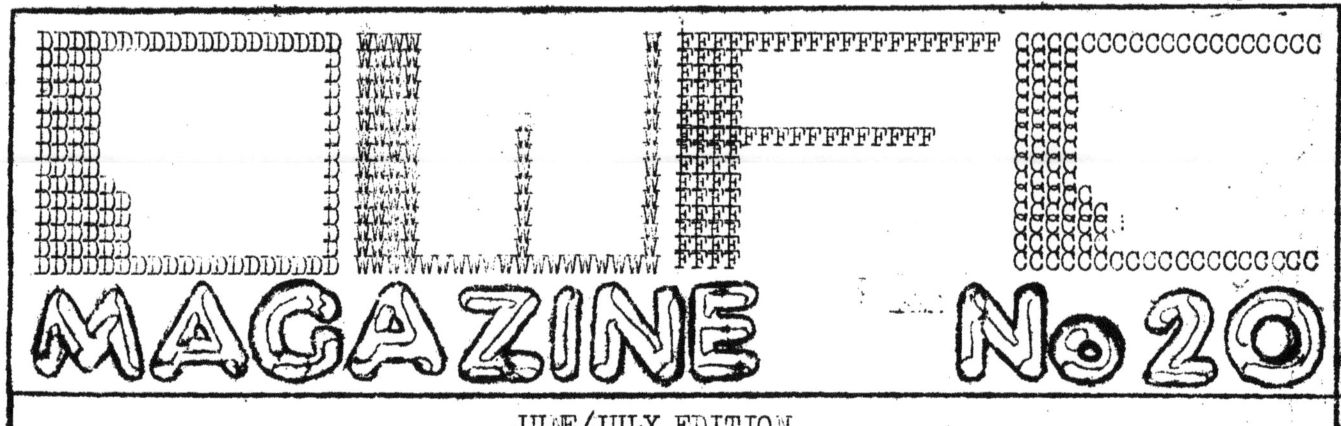

JUNE/JULY EDITION

DR. WHO

WELCOME BACK!,

Here I am again, very pleased that I can at last talk to you again. A lot has happened since last I set to work on the mag, so let's try and catch up.

Well, it's goodbye to Jon Pertwee as the PLANET OF THE SPIDERS draws to a close. It's a very sad occasion when someone you've come to know so well leaves, but that's the way it goes I suppose, but in the meantime, you can re read my farewell interview with Jon on pageThree.

You'll find a lot had changed in the mag since issue 18, so please write and tell me what you think of it.

DWFC LIBRARY NEWS: DWFC 11 is now available! It's "INVASION" which tells the story of the last Cyberman invasion attempt to date. Pat Troughton stars as the Doctor. If you would like this title added to your list, please send you order on a postcard, please.

Four new Dr Who jigsaws are out now! They are made by Whitmans and show excerpts from THE THREE DOCTORS, DAY OF THE DALEKS and THE GREEN DEATH. Each one costs 30p.

Another Dr Who product is a new model Dalek which is about to go on sale (sometime in July). It is made by the original Dalek model makers - Marx And Co.-and is coloured yellow and black, rather like those featured in DEATH TO THE DALEKS. They are battery operated.

Now for Dr Who Publications:

THE DOCTOR WHO HOLIDAY SPECIAL is again on sale this year. Let's hope it is as good as last years. Published by Polystyle Publications, it cost 13p. (Review next issue)

There has been a delay with the two new Dr Who paperbacks DAY OF THE DALEKS and THE DOOMSDAY WEAPON but Target hope to publish them by the beginning of June. If they are succesful, a Review will follow next issue.

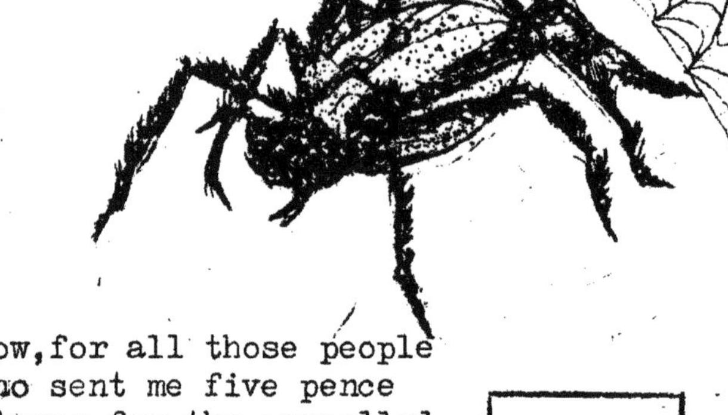

Now, for all those people who sent me five pence stamps for the cancelled DIMENSION OF DR WHO, your stamp should be returned opposite ——————————

To promote the new series of Target Books, Jon Pertwee journeyed to Birmingham to Smith's Bookshop and it was a staggering success! At ten in the morning, there was a queue of 2,000!

And talking of Dr Who publications, I wrote to TV Comic asking if there is any chance of a Dr Who Weekly being produced due to the success of the Dr Who Holiday Specials. I recieved a letter from Mr Hooper, the Editor saying that the programme is too old and hasn't enough novelty for a publisher to start up a mag on a weekly basis. Emph! I for one would think it would sell...what do you think?

At the end of this issue, you'll find an Application Form. This is for the new filing system up here, so could you fill it out as soon as possible please. Ta!

In case any of you are wondering where DR WHO DICTIONARY has got to, it'll be back when there's some space. The mag is so packed and will be for the next few issues that I really couldn't say exactly when it'll be back.

Did anyone see Tom Baker in the Sun newspaper report about the time travelling experiments? Quite a good photograph was with it. Anyway, did anyone try the experiment? Would be glad to hear from you if you have. Well, I'll sign off now and see you next ish.

REPORT

I arrived at the BBC entrance hall at around one o'clock and checked in where I was told recording was taking a little longer than usual so I would have to wait. While waiting, Richard Franklin (alias Mike Yates) appeared, then promptly disappeared as he was late for the filming. After Michael Parkinson, Ronnie Barker and Philip Jenkinson walked past, the doors to the foyer swung open and the tall figure of Jon Pertwee strode through the entrance.

He said that recording would still take a little time to complete, so I went of and had lunch.

Afterwards, I met up again with Jon where we walked through the corridors of the BBC to his dressing room, where the TALK-ABOUT interview opposite was recorded.

This isreally just a prologue to the Report of PLANET OF THE SPIDERS which I hope will be in the next issue. In the menatime here's:

REVIEW

PLANET OF THE SPIDERS
by Robert Sloman

Well, what can I say? This adventure was absolutely fantastic! It brimmed over with emotion, sadness and adventure.

Ep.1: The first thing that struck me were the pathetic jokes in the cabaret, but they were merely time fillers until we met up with Prof. Clegg. When the Prof visited UNIT HQ, the excerpt with the floating tray was quite good. Before I go further, I think it should have been explained that Yates conecrn in the Golden Age was due to the effects the blue crystal had on his mind from THE GREEN DEATH. The test with the Brigs watch was quite amusing. It was good to see the Drashigs again on the IRIS machine. Itneresting to note that Cho-Je was played by Kevin Lindsay, alias Linx alias the have-an-extra-pinta-milkman. Also John Dearth was the voice behind the Boss. Good to hear from Jo again. The "Exorcist" type scene with the objects being thrown about the room was very well done.

Ep.2: Began rather well with one oof the group behind "webbed" by the Spider. And the Spider voices were superb! The Spider sinking into Luptons back was very well done. The Dr. then went on to repeat the story he told Jo in the dungeonin Atlantis It was good to see the Whomobile again. I liked the effect when people got webbed - the lightning shooting from their fingers. the chase that followed was superb (more about that over the page). One thing that did surprise me was that the Whomobile could fly.

Ep.3: The cellar scene when Sarah Jane was transported to Metebelis 3 was unusual with the background disappearing instead of the subject herself. The large crystal guns of the Spider Slaves were good looking. Thank goodness they've brought back the key to the Tardis. The ending fight was very well done and it concluded well with the Dr being webbed and reaching for the Tardis.

Ep.4: I thought the end was good, but not that good that it had to be repeated in full in the beginning of this episode. A thoughtless waste of time considering we only get 25 minutes a week. Now for Tommy. I thought John Kane took the part very well as the retarded caretaker of the meditation centre. The crystal transformation he handled very well. The council of Spiders looked very good. The village scenes were not too bad with the Tardis being situated in the courtyard. I liked Sarah Jane and Sabor being coccooned in the Spiders "larder". The ending wasn't exactly startling with the Dr simply pointing behind him at the guard.

Ep.5: I liked the Dr's uncertain reference to Harry Houdini. The voice of the Great One was quite frightening and it left us wondering just what she looked like. The G.O. power was well demonstrated when she made the Dr turn around. "Is that fear I sense in your heart, Dr? You're not accustomed to being frightened are you, Dr?" It was stated that Tommy was saved from th the webbing by his innocence and Cho-Je by his compasion, but what saved Mike Yates? He was webbed twice, and still lived. The surprise attack when the Dr and Sarah returned to Earth in the Tardis was quite exciting. Another old friend then turned up. George Cormack (who's birth place is a short distance from the DWFC) was also the King from the Time Warrior. The threatening long sequence with Barnes walking ever so slowly backwards then webbing Tommy added a good atmosphere.

PART TWO OF THIS REVIEW NEXT ISSUE!

talkabout JON PERTWEE

To mark the beginning of this new series of interviews with the stars of the programme, we begin by talking to the one and only Doctor himself JON PERTWEE.

I met Jon at the BBC TV Studios in London (see Report) and we sat down in his dressing room for this two part interview...

Q: "What are your immediatte plans for the future, Jon, now that your long term as Doctor Who is drawing to a close?"

JON: "Well, I open in a new play, 'The Bed Winner' at the end of July and we open in Norwich, then we go to Leeds, Liverpool, Preston, Richmond, Bournemouth and so on."

Q: "How are you going to change over from yourself into Tom Baker?"

JON: "Well, I go to face my 'fear'...you remember I gave Katy, Jo, the crystal from Metabellis Three and she sent it back to me as it was causing her a lot of problems up the Amazon and it gets nicked from me and we find it is desired by the Great One, the Queen of the Spiders and I have to return it to her and in doing so my present life is forfeited, I die but being a Time Lord I'm taken over by Tom, just like the William Hartnell/Pat Troughton changeover."

Q: "You said you had a lot of chase sequences in PLANET OF THE SPIDERS..."

JON: "Yeah, there really is a magnificent chase sequence with Barry letting me loose with my love of gadgetry. We have a speedboat chase in a lovely speedboat which I was so impressed with that I have now bought. I chase it in a Hovercraft, then we have the Whomobile in it, my new space car and Bessie...So I'm going out in a blaze of glory. We also have Gyro-copters in it. In fact where we were making the scene, the Gyrocopter crashed! He started the prop-up, the pilot, and it took off with him sitting on the end, but he managed to jump clear and the thing went charging along, tipped up and wrote it off so one of our shots looks very peculiar with a bent rotor arm."

Q: "Have you got any favourite Doctor Who adventures?"

JON: "Oh, undoubtedly the one we did at Malborough, the DAEMONS. The other one was the one with the Drashigs, CARNIVAL OF MONSTERS, I liked that one very much indeed. THE GREEN DEATH, I liked, although it was a sad one to do."

Q: "How much say do you have in the script, say there was something you didn't like, could you cut it out?"

JON: "Yes, very much so. But it doesn't happen all that often, it depends on the writer. The writer on this one (SPIDERS) is very good, both Barry and myself like the way Robert Sloman writes. I don't like a lot of scientific jargon I never have done becuase I think, well I know what I'm talking about as Dr Who, but as Jon Pertwee I'm sure I wouldn't be able to understand all the futuristic equasions and so on."

Q: "Could you tell us how you got the part of the Doctor?"

JON: "It actually happened by Tenniel Evans who plays Taffy Goldstein in the Navy Lark when he said "Why don't you put yourself up for Doctor Who?" and I said "Why? What's wrong with Patrick Troughton?" and he said "He's leaving, I hear." So I rang up my agent and said "I've got a pretty silly idea to suggest but I don't think anyone would want an eccentric comic to play Doctor Whobut do think I could do it?"

Well he thought it was as silly an idea as I did but he said "I'll do it if you like" and so he rang up and spoke to the then producer which was Derek Sherwyn and Peter Bryant and said "I've got a suggestion to make" He said, "Jon Pertwee." There was a pause then he said "All right, forget it, I agree with you..." "No..no, wait a minute" said Derek, "Could I read you our short list?" My agent said of course not and read it out. The first name was Fred Flange or something like that, and the second name was Jon Pertwee. They had thought of to play Doctor Who some four years previously, which I never knew at all!"

(We'll have to leave it there I'm afraid, but the second part will be printed next issue.)

starring
JON PERTWEE as DOCTOR WHO
and ELIZABETH SLADEN as SARAH J.SMITH
in
"THE COMING OF THE REVELASIANS"

The story so far: Rick Warrington and Paula Martin have stumbled into the Tardis after seeing a serious road accident.Trying to open the doors,Rick operates the Tardis,fusing the controls into place. The Doctor,Sarah and their two new companions step outside to see five small flying saucers gliding towards them!

Chapter Two

The saucers manouvered themeselves around the party,making them step back up against the side of the police box.

"What...what are they,Doctor?"questioned Sarah.

"I'm not sure,"whispered the Time Lord, "But if they are what I think they are,we are in very serious trouble."

Sarah Jane shot a worried glance at the Doctor.Then she felt one of the machines communicating.It was as if their voices were inside her head,speaking in soft but threatning tones.

"Where have youcome from?"

"Tell me,"answered the Doctor,ignoring the machines remark,"Do you know the way to Trafaquar Square,we seem to have lost our way."

"Do not try to evade our questions,alien

Alien?thought the Doctor,then they're not man made anyway.Seams as if they are who he thought they were.

"When I say,everyone into the Tardis as quick as..."

"What are you saying?"demanded the machine.

"NOW!"shouted the Doctor as the party spun into action.

Suddenly,the slit in the dome of the machine which the Doctor presumed was their viewing apparatus,glowed with an ominous blue light,sending a lightbeam coursing into the back of Ricks neck.He stretched an arm out in front of the Tardis doors,barring his companions from entering Before the girls knew what was happening, the Doctor suddenly swung his arm round and buried it in the stomach of his young companion.

"Doctor?!"screamed Paula,"What...?"

"Into the Tardis,both of you!"he shouted as Rick steadied himself from the attack. No pain registered in his face,only a blank stare curtained his features.

The Doctor kicked his heel up onto Ricks chest with an ear-splitting "HIAT!",sending the man staggering backwards a few paces but with inhuman skill,he regained his balance and charged towards the Doctor. Ripping his cloak from around his shoulders he spread it quickly in front of him, sending Rick into a veil of darkness.As the young man struggled to get free from the cloak,the Doctor started back towards the Tardis,only to find one of the domed saucers had glided in front of the open doorway.

Suddenly,another beam of light shot from the slit in another of the machines domes, striking the Doctor directly on the forehead.The Time Lord braced himself for the impact...but felt nothing!

By this time,the machine slid away from the doorway and the Doctor sped through into the control room where a puzzled Sarah was trying to comfort a very frightened Paula Martin.The Doctor slammed his fist down onto the door control and they closed.

"But Rick is still out there!"sqealed Paula.

The Time Lord propped himself up against the console,trying to regain his breath.

"There is no in which we can help him... for the moment at least."

"How do you mean,Doctor?"questioned Sarah

"The saucer domes out there...the metal machines...they are called Revelasians. I've never encountered them myself before, but I know them by reputation."

"Revelasians?"asked Sarah.

"Yes,so named after the last book of the Bible."

"But that only deals with..."

Sarah paused.

"Yes,"answered the Doctor," It deals with the end of the world!"

"But what happened to Rick?"asked Paula, "Why did he try to stop us getting back in here?"

"The dome section of the creature houses a pulsating blob of intagible life... almost pure energy.Through their viewing slit,they can discharge that energy by a beam into the brain of human or other specialized species.Rick was taken over, possesed if you like,by one of those monsters out there!"

"You mean to say there's some alien life force in Rick now...controlling him?"stuttered Paula.

"Yes...but the "possession" only lasts one Earth hour.By that time,the human mind manages to build up a resistance to it and takes over,this also gives immunity."

"So those things can only attack once, for one hour?"asked Sarah.

"Yes,"replied the Doctor,"But think of what could happen in a hour.He could kill someone,build a bomb,anything.Let's see where he is now..."

He pressed a control button on the console and the scanner activated to show the Revelasians disappearing down the deserted London street with Rick following like a pet dog behind.

"Can't we get back to our own world, get the Brigadier and his troops and come back to deal with these Revelasians "asked Sarah.

The Doctor turned and gazed dispairingly at his companion.

"There are only three things wrong with your suggsetion. a)There are probably more than the five Revelasians we saw outside gliding about London somewhere b)That means they could take over the UNIT troops and order them to kill each other and c)The Tardis controls are fused together.We can't move anywhere until I can find something to melt the solder inside the console.Besides,we are in your own world by the looks of it."

"Then where is everyone?"

The Doctor ignored the remark and opened the doors.

"Come on.We'll have to follow those metal menaces to see where they are taking Rick.Once the Revelasians hold is broken,he'll need help to get away from them."

"Doctor?"said Paula as thet stepped outside and the Doctor locked the doors. "Why weren't you taken over?The beam hit you head on and you said it could take over any human?"

The Doctor smiled a knowing smile at Sarah who returned the grin,and then decided that the truth may be too much for her at the moment.

"Luck,my dear.Just luck."

They hurried down the empty London streets,taking care to keep a steady distance behind the aliens.Winding their way through the maze of streets, they made their deeper and deeper into the heart of the city.On their way, Sarah stopped then pointed to a newspaper stand.

"That should tell us something."

She ran over,lifted a newspaper from the rack and returned to the Doctor and Paula who continued following.

"There,Doctor",said Sarah pointing to the title 'LONDON EVENING NEWS',"It seems as if you were right.This is London."

"The date,Sarah,"said the Doctor,"What's the date?"

"The 16th of July 1974."

"We've jumped a day!"exclaimed Paula.

"One day,"sighed the Doctor,"And the whole of the human race has disappared. What on Earth happened?"

Suddenly,Sarah gasped and Paula sqealed. There in front of them,balanced on three stilt-like legs in a clearing where Nelsons column once stood,was a huge saucer craft,towering high above them and stretching for hundreds of yards in each direction.It was divided into three gigantic sections.The top section was a tranparent dome where they could see millions of Revelasians glided back and forth,each one with it's own individual task to complete.The middle section was bigger then the other two,but this was made up of a steel looking hull with four rows of portholes,each on top of the other,sigifying four floors.The bottom section,the Doctor deduced,was the propulsion unit - a vast area of four glowing half-spheres which was partly hidden by the metal ramp running up and into the ship.The five Revelasians and Rick were climbing up the huge metal ramp when they joined were joined by four more of the creatures before the congregation vanished inside.

"What do we do now,Doctor?"whispered Sarah as the Doctor ushered them behind a rubble wall.

"I want you to remain here..."

Sarah opened her mouth to protest but the Doctor held up his hand.

"Please,Sarah,no arguments.I'll be back as soon as I get Rick."

He glanced at his watch.

"He should be breaking out about now, so I suppose they've got him locked away somewhere.I'm going to go in there to get him and find out what's going on here."

"Look after yourself Doctor."said Sarah.

"Please bring Rick back,Doctor,"said Paula softly.

"Don't worry,my dear."

The Doctor stood up and peered up the ramp,the end of which was only a few yards away.

"It seems deserted.They must all be up in the top section.Well,here goes," said the Doctor jumping over the wall, up the ramp to dissappear into the

RETURN OF THE POPULAR SERIES

DR. WHO - FROM THE BEGINNING

AND TO CELEBRATE IT'S RETURN, THE DWFC PROUDLY PRESENTS A SUMMARY OF THE STORIES PRINTED SO FAR CALLED

GENESIS

The series opened with a story entitled UNEARTHLY CHILD Ian and Barbara, two school teachers from Coal Hill School were worried about Ssusan, a strange child with an amazing knowledge of history. They follow her to a scrap yard in London where they rush into the Tardis, which belongs to a white haired aged man called the Doctor. Pinning the Doctor to the control table, Ian accidentlly operates the controls and they set off back in time to the Stone Age where they encounter fire seeking natives but manage to escape to the Ship.

THE MUTANTS saw the Tardis land in a strange stone jungle and the Doctor says that they are many light years away from Earth and in the far distant future. Seeing a city, the party go to investigate only to be captured by the Daleks, a pitiless race of creatures, who share the planet Skaro with the Thals, a peaceful race of humanoids who help the Doctor destroy the Metal monsters.

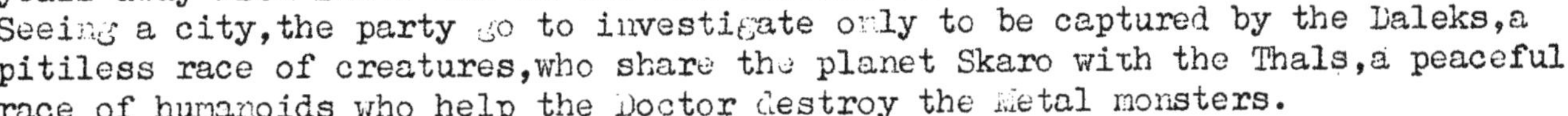

The next two episodes had no title collectively, but they concerned the Tardis as it spun through space, the controls locked. There were arguments flaring inthe control room, but it is found that the Tardis was on course for the sun and it was this that was causing the malfunction.

The controls reset, the Ship lands at the encampment of Kubla Khan where the Doctor narrowly misses losing the Tardis by gambling. This adventure was called DR WHO AND MARCO POLO.

THE KEYS OF MARINUS saw the party desperately trying to find the keys which operated a machine which would rule the planet wisely and fairly. The evil Voords invade and try to take over the machine, but the Doctor had substituted a false key, blowing up the machine and the Voords with it.

DR.WHO AND THE AZTECS began with the travellers being shut off from the Tardis as they made their out of a tomb by a wall of stone. After Barbara was heralded as a Queen and a God, Ian being set for sacrafice and the Doctor finding out how to get back into the Tomb with information from the Elders, the party escape and journey to the planet of THE SENSORITES.

Here, the Doctor managed to help the inhabitants by curing them of a deadly disease which was killing them. He found it due to early space travellers who had crashed and their minds had deranged, and were feeding deadly nightshade into the planets water supply.

The Tardis once again went back in time to THE REIGN OF TERROR where the travellers become involved with Robespierres' downfall.

Travelling back to Earth in 1963, the Doctor and his companions find that they have been reduced in size to only one inch tall, and after terryfying encounters with giant spidersand tidal waves of sink water, they escape to the Tardis where the Doctor operates the controls on Time Warp only, sending them into a devastated London and a frightning future!

NEXT ISSUE: The complete story of THE DALEK INVASION OF EARTH (which is also available in Paperback form and in more detail in the DWFC Library, Number DWFC1)

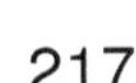

One of the perks of the job were the freebies! I liked the sweets best of all - I got a whole box of chocolate bars from Nestle. Yum. But there were other things too:

LOUIS MARX & COMPANY LIMITED

PRFB/EH

Swansea Industrial Estate Swansea SA54JD Swansea 32651/5

24th June, 1974

Dr. Who Fan Club,
Mr. K. Miller,
109, Moredun Park Road,
EDINBURGH. EH17 7HJ.

Dear Mr. Miller,

We will be most happy for you to mention details of our Model Dalek. If you contact Deeson Press Services, they will provide you with a photograph of the Dalek storming the Houses of Parliament. The telephone number of Deeson Press Services is 01-733-6201. We will be happy to let you have a Dalek free of charge for a prize in your magazine.

Yours sincerely,
LOUIS MARX & COMPANY LIMITED

P.R.F. BROWN
MARKETING MANAGER

Directors: R. J. Beecham JP (Chairman), J. C. Williams FCA (Vice-Chairman), Rt. Hon. Lord Westwood, B. S. Feldman, I. Shulman FCA, M. A. Fletcher MA BSc (Managing), A. Stephens, A. D. Morris, Secretary J. T. Evans ACA

PUBLISHERS AND DISTRIBUTORS OF
BOOKS, PAPERBACKS, MAGAZINES, AND PART WORKS

NEW ENGLISH LIBRARY

TIMES MIRROR

10 July 1974

Mr Keith Miller
Dr Who Fan Club Secretary,
109 Moredun Park Road,
Edinburgh
EH17 7HJ.

Dear Mr Miller,

Thank you for your letter concerning SCIENCE FICTION MONTHLY. We shall be publishing as many as possible in the magazine. Thanking you for your interest.

Best wishes,

Julie Davis

Patricia E Hornsey
EDITOR
SCIENCE FICTION MONTHLY

PS Could you send another sample copy of your fanzine, as we may possibly feature it in our series on fan activities.

NEW ENGLISH LIBRARY LIMITED. BARNARD'S INN. LONDON EC1N 2JR (Registered office) TELEPHONE: 01-405 4614 CABLES NELPUBLISH LONDON. TELEX 21924
Registered in England No 586668 Directors: H. P. Tanner (Managing) Martin P. Levin (U.S.A.) A. R. Jollye T. R. D'Cruz F.C.A. Nicholas G. Chantiles (U.S.A.) Associate Directors: R. G. Gray C. Smith J. O'Leary
Vat No. 232902878

115 Castelnau,
Barnes,
London SW13 9EL.

15th August, 1974.

Dear Keith,

Now that Jon has finished with "Dr. Who", he intends starting up his own personal Fan Club. To help get this started, he is wondering if you would let him have the names and addresses of all members over the age of fourteen who belonged to his "Dr. Who Fan Club".

Your assistance would be much appreciated, and I am enclosing a stamped addressed envelope for your reply.

Yours sincerely,

J. Evans (Mrs)

Secretary

Keith Miller, Esq.,
109 Moredun Park Road,
Edinburgh,
EH17 7HJ.

SCIENCE FICTION
MONTHLY

August 19 1974

Mr Keith Miller
DWFC Secretary
109 Moredun Park Road,
Edinburgh
EH17 7HJ

Dear Mr Miller,

Thank you for sending me all the copies of the Dr Who magazine, I found them very interesting; I must apologise for taking so long in replying to you.

I am hoping to publish some details of the fanclub in either the News page or in our new feature on fanzines although the first few articles will pay homage to the established fanzines like Speculation, Zimri and Cypher.

You may also be interested to know that an article is at present being prepared about sf on TV and it will of course feature Dr Who.

Thank you for your co-operation and again I apologise for the hold-up in actually using the material you have sent. I am enclosing the copy of the book 'The Dimensions of Dr Who' and the cover of 'Dalek Invasion of Earth'.

Sincerely yours,

Julie Davis

Julie Davis
Assistant Editor SFM

NEW ENGLISH LIBRARY LIMITED. BARNARD'S INN. LONDON EC1N 2JR (Registered office) TELEPHONE: 01-405 4614 CABLES NELPUBLISH LONDON. TELEX 21924

Registered in England No 586668 Directors: H. P. Tanner (Managing) Martin P. Levin (U.S.A.) A. R. Jollye T. R. D'Cruz F.C.A. Nicholas G. Chantiles (U.S.A.) Associate Directors: R. G. Gray C. Smith J. O'Leary
Manuscripts or other material submitted to NEL are received exclusively at sender's risk.

The Doctor Who Annual featuring my story, "The House That Jack Built", then hit the shops. I had left school by this time, and my first job was working in a bookseller in the centre of Edinburgh. It was a very odd feeling, seeing people picking up and buying a book that you had partly written.

THE DR WHO

annual 1975

Starring JON PERTWEE
as DR WHO

Authorised edition
as seen on BBC tv

THE HOUSE THAT JACK BUILT

Jo Grant sat watching the tall figure of the Doctor as he tinkered at one of the control panels of the *Tardis* console which she had helped him drag out of the police box a short while before.

"Any luck?" she asked, jumping down from her seat on the table.

"*Mmm?*"

The Doctor raised one eyebrow but otherwise ignored her question. She stood beside him and peered at the intricate piece of circuitry in his hands as he steadily pushed his sonic screwdriver into a small aperture in its side.

"I said, have you had any luck in repairing your compass?"

The Doctor looked up from his work annoyed. "I wish you wouldn't keep calling it that, Jo. This is the dimensional direction unit, which is essential if I want to programme the *Tardis* properly."

"That's what I said . . . a compass!"

The Doctor sighed, then returned to his work as his young female companion shrugged her shoulders and propped herself up against the hexagonal shape of the control console. She ran her finger around the switches idly and made them jump over the meters which lay dormant under the thick glass.

"Watch what you're doing, Jo, we don't want a . . ."

Suddenly the room shook violently and the Doctor dropped his workpiece on the floor. Jo reached for the console to steady herself, but it shimmered as if through a heat haze . . . and her hand passed right through it.

She screamed to the Doctor but no sound came from her lips. Instead a loud swishing sound filled the air and the walls began to spin in front of her eyes. She reached out for the Doctor's arm, but Jo was suddenly wrenched from the room together with her companion, and hurtled through the walls into a black void. She felt herself being propelled through time and space by some unknown force, with the Doctor's voice calling to her from somewhere in the distance.

As she sped through the unknown void, unconsciousness began to cloud her mind, but before falling completely into a deep sleep she could see that it was getting lighter . . . and the Doctor was ahead of her as they sped along an endless corridor, as if carried on a cushion of air. Everything grew confused, and she slipped into the sleep of the unconscious mind.

Jo Grant's eye lids fluttered open as she emerged from the darkness to see a black, cloaked figure towering above her. Her eyes grew used to the light and she could see it was the Doctor who was smiling down at her. He bent down and helped the girl to her feet. She swayed for a moment, but then found her legs were growing more steady by the second.

"Well, Miss Grant, we seem to have arrived," announced the Doctor, waving an arm around.

She peered around her to see a brilliant white room, with no decor apart from a heavy oak door set in the furthest wall.

"Where are we?" she gasped.

"That," announced the Time Lord, "is what I intend to find out. Come on."

The Doctor strode over to the door and grasped the handle. He shot back as a charge of electricity crackled up his arm. Laughter echoed from an unknown source around the room.

"Who is the prettiest one of all . . .?" boomed the voice, then erupted into a thunder of laughter as before.

As suddenly as it came the sound stopped, leaving Jo and the Doctor speechless. The Doctor was the first to break the silence.

"Seems this place is inhabited then . . . by a lunatic, by the sound of it."

He bent down and examined the menacing handle.

"Single wire electrocution . . . very ingenious," remarked the Time Lord.

"It seems our captor is on that often quoted border

between genius and madness. Now let's see what I can do about getting us out of here."

Jo watched as the celestial alien delved into his pockets and extracted a long piece of machinery – his sonic screwdriver.

"Shield your eyes, Jo," he said.

The young girl obeyed, covering her eyes with her arms.

The Doctor lifted his cloak up over the lock and behind the black curtain pressed the blade into the lock and touched the ornamented handle with the shaft. There was a loud bang and thunderous crackling as the Doctor's cape blew up into his face in a cloud of smoke.

Jo Grant peeped through the space between her arms to see the Doctor dropping the veil of black to reveal a burnt-out lock with a black streaked handle which had slightly melted above.

"What happened?" asked Jo in a shrill voice.

"As I said," began the Doctor, "the lock was electrified by a single wire system. That means that the lock and handle were both positively charged, so when I connected the two with my screwdriver . . . *kaboom!*"

He then turned and pressed the handle down, somewhat gingerly. The door swung open and the Doctor shot a quick smile at his companion. They stepped through the frame into complete darkness. It was as dark here as it was bright in the room they had just left.

The duo entered and the door behind them slammed shut, cutting off their only source of light. Jo was about to ask the invisible Doctor what they were going to do now, when the floor began to vibrate, the whine of engines started up, and something could be felt moving in the centre of the room.

Suddenly light began to flash throughout the room, and between the brilliant flares Jo could see a carousel, highly decorated with a large mirrored ball on the roof, which spun in rhythm with the revolving horses, which spun faster and faster as the engines rose into higher speeds. The horses began to blend together as the spinning made the wooden animals into a pink and white blur of movement. The ball at the top of the chaos spun faster, throwing light from its face to splash against the amazed duo standing below.

"This is a madhouse," hissed the Doctor over the engine noise.

He looked over to his companion to see her staring at the large mirrored ball which spun frantically in the air. The lights swept across her face to pause a moment in her wide eyes then disappear to be replaced by another brilliant outburst. The hypnotic spinning increased as a voice whispered to her: ". . . who's the prettiest one of all? Come to me . . . come to me. . . ."

Jo paused and stared at the wall of movement shimmering in front of her. The conscious side of her brain battled to tell her that to go any nearer the carousel would be instant death, but her subconscious triumphed, with the voice as an ally.

"Come to me."

"Yes, I must come to you . . ." echoed the girl, her eyes glazed and fixed on the ball spinning in the air in ever increasing and decreasing throbs. She took a step forwards and could feel the current of the air created by the mad machine blow her hair out behind her. Then a hand reached out, grabbed her arm, spun her round and another hand drew a sharp smack across her cheek.

Jo Grant staggered forward, to be caught by the Doctor. "What . . . what happened . . .?"

"I'll tell you later," urged the Doctor," but we must get out of here before this machine does any more harm!"

Then the whine of the engines ceased and the carousel skidded to a halt.

"Our host has found that little game useless," remarked the Doctor.

"Just what is this place?" squealed Jo. "It seems full

of deadly devices and voices asking us 'who's the prettiest one of all?' "

The Doctor pinched his lower lip thoughtfully.

"Yes, I had been thinking about that, but I can't make out anything logical from it."

"Oh, I wish I had stayed where I was," groaned the girl.

"What do you mean?" puzzled the Time Lord.

"Well, if I hadn't fiddled around with the *Tardis* console, we wouldn't be here, would we?"

"My dear Miss Grant, you had nothing to do with getting us here! The console had been disconnected. No, someone or something has drawn us here for some purpose only known to themselves."

Jo Grant's eyes widened.

"Then how are we going to get out of here?"

The Doctor looked grave.

"Let's see what's behind the next door," he said, ignoring Jo's question.

They crossed over to the door, past the now stationary carousel, and the Doctor touched the handle lightly. Finding it safe, he pushed down and slowly opened the door.

The room beyond was dimly lit, with no furnishings except two full length mirrors on the far wall which seemed to glow around the frame with a silver radiance.

"Nothing menacing here, I think. Let's try the next room." They walked past the mirrors, their reflections following them as they travelled past.

Jo reached out and grabbed the Doctor's arm. "Here!" she shouted, then said more quietly, "Here."

The Doctor looked puzzled.

"What is it, Jo? What's wrong?"

Jo Grant waved a finger in front of her.

"Something about this room. Something in here . . ."

"There's nothing in here except two mirrors. Now come on, I want to get out of here."

Jo shook her head as if to rid herself of cobwebs which clouded her mind, then she followed the Doctor to the next room. Yet another heavy oak door creaked open and they stepped into a huge hall with subdued lighting similar to the room with the carousel, except that this time, instead of the colourful roundabout, there was a blue police box standing in the centre of a huge chess board, each black or white square being at least four feet across. Behind the blue box stood an army of chess pieces, each one black and menacing, and ready to do battle.

"I hope you know how to play chess, Jo."

"But, Doctor, look! It's the *Tardis!*" Jo shrieked, standing on the first square of the giant games board.

"Who's the prettiest one of all?" boomed the voice, as if to signify the beginning of the duel.

Jo skidded to a halt. She was on the first square at the left hand side of the board. The corresponding section at the other end of the room lit up, and the black Queen's Castle slid from its position. Below the turrets of the piece sprang two sharp blades which glistened fearfully in the dim light. As it manoeuvred itself on the board, the blades began to spin round at an alarming rate. Jo stood there, petrified, as the chess piece shot

across the board towards her, the blades whining like some primeval war cry.

The Doctor sprang from his position at the safety area towards Jo and grabbed her, throwing her two squares into the board. The castle shot past them until it met the safety area, where it faded from sight.

"Doctor, what are we going to do? There isn't another door out of here!" shrieked the young girl.

"The police box obviously represents the prize for the winner of this barbaric game. Head for there."

By this time another square had lit up and a Bishop was hurtling towards them, its outline glowing from the highly-charged electric current it carried, which meant death to anyone it touched. The Doctor propelled Jo away from him as the piece slid between the two of them to fade into the safety area behind them.

"Run, Jo!" yelled the Doctor as he raced across the board towards the large blue police box.

As they scurried towards the prize the sequence of squares lit up at the other side and the pawns and pieces moved forwards towards their victims. More squares lit up with each step they took towards the box and slid in an army towards them.

"Jo, look out!" warned the Doctor as an electrified Knight skimmed past her side.

It made contact and the girl screamed as a charge of electricity shot into her side. Dodging another Rook, the Doctor picked the girl up from the board and dragged her to the police box. The huge King lumbered towards them, its crown a myriad of razor sharp blades which spun towards them.

The Doctor hammered his fist onto the doors of the box and dragged his unconscious companion into the darkness of the interior. He found the dimensions were exactly the same inside as out, unlike his own machine. The double doors slammed shut and the Doctor could feel the floor moving, carrying him and his assistant towards a light far above them.

The Time Lord bent down and felt Jo's pulse at the side of her neck. He could feel the blood pound against his fingers and he sighed with relief.

The girl moaned as she struggled to regain consciousness when the square section of floor that carried them upwards emerged into a brightly lit control room which hummed with electronic activity. The elevator jerked to a halt and the Doctor stepped from the conveyor into the control room which flashed on and off with irregular pulses as the collection of machines each carried out its individual function.

"We've escaped your little games," shouted the Doctor. "Now . . . show yourself!"

His voice echoed throughout the complex and died away before the strange noise floated through the air. It was like a heartbeat, but was also filled with the noise of a computer read-out, a gentle purring or ticking. A section of wall slid upwards and the Doctor spun round to the source of the noise and movement.

A giant computer was revealed, its tape spinning left, and then right, its gauges showing life and then stillness, its giant viewing screen throbbing red and blue and white.

"Why have you brought us here?" asked the Doctor, automatically thinking this was the entity that had kidnapped them from Earth and brought them here.

There was a low whirr as the computer digested the question, then a grating, inhuman voice replied, "It amuses me."

The statement was so unexpected and short that the Doctor was momentarily lost for words. A computer that had developed a sense of amusement was something he had never encountered before in all his voyages through the fourth and fifth dimensions.

"Amusement!" hissed the Doctor. "But . . . but why us?"

"You are above human intellect," it said, then after another whirring of calculation added, "It was unfortunate your friend was involved."

"Unfortunate!" growled the Doctor. "You very nearly killed her!"

The computer remained silent.

"What do you plan to do now?" enquired the Doctor sharply.

"You must remain here until you find the way back to your planet."

"There *is* a way, then?"

Somewhere behind him a tape recorder spool began to revolve and the lunatic voice burst into the room: "Who is the prettiest one of all?!"

"Stop playing that ridiculous quotation!" bellowed the Doctor.

"Mirror, mirror on the wall . . ." hissed a voice from behind him.

The Doctor spun round to see Jo, one arm propping her up while her free hand ran through her sandy hair in exasperation.

"Of course!" she exclaimed. "'Mirror, mirror on the wall, who is the prettiest one of all'."

She leapt to her feet and hurried over to the Doctor.

"That's it! That room we past through, the one where nothing happened! That must be the way back. Don't you see? The two *mirrors!*"

The Doctor snapped his fingers.

"Of course! Jo, get back to the lift!" urged the Doctor, then turned to the computer.

"What is your function?" asked the Doctor simply.

"To capture species from other planets and set them numerous tests."

"If they fail," interrogated the Time Lord.

"If, during one of the games, they sustain damage and cease to function, their bodies are returned to their own worlds, death by natural causes being established . . . after they have been processed."

"Processed?" enquired the Doctor.

"All knowledge of tests of skill and strength are collected and stored from their intelligence organs, for future reference."

The Doctor rubbed the back of his neck thoughtfully.

"You mean you collect as much information as possible about the games and trials of the inhabitant of that particular planet and test them out on a chosen subject?"

"That is correct," whirred the machine.

"Very well," announced the Time Lord. "Try this."

The Doctor looked back at Jo who stood on the elevator square then returned his gaze to the computer.

"Checkmate at three dimensional chess in six moves."

The computer whirred for a few seconds then grated "It is illogical. It cannot be done."

The Doctor smiled slyly. "Oh, yes it can."

The machine whirred again, and this time the Doctor could hear that the noise had increased in tone considerably.

"It . . . cannot be done," repeated the machine.

Its voice was higher, thought Jo, but put it down to imagination.

"Checkmate in six moves!" shouted the Doctor.

The viewscreen on the computer glowed a blood red as the whirring continued to rise in pitch. The Doctor hurried over to Jo and stood beside her on the platform.

"Six moves!" repeated the Doctor as the elevator began to descend. His last view of the computer showed thin whisps of smoke seeping from beneath the view screen as the computer tape began to spill onto the floor.

"But, Doctor," said Jo, "we'll have to go through that chess set again!"

"No, somehow I think the Jack that built this house is a little preoccupied at the moment."

The conveyor descended with the police box, and the Doctor pushed the doors open stealthily. He peered

into the hall and saw the pawns and pieces spinning furiously around the sides into the safety area, where they disappeared. After a few moments all was silent, and the duo stepped from the box and ran over to the door.

The Doctor wrenched it open and he ushered his female companion into the room of mirrors. By now the high pitched whining of the computer could be heard throughout the entire complex, as the computer battled for a solution to its problem. "Jo!" cried the Doctor over the noise. "Search around the frames of the mirrors for any control studs that might open them up. The door might be behind them!"

Jo Grant's fingers fumbled at the sides and found two hinges on the left. She nervously felt around for the control stud at the other side and found it. The floor began to tremble as the Doctor helped her pull back the mirror . . . to reveal a blank wall. The Time Lord smashed his fist against it until his knuckles bled.

"Doctor!" screamed Jo, "This place'll go up at any moment."

The Doctor ceased his futile attack and ran his fingers through his silver hair. The whine of the computer seared through his brain, jumbling up his thoughts so that he couldn't think straight. Then he looked at Jo and saw behind her that the hinges on the other mirror were at the right hand side . . . the *opposite* to the other one. He scrambled over to the glass and heaved it out until it was parallel with its neighbour. The two mirrors shone from yellow to blue as each mirror reflected the other, creating a never ending corridor to eternity.

The Doctor's eyes widened as plaster began to crumble from the ceiling as a large crack shot across the far wall. He stepped between the two mirrors, and found that the corridor wasn't a reflection at all, and that he could pass his hand through the glass as if it wasn't there!

He grabbed Jo by the arm and stepped through the glass as the roof collapsed and a gigantic explosion demolished the two mirrors and the remainder of the complex.

The Doctor and Jo were picked up by some invisible force and hurtled down the vast corridor at incredible speed. Jo then remembered this was how they had been delivered to the house of tests, this was the corridor she had seen before she had passed out.

Their journey seemed to take an eternity.

Jo tried to talk to the Doctor but no sounds left her lips. Then, staring down the corridors, she could see a tiny pinpoint of light speeding towards them. Suddenly they burst through an invisible door in the wall of the Doctor's lab and landed with a thud on the floor.

The Doctor grunted as he picked himself up from the floor and commented that they would never see that place again.

Jo stood up and brushed the crumbling plaster from her trousers, the only evidence she had that the adventure had truly taken place. Looking up, puzzled, and balancing her hands on her thighs, she asked "Doctor? *Can* you checkmate in six moves?"

The Doctor's face burst into a broad grin. "Of course," he remarked, as his tongue slid mischievously in his cheek.

Years later and I was reading a copy of *SFX*, reviewing the latest *Doctor Who New Adventure "Verdigris"* by Paul Magrs. "Ooh, a Doctor Who story done in the style of The Avengers, I like the idea of that " and promptly bought it. As I read on, I had the distinct feeling I had read the part where Jo breaks into a house containing a large merry-go-round with a disco ball above it somewhere before. Of course, that's why I liked the idea of a *Doctor Who/Avengers* crossover, it was *my* idea! *The House That Jack Built* had been an episode of *The Avengers* where Mrs Peel finds herself in a house she can't escape from. I used that idea for the basis of my story and stole the name. Even the "yellowing peice of paper" Jo finds in *Verdigris* is covered in direct quotes from my story. I was really chuffed!

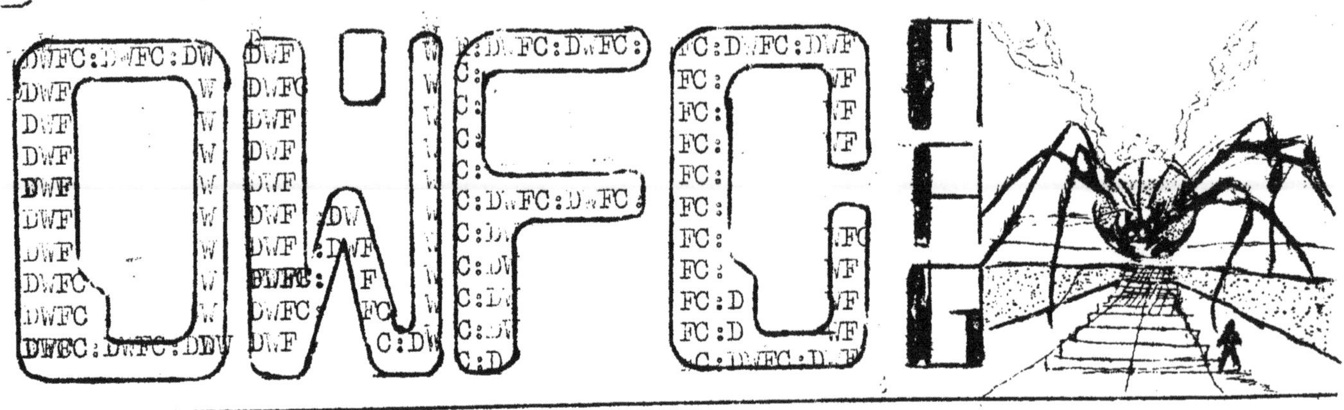

Number 21 August/September Edition DWFC

REVIEW :PART TWO

REVIEW :PART TWO

PLANET OF THE SPIDERS

EPISODE SIX

Again a huge chunk was taken from the ending of episode five, but this time it was mingled with new sequences. This made it slightly better, but was still a waste of viewing time. The revelation that Sarah-Jane had been taken over by the Queen Spider was very good, with Liz acting it out very well with the Spiders' voice. I liked the way the spider curled up when it fell off her back.

The Doctor reveals that Kan Po is the mysterious Guru he always remembered from his childhood and that Cho Je is, in fact, a projection of himself. It could have been more than a little confusing if you didn't concentrate! As the Doctor disappears to Metebelis Three, poor old Kan Po gets webbed by Barnes and company but it was good to get a taste of things to come when he rejuvinated into Cho-Je.

Meanwhile, the Doctor is back on Metebellis Three and it was a surprise to see that the revolution hadn't been a success.

Then came the moment when the Doctor returned to the cave of crystal and that absolutely awsome sight! That gigantic Spider on top of that equally huge flight of stairs was indeed a fitting visual spectacle for the Great One.

The fitting of the crystal into the web was well done while the Doctor desperately tried to make the Great One see the folly of her ways but to no avail. The power maddness of the Great One which followed was somewhat horrifying and when the power became too great and fused into nothing, it was a very good twist.

The flashback to the Council of the Eight Legs was great, with the whole web rocking and the Spiders coiling up like their Queen before them. Then came that fantastic explosion of the mountain. I have noticed that usually the BBC explosions aren't very good, (except for the odd exception like the church in the DAEMONS) but this one was very well done indeed.

And so it draws to a close. It is three weeks later and the Doctor lands at last at UNIT H.Q. just as Sarah-Jane explains to the Brigadier that she thinks she won't see him again. The doors hum open and the Doctor falls out after having been lost in the Time Vortex. The Doctor lies dying and Sarah cradles his head in her arms as she begins to cry...then comes the transformation. Jon Pertwees hair darkens, his wrinkles smooth out...Jon Pertwee is an older Tom Baker!

talkabout JON PERTWEE

JON PERTWEE INTERVIEW PART TWO

Q."We've had an adventure called the Three Doctors.If they ever had the Four Doctors,would you return?"

JON:"We got away with the Three Doctors but I don't think you'd get away with the Four Doctors.Poor old Bill (Hartnell) is getting on a bit,but I suppose it's possible.I mean,because I'm leaving now doesn't necessaraly mean I'm leaving forever.The great of Dr Who is that you can always come back...that's if the BBC want me and if I want to do it.At the moment,I feel I want to go away and do new things,tread new ground but I never know how I might feel in two or three years time.So maybe if nothing else has come up I'll come back.But I have some interesting plans for the future."

Q "Have you any idea what's happening to Dr Who next year?"

JON:"No idea at all...I don't want to know either as I might upset myself..."

Q:"Is Liz staying on?"

JON."Oh,yes,Liz is staying on with the Brig,John Levene and Richard Franklin. He's in disgrace of course."

Q."Have you any favourite locations?"

JON:"Yes,I think the best location work was in the last one we did "DEATH TO THE DALEKS".It was a marvellous location... a sand pit down in Dorset near Lullwell Cove and it was down about 70 feet below ground level...it was like the Grand Canyon and if you can remember some of those high shots,marvellous ones where we were walking through those pinacles that looked like rock:that was sand.You need only lean against it and it would topple over.When it rains,the water runs down and makes cracks and rivulets down the sides and makes it look absolutely marvellous."

Q:"What is the best thing you enjoyed in doing Dr Who?"

JON:"Locations.I love doing locations. As long as it's not too cold...we are usually up to our necks in mud which is a bit irritating.In fact,when we were doing COLONY IN SPACE we were in the China Clay pits in Cornwall and I got the stuff all over the inside of my car.So when I washed the outside,I didn't bother with the interior so that when I got back to London,the heat of the car had baked all the clay on the chassis and it cost me about a hundred quid to get it chipped off with hammers and chisels. But I like location work because that is where I get free reign to race motor cycles about and have speed boat chases and things like that."

Q:"Which story were doing when you were chosen for THIS IS YOUR LIFE?"

JON:"It was my second season during COLONY IN SPACE.I remember Barry (Letts) saying that there was this little trailer they were going to show and there were heaps of things that should have told me it wasn't true but I never twigged it at all.Then Barry said "Keep looking to the right and whatever you do,don't look round." Then I heard something drive up and there was Eamon sitting on the jeep like a perishing pixie with that duffle coat and a hood on,then I saw that red book in his hand and I realized I had been caught,but it was great fun...I enjoyed it tremendously."

Q:"Could you give us some info on the Whomobile?"

JON:"It was designed by me and Pete Farries and it's my own car so I'm afraid it won't be in any more Dr Who's unless I lend it to the BBC."

Q:"Were you pleased with the end result? Was it just what you wanted?"

JON:"Oh,yes.It drives beautifully...over 100 mph and sticks to the ground like a limpet.We had a lot of teething troubles but after a bit of redesigning,it was fine."

Q:"Do you find it draws a lot of notcie?"

JON:"Yes,too much!Cars crash into each other all over the place when I've got it on the road.I remember once when a German Volkswagon bus full of students stopped dead when they saw it and a big EVENING STANDARD delivery truck ran straight into the back of it.It happens all the time!"

THE COMING OF THE REVELASIANS
with
JON PERTWEE as DOCTOR WHO
and ELISABETH SLADEN as SARAH JANE SMITH

Chapter Three

The Doctor carefully peered round the hull of the spacecraft into the long, spacious corridor leading to a lift at the end.Hardly daring to breath,the Time Lord edged along the tunnel until he came to a cross-corridor where he slowed down.Pressing himself up against the wall he leaned out a little,only to see six or seven Revelasians gliding down the corridor opposite.Both of his hearts leapt as his brain quickly decided upon a harsh course of action.Sprinting from his hiding place,he darted across the openings to the corridiors and leapt into the lift.The Revelasians,he could see, were giving chase as their metal saucers slid around the corner at an angle and rushed towards him.Jabbing at the lift controls,the Doctor waited for the doors to close...nothing happened!As the monsters slid nearer,he desperately tried to operate the conveyor,but to no avail... until he notcied the microphone jutting out from the wall of the lift.

"Lowest Level!"he shouted as the doors slid to close and his stomach told him he was shooting downwards into the heart of the spaceship,leaving the Revelasians on the ground level to sound the alarm he could now hear echoing through the network of corridors.

The conveyor slid to a halt and the doors opened.Far away down the corridor, he could see three or four of the metal monsters huddled around a viewscreen, presumeably getting instructions on how to deal with the intruder.The doors to the lift closed and it went shooting upwards towards his pursuers.He would have to hurry.Suddenly,he heard a voice.

"Doctor!Over here!"

The Doctor looked round to see Rick peering at him from a small opening in the door opposite the lift.

"Why on Earth have they shut you up in here?"whispered the Doctor as he surveyed the scene behind the young man.

"They mustn't have counted on taking any prisoners so I don't suppose they have any cells."

"Mmm...possibly.Have you found out anything else?"

"Nothing...only that it's the same day we left 'our' Earth."

The Doctor smiled.

"I'm afraid you're wrong there.This is the day after."

"But I heard those metal creeps making some time calculations and they quoted today as being the fifteenth!"

"The fifteenth..."he Doctor hissed.

"Listen,Doctor,can't you get me out of here?"

The Doctor Ran his fingers over the lock,all the time glancing back at the Revelasians who were still at the end of the corridor.

"I'm afraid not.This kind of lock is completely unknown to me...wait a minute,isn't that a thermal lance behind you?"

Rick looked mystified.

"What?"

"That long,rod-like structure...pick it up."

Rick managed to free the machine from the pile in the corner and brought it over to the door.

"Set it to mark F...yes,that's it...now point the crystal towards the door."

Rick did what he was told,pointing the large,red stone towards the door.

"Now,press the lever at the side..."

Rick was suddenly thrown of his feet and smashed into a wall as the machine burst into life,melting the door in a hiss of vapour in seconds.Still dazed, the Doctor helped the man to his feet.

"Come on!We've attracted our metal friends attentions!"

The two men stepped from Ricks prison and the Doctor glanced at the lift indicator.It was stationary.

"They must be leaving the beings down here to deal with us."said the Doctor, jabbing the button,sending the lift downwards towards them.The Revelasians were gliding quickly along the corrdior towards them.

Just in time,the doors slid open and the Doctor pushed Rick inside,throwing the Thermal Lance into his hands.

"Get back to Sarah and Paula and get them back to the Tardis..."

"Doctor..!"

"No time to explain.I'll meet you back there.Take care of the lance!"

The doors slid to a close,and almost at once,the Doctor was surrounded by Revelasains.

"You are the alien discovered in Sector 5..."hissed one.

"I am."stated the Doctor simply.

"You will come with us."

The machines slid around the Doctor, providing an exit from their circle. He was taken deeper and deeper into the ship through corridors upon corridors of metal domes, gliding back and forth on top of the silent, gleaming saucers. His journey came to an end when the circle closed round him again, signalling him to stop in front of a doorway which the Doctor guessed at being the very heart of the ship itself.

The door slid away, and to the Doctors amazement, it revealed a huge metal room, the size of a cathedral, filled with instruments of all shapes, sizes and descriptions. Around them, the Doctor could see at fifty Revelasians busying themselves with all important tasks. But in the centre of the room was greatest spectacle of all.

Hovering seven feet in the air, was a brilliant white Revelasian, it's shell gleaming with alien brilliance, twice the size of any of the other domes...but this one wasn't exactly a dome, but a perfect sphere with it's saucer running stright through it's diameter.

It swung round until the Doctor could see a slightly duller viewing slit traverse it's face.

"COME CLOSER!"it hissed inside the Doctors head, "I WISH TO SPEAK WITH YOU."

FINAL CHAPTER NEXT ISSUE

BOOK REVIEW

DOCTOR WHO HOLIDAY SPECIAL 1974

Hmm...yes, well, not exactly the same as last years, was it? The front cover was fine and the introduction the same, but thos awful picture stories.

The dossiers on Lis and Jon were pretty good, but weren't long enough and not enough photos.

The pin-ups were okay but the one of The Doctor looked as if it had been taken with an ordinary camera and flash-cube.

Godd grief. Spiggy Sace Bug and Spog... didn't add to it in any way, did it?

The Dalek story was good, but as before it was a reprint from TV 21.

Then four pages of Stepping into Space. Okay, an educational article is okay if given in the correct quantity, but four pages worth was too much, and two of those were the colour photo pages which were few and far between.

I'm afraid you let us down this time, Polystyle! Now on to better things...

DOCTOR WHO AND THE DOOMSDAY WEAPON

by Malcolm Hulke: Target Books: 30p.

Wow! What a superb version of COLONY IN SPACE. I thought the introduction, A Missing Secret was good, with the Old Keeper telling the young Time Lord about the Doctor and his escapades.

On thing I didn't like was that Malcolm made this Jo Grants first adventure with the Doctor, while we all know that it was Terror of the Autons.

Then, the Doctor and Jo journey to the planet of the Colonists. It was the good the way Malcolm kept reffering back to life on Earth; the terrible conditions, the way you had to pay to get sunshine, how every inch of the ground had been built upon and so on.

Good touch when Ashe remembered "the terrifying creatures space-travellers had found over the centuries-Monoids, Drahvins...Daleks".

The sequnce where the Colonists find themselves facing the ritual of the dead when the two Colonists were murdered was very well handled and again, this didn't crop up in the TV series.

Then the Master makes his debut and when he gains control of the Doomsday Weapon, I liked when he said that with the weapon he could even control the Daleks.

The ending was very good, with the Doctor and Jo slipping away back to the Tardis and arriving at UNIT just a few minutes after they had left. Jo's ending statement was very good.

All in all, I think it is the best original Target have brought out so far.

DOCTOR WHO AND THE DAY OF THE DALEKS

by Terrance Dicks: Target Books: 30p.

I don't know why this story has fascinated so many people, what with the TV serial, the 90 min. special, jig-saws and now a paperback, but Terry has managed to make a good job out of a not-too-exciting story line. As Malcolm did in Doomsday, Terry has added a few details to the story, mainly the life of a Dalek slave in the future.

Now it only remains for me to say that although the covers are always great, why dosen't Chris Achilleos ever take as much care over the illustrations inside? After all, the drawings of Jon etc. are horrible! So, Chris, either you better your drawings in the inside or don't bother with them at all!

NEXT:-

DOCTOR WHO AND THE DAEMONS

DOCTOR WHO AND THE SEA-DEVILS

(Not yet published)

NEW SERIES

No.1;THE DALEKS

Q.Can the Daleks see behind them without turning round?Philip Veacock

A:No.The eye stick must train upon the subjext before it can be seen,but they can sense someone/thing is behind them if the person touches the black band surrounding the base of the Dalek.

Q:Ho do the Daleks talk?Andrew Dutch

A:The Dalek actually communicates by telepathy.It just needs to think it's message and the subect it is talking to will pick it up in it's own language.

Q:I would like to know the order of the Daleks.Michael Gittings.

A:A very difficult request!At the top is the Emperor,second in command is the Gold Dalek,third in command (but first if the Gold Dalek remains on Skaro when the Daleks journey to another planet) is the Black Dalek,fourth is the Red Dalek, then the lowest blue Dalek.The last order can be changed if they are Dominators. When a battalion of Daleks are sent to conquer a planet,they are sprayed a different colour from the rest to avoid confusion on Skaro (e.g.the yellow and black on Exxillon,the dark blue on Spiridon.)Whew!

Q:Does the Emperor Dalek have a gun for exterminating?Nicky Ingham

A:No.The Emperor Dalek is never left alone,so ther is always a Dalek around to defend it.

Q:As the Daleks have a flat base,when hunting humans on rough terrain,just how do they accomplish movement? Mark Bentam

A:The Daleks actually glide over the ground using a form of telekinesis (thought travel)which they harness with the help of static electricity.They propell themselves along the ground on a very thin cushion of thought power.

Q:In the old Doctor Who adventures starring William Hartnell,the Daleks used to say "You will be exterminated" and fire a gas.What was this gas?

A:It wasn't really a gas at all.It was in fact a radioactive mist which used to shower the body of the intended victim and kill him.Now the spray is invisible.

Q:The Daleks we know are alien creatures but in some adventures they are called robots.Could you explain this?Colin Gunn.

A:The Daleks are actually a mixture of both.From the outside they are robots, but in the inside sits a living creature.

DR WHO

Here we are again,Timelord,

First of all,I'd like to thank all of you for writing and telling me how much you like the new format of the mag. "The Coming of the Revelasians" has made a big impact with a lot of you, so it is rather sad that next issue sees the end of the story,but one word of advice.When issue 22 arrives, read the story from issue 19 again, otherwise,the ending will seem a little complicated.Have any of you guessed the Revelasians secret?All will be revealed next ish!

Now,Jon Pertwee has asked me to inform you of his own personal fan club.So if you are over 14 years of age and would like to become a member of the JPFC, just send your name and address to me and I'll forward them down to him.

As all you know,the mag is nearly always late.Thid is usually because of the complicated postage system we have for getting them to you.So,if you want your mag on time (or early in some cases), then send six 4½p stamps to me.You could get the mag up to a month earlier!

I've had quite a few letters telling me that you agree with me about a DR WHO WEEKLY.Well,I've done my bit,so how about everyone,and i do mean everyone, writing to Dennis Hooper,the editor and say that you would like a DW Weekly.If everyone does this,I'm sure he'll have second thoughts!Send your letter to The Editor,TV Comic,Polystyle Publications, Polly Perkins House,Paddington Green, 382-386 Edware Road,London W2 1EP.Onward Timelords!

Look out for a special DR WHO article in SCIENCE FICTION MONTHLY in the near future.They are running a series on SF on TV and the Doc will feature in one of the chapters.Also,there is a possibility that the DWFC will get a mention.Look out for it at your newsagents!

There is a book out at the moment called Movie Monsters (or something like that) and in it are photographs of the Daleks, the Cybermen and the Ice Warriors.Rather expensive,though,at £1•90.

Actually,I was hoping to bring you the fifth Fact Sheet on the Cybermen this issue,but I've ran out of space.I'll try and fit it in next issue.

In closing,I have had an idea being kicked about in my mind and I would like your advice.If the DWFC was to bring out a Photocopied mag (with photos)at say 30p every two or four months,how many of you would buy it?Write and tell me!Until

DOCTOR WHO-FROM THE BEGINNING presents

DALEK INVASION OF EARTH

SERIAL:K Written by Terry Nation Directed by Richard Martin Produced by Verity Lambert Stars William Hartnell as Dr Who

1;"WORLD'S END"Transmittion date 21/11/64.The Tardis lands by a bridge over the Thames and Ian and Barbara are overwhelmed at being returned home.Whilst exploring,Susan slips and send girders crashing down in fron of the Tardis.While Barbara and Susan go down to the river to bathe Susans ankle, Ian and the Doctor look for tools to remove the girders in an abandoned warehouse.Meanwhile,Barbara and Susan see a huge flying saucer glide over the city and are ushered to safety in an Underground Station by a group of people headed by the crippled scientist,Dortmun.The Doctor and Ian are suddenly confronted by four Robomen,human who have been processed to obey,and they escape down to the river only to see the water bubble and boil as a Dalek rises from the water.

2:"THE DALEKS"(td28/11/64)The Dr and Ian are escorted back to the giant saucer which has landed in Trafalgar Square.There they learn that the Daleks have conquered Earth and mining deep into the Earths crust.The resistance attacks with a bomb that Dortmun has devised.Menawhile,the Doctor has been led into the saucer for Robotisation.

3:"DAY OF RECKONING"(td5/12/64)The Dr is rescued,but the bombs are useless and they make their way back to the hideout where the party are reunited.They decide to split up and try to attack in indivdual groups.Barbara accompanies Dortmun,Tyler and Jenny,the Doctor and Susan take a different route and Ian makes his way aboard the saucer.The saucer takes off for the mine workings and Ian meets Larry who is trying to find his brother.Dortmuns party meet the Daleks in a museum and the cripple sacrafices himself to save them by propelling himself forward with a bomb,bringing the roof of the building down on top the Daleks.His notes are left with Barbara.The saucer arrives at its destination and Larry tells Ian that the Daleks are planning to mine down to the magnetic core of the Earth and ship the whole planet back to Skaro.

4:"THE END OF TOMORROW"(td12/12/64)Barbara and Jenny lose Tyler at the museum but he manages to join up with the Doctor.The two girls then break through a Dalek cordon in a dustcart.Ian and Larry manage to drop from the saucer where they are pursued by the Slyther,the Black Daleks 'pet',but find themselves on the edge of a precipice.

5:"THE WAKING ALLY"(td19/12/64)The two men manage to dodge the monster and it falls to it's death.They jump onto a conveyor which takes them underground to the bottom of the shaft.There,they are spotted by Larry's brother,but he has been turned into a Roboman.Larry sacrafices himself by throwing himself at his brother and they both fall into the bottomless shaft.The Doctor and his party reach the mine.Barbara and Jenny are taken prisoner and led to the control room where they find that the Daleks are withing four miles of the Earth's core.Ian climbs aboard the bomb capsule which will be used to blow the remaining four miles up.

6:"FLASHPOINT"(td26/12/64)Ian manages to break out of the capsule but falls down to the bottom of the shaft.The Black Dalek orders that all humans have to be herded into the lower galleries where they will be destroyed by the explosion.Barbara manages to garb the control microphone and orders the Robomen to attack the Daleks.Susan and a young man called David plant explosives around the radio masts where the Daleks draw their motive power.The Dr and Tyler make their way up to the control room of the saucer.Ian builds a barrier across the shaft of the bomb. The radio masts are destroyed and the Daleks slide to a halt,but not before the Black Dalek can release the bomb.The humans make their way to the surface where they are reunited.The mine is evacuated and the bomb explodes,destroying the Daleks and their saucer.Recovering their senses,the group congregate around the Thames and discuss the task of rebuilding while the Doctor,Ian and Barbara reenter the Tardis.Susan decides to stay with David much to the annoyance of the Doctor,but the Tardis dematerializes,leaving Susan to her new life on a new Earth.

BRITISH BROADCASTING CORPORATION

TELEVISION CENTRE WOOD LANE LONDON W12 7RJ

TELEPHONE 01-743 8000 CABLES: TELECASTS LONDONPS4

TELEGRAMS: TELECASTS LONDON TELEX TELEX: 22182

September 2nd, 1974

Dear Keith Miller,

I am sending on the enclosed letters to you as I think it is quicker than writing to them to tell them your address.

Philip Hinchcliffe and I are in the process of taking over from Barry Letts and Sarah Carroll so I expect we shall be in touch fairly frequently from now on.

Yours sincerely,

Ann Burnett

Ann Burnett
Secretary to Philip Hinchcliffe

Keith Miller, Esq.,
109 Moredun Park Road,
Edinburgh EH17 7HJ

December 1974

End of an Era, and Genesis of Another

And that was it. No goodbyes. Sarah and Barry just... stopped. Decades later and I was listening to the commentary on *The Monster of Peladon* DVD moderated by my good chum, Toby Hadoke (of *Moths Ate My Doctor Who Scarf* fame) and during a lull in the conversation (there were lots of them during *Monster*!! Boring doesn't cover it...) Toby swerved the conversation round to fans and fandom. Gosh, I thought, was I going to get a mention? "How close did you get to fandom during the 70's, Barry?" You could almost hear Barry scowl. "Fan clubs? We had nothing to do with them..." Eh? Have the past 230 pages been made up? For goodness sake...

So a completely new era was starting. This was going to be something new for me, to be in at the beginning with a completely new Doctor and new production team. Things were changing... and it soon became clear - I was going to have to change as well...

NEXT TIME

The Official Doctor Who Fan Club Vol 2: The Tom Baker Years

The story continues with a brand new Doctor, a reinvention of the club magazine, and set reports from *Genesis of the Daleks*, *Terror of the Zygons* and *Masque of Mandragora*. Due for publication late 2012. Keep up to date on www.odwfc.com

www.ingramcontent.com/pod-product-compliance
Ingram Content Group UK Ltd.
Pitfield, Milton Keynes, MK11 3LW, UK
UKHW050615260726
13967UKWH00008B/2875